Educating for Sexual Virtue

Religion, Education and Values

Volume 12

PETER LANG
Oxford • Bern • Berlin • Bruxelles • Frankfurt am Main • New York • Wien

Educating for Sexual Virtue

A Moral Vision for Relationships and Sex Education

Olwyn E. Mark

PETER LANG
Oxford • Bern • Berlin • Bruxelles • Frankfurt am Main • New York • Wien

Bibliographic information published by Die Deutsche Nationalbibliothek.
Die Deutsche Nationalbibliothek lists this publication in the Deutsche Nationalbibliografie; detailed bibliographic data is available on the Internet at http://dnb.d-nb.de.

A catalogue record for this book is available from the British Library.

Library of Congress Control Number: 2017955872

Cover Photography & Design by Silje Lilly.

Series design by Peter Lang Ltd.

ISSN 2235-4638
ISBN 978-1-78707-128-5 (print) • ISBN 978-1-78874-097-5 (ePDF)
ISBN 978-1-78874-098-2 (ePub) • ISBN 978-1-78874-099-9 (mobi)

Published by Peter Lang Ltd, International Academic Publishers,
52 St Giles, Oxford, OX1 3LU, United Kingdom
oxford@peterlang.com, www.peterlang.com

This publication has been peer reviewed.

Printed in Germany

Contents

Acknowledgements

Research and writing is more often than not a solitary task, yet one that is constantly enriched by the cheerleaders and companions along the way. As this book is the culmination of ten years of study and research, there have been many such individuals and groups.

This book is largely the reworking and updating of my PhD thesis which was completed at London School of Theology (LST). Particular thanks must therefore go to the faculty and community at LST for the opportunity to grow and learn amongst you, both academically and spiritually. Special thanks to my fellow researchers in the Guthrie Centre for the intellectual sharpening, the spiritual companionship and the tonic of laughter – all of which were readily available and much needed. In this regard, extra special thanks must go to my PhD companion, Dr Chloe Lynch. I extend my thanks to my PhD examiners, Professor Tony Lane and Professor John Sullivan, for their critical and constructive feedback and encouragement. Finally, to my PhD supervisor, Professor Anna Robbins: thank you for helping me to sharpen my own voice, and for continuing to use yours with such strength, sensitivity and wit.

My appreciation must also go to the lecturers on the MA in Bioethics and Medical Law course at St Mary's University, Twickenham, with particular and sincere thanks to Dr Trevor Stammers for the careful and courageous attention that he has given to many of the issues discussed in this book. I also wish to thank Professor Trevor Cooling at Canterbury Christ Church University for his own contribution to Christian education and for his personal and professional support and encouragement.

I offer warmest thanks to my extended family and friends who have blessed me in numerous ways over the past years – you know who you are! In particular, to my church families at Hill Street Presbyterian Church, Lurgan and Northwood Hills Evangelical Church. To my colleagues and friends at Love for Life: I am honoured to have worked alongside so many exceptional individuals with such a heart and passion for the welfare of children and young people. In particular, I wish to acknowledge the courageous and compassionate leadership of Dickie and Janice Barr and Judith Cairns.

My thanks must also go to Willie Barton for proofreading this manuscript, and doing so with such patience, care and diligence. Also, to Silje Lilly for designing the cover of the book and inhabiting the image so beautifully in her own life.

My final and most heartfelt thanks must go to my own immediate family: my mother, Alison, along with Jonathan, Lucy, Joshua, Zack, Catherine, Andrew, Punita, Cian, David, Ruth, Cillian, Finley and Peter. Remembering, too, with deepest love, my late father, Douglas, whose love and encouragement was unstinting, and who is now caught up with the 'great cloud of witnesses'. To God be the glory.

Earth's crammed with heaven,
And every common bush afire with God;
But only he who sees, takes off his shoes;
The rest sit round it and pluck blackberries ...
— ELIZABETH BARRETT BROWNING

Preface

In the weeks leading up to the completion of this manuscript, a public campaign was launched against a neon sign inside a clothes shop in London – the sign read 'Send me nudes x'. The petition against the sign, which received over 9,300 signatures, asked the clothes shop, which tailors for teenage girls and young women, to remove the sign on account of the culture of exploitation and coercion that it legitimized. As a result of the campaign, the sign was removed.

In a moral climate that is still particularly sensitive to the sexualization and exploitation of children and young people, many celebrated the success of such a short and sharp campaign; however, the challenge and questions that it raised for our public moral conscience linger on – questions, for example, concerned with how and why such a message was ever deemed to be a morally legitimate one for a popular and mainstream retail outlet to display.

How many people had fitted, worked under and passed by this sign, and perhaps others like it, unmoved by the implications of the message for the teenage shoppers? If their consciences had been pricked, would they have hesitated in questioning its appropriateness for fear of appearing prudish or judgemental about behaviours, like sexting, which increasingly shape young people's sexual lives – even when such behaviours are illegal for under-18s?

After all, it is largely accepted that what adults and increasingly young people do in their private sexual lives – within the moral bounds of mutual consent and respect, of course – is nobody else's business. However, this moral judgement, while appearing to be a morally 'neutral' one, cannot be so. It is inevitably conditioned by cultural norms and values around sex and relationships that at least determine the moral bounds of consent and respect.

In spite of concerns expressed over the need to protect children and young people from undue sexual pressure and targeted sexual exploitation, culture has progressively affirmed the sexual subjectivity of young people and their right to make their own 'informed' decisions and pursue their own sexual script. The result has been the creation of a climate of moral ambiguity and confusion, not least for young people. For in order to make an 'informed choice' around relationships and sex, a young person needs to have at least the moral resources to draw on in order to do so. In a culture increasingly defined by expressive individualism, young people themselves are drawing attention to the fact that they are lacking the moral and spiritual resources necessary to make their choices.

This appears to be part of a wider and deeper crisis in moral education. Research among emerging adults in the US, for example, indicates that young people are morally adrift: no longer believing that objective moral truth exists, 'they think that people believing something to be morally true *is what makes it* morally true' (Smith et al. 2011: 61, italics in original) Such thinking leads to 'moral scepticism, subjectivism, relativism, and, ultimately, nihilism' (2011: 62).

This book, therefore, calls for an urgent re-engagement with the moral vision shaping our approach to moral education and our understanding of sex and relationships – a moral vision exemplified in government policy on Sex and Relationships Education (SRE) in England. The arguments that this book presents are particularly timely in view of the recent announcement that Relationships Education and Relationships and Sex Education (RSE) will become a statutory requirement of the curriculum for all schools in England from 2019. Indeed, considered policy discussion will have no choice but to engage with the moral vision of Relationships Education and RSE, for there can be no neutral account of relationships.

In Part I, we will give particular attention to tracing the shifting moral narrative in SRE policy discourse, in particular changes in the moral and spiritual content. In arriving at the current 'informed choice' approach, we will explore key concepts and arguments associated with this liberal metanarrative as outworked in the current moral framework of public health, health education and moral education. This is a metanarrative that legitimizes the autonomy and self-determined nature of young people's sexual choices within the bounds of a socially constructed understanding of 'harm' and 'wellbeing'.

In light of the implicit moral judgements being made within current discourse around young people's sexual behaviour, we will in Part II give particular attention to the moral narrative currently scripting our understanding of sex and relationships. We will engage with philosophical questions and answers concerned with the meaning of sex and love and examine the naturalist presuppositions on which such judgements are founded. We will also engage with the adequacy of current legal parameters on sexual behaviour, largely defined by a socially constructed understanding of consent.

Two-thirds of this book are given over to scrutinizing and critiquing current moral norms and values surrounding SRE in order to make a compelling case for why a politics of moral engagement is a necessary prerequisite for future RSE policy and practice, as well as why the current moral vision is incoherent and inadequate. The discussion in Part III will present virtue ethics as an enriching moral narrative for moral education. A Christian vision of a sexually and relationally educated young person, a vision informed by the virtues of Christian love and chastity, takes account of the embodied nature of the learner in community and presents an account of sexual virtue that leads to human flourishing. It provides children and young people with a richer and more coherent moral language and vision within which to understand their sexual nature and choices.

The discussion in *Educating for Sexual Virtue* is only the first step in opening up a wider discussion on the moral and spiritual content of Relationships and Sex Education policy, practice and programmes. It is right from the outset, therefore, to acknowledge a couple of limitations. First, in engaging with disparate fields throughout the course of this book – including philosophy of education, ethics, theology, political theory and social and health policy – the purpose of doing so is to build a comprehensive and compelling public moral argument against the current liberal metanarrative. The danger of doing so, however, is that not enough critical attention or depth of reflection is given to the relevant ideas presented within each field. Nevertheless, while my discussion is primarily directed through a theological lens, drawing on disparate fields to underpin the core tenets of the argument opens up the opportunity for the ideas presented to be critiqued and developed in different directions and for different audiences.

This is a particularly compelling prospect in view of the 'live' nature of the policy issues being discussed.

Secondly, the discussion is grounded in the theoretical and therefore gives only limited attention to the practical implications in terms of the outworking of the moral vision for, among others, teachers, pupils, education policy-makers, politicians, religious bodies and teacher-educators. This is the inevitable result of the need first to build a compelling case for the recasting of the moral vision for RSE, doing so with a particular focus on character and virtue. As such, the relevant concepts and arguments that substantiate this vision are the main focus of this discussion. The practical implications must flow from the vision.

PART I

The Moral Framework of Sex and Relationships Education (SRE)

CHAPTER 1

Relationships and Sex Education Policy: A 'Politics of Moral Engagement'?

> To inform and advise young people on these matters calls for wisdom, understanding and tolerance, and parents, teachers and all who enjoy the confidence of young people, share a responsibility for seeing that they are not left in dangerous ignorance, nor alternatively left to acquire knowledge in ways which are likely to distort or degrade their outlook upon sex, and their sense of responsibility in regard to it.
>
> — BOARD OF EDUCATION (1943: 4)

> We will ensure our work results in a clear understanding about the full set of knowledge and life skills that Relationships Education, RSE and PSHE should provide for young people to support them to be safe, healthy, happy and successful.
>
> — DEPARTMENT FOR EDUCATION (2017: 2)

On 1 March 2017, the Secretary of State for Education in England announced the government's intention to make Relationships Education in primary schools, and Relationships and Sex Education (RSE) in secondary schools, a statutory requirement for all schools.[1] The announcement was warmly welcomed by many organizations and campaign groups who had long called for successive governments to guarantee delivery on this subject.

1 This announcement marks a change in the name of the subject from SRE (Sex and Relationships Education) to RSE (Relationships and Sex Education). The discussion in this book will mostly use the term 'SRE' to acknowledge its use in policy discussion and surrounding discourse to date; however, in Part III (chapters 8–10), I will more often use the term RSE in casting a vision for current and future RSE policies and programmes.

However, this was not an innovative or unanticipated policy move, for sex education has long been a subject of public and political concern. In fact, the first policy advice on sex education in England was published by the Board of Education in 1943. At that time, the 'stress of war' and the 'social dislocation' that arose as a result were credited with raising the importance and necessity of government advice for teachers and youth leaders alike on the subject (Board of Education 1943: 3). Since then, the social and sexual lives of citizens have changed in revolutionary and unprecedented ways. This sea change has inevitably impacted the government's rationale for education on this issue, and the content of the information and advice offered to young people; it has not, however, diminished the need or the demand for it.

The government's reason for putting the subject on a statutory footing was, in the end, an 'ambition to support all young people to stay safe and prepare for life in modern Britain' (Department for Education 2017b: 1). The policy statement notably emphasized a paternalistic concern for the wellbeing of children and young people in view of the dangers that they faced within modern culture: 'Given the increasing concerns around child sexual abuse and exploitation and the growing risks associated with growing up in a digital world, there is a particularly compelling case to act in relation to pupil safety' (2017b: 2). Yet, despite the explicit moral rationale of this policy announcement, and the widespread warmth with which it was received, the government's expressed ambition may well obscure the extent to which multiple moral judgements – both explicit and implicit – have shaped, and will continue to shape, policy discourse and content around Relationships and Sex Education. For while it has previously been suggested that 'SRE is not and should not be controversial' (Blake 2014), this is a simplistic and misguided assumption; within a liberal and diverse society, it is difficult to conceive how an issue that cuts to the heart of how we understand ourselves and our relationships can ever become anything but controversial.

For a start, each possible approach to SRE adopts a view on the appropriate level of state involvement in what is rightly perceived to be a sensitive subject area, one in which the state endangers infringing individual liberty and the boundary between the home and the state. A common criticism raised against the teaching of school-based SRE is that it is a subject that should remain the sole domain of the home, and despite fears and accusations of parents' moral abdication on this subject, it is argued that parents still retain the normative role of primary educators, including the right to pass on beliefs and values to their children. This is recognized as a critical building block of society, particularly when it comes to establishing boundaries between the moral responsibility of the state and the freedom of the individual, and is regarded as a necessary prerequisite to protecting the institution of the family (Almond 2006). Indeed, even those who advocate for the moral autonomy of the child must yet concede that when it comes to the appropriate context for raising children, the family remains, on balance, 'the most feasible and desirable' (Archard 2010: 99).

What the concerted campaign for statutory SRE, both within and outside of government, evidenced however is that a questionable level of importance and influence continues to be assigned to the place of school-based SRE in tackling what are judged to be the sexual and relational 'harms' evident in wider society. In light of this, the ever-present danger exists that the liberal state is unfairly apportioned a level of responsibility for aspects of individual and societal wellbeing that it has no authority over or, indeed, ability to dictate or control. As political theorist Bernard Crick observed: 'No state has the capacity to ensure that men are happy; but all states have the capacity to ensure that men are unhappy. The attempt to politicize everything is the destruction of politics' (2000: 151). Thus, the dynamic intersection between the various social actors and their role in SRE is bound to incur at least some controversy. This will become more explicit as moral engagement over the meaning and purpose of SRE is explored.

Upholding the rights and responsibilities of the family and the individual does not, at the same time, completely exempt the school from its role in addressing value-laden subjects like SRE. For notwithstanding the values and virtues taught in the home, David Carr points out that it may yet be 'reasonable' to suggest that schools teach 'a common "core" of values and virtues for the purposes of moral, social and civic education and as a basis of moral sensibility and order for the common school' (2003b: 70). In doing so, the interests of society at large are recognized, including the need to provide a basic education for its children in order to ensure its own future stability and security (Archard 2006: 10). As a result, it is not the existence of a relationship between citizenship and moral education that is 'seriously questioned', but what is up for discussion is the 'nature and limits of this relationship' (Halstead 2010: 255).

The purpose of our discussion in Part I, therefore, is to identify and explicate the moral narrative in SRE policy discourse and critique the moral judgement evident therein. When it comes to exploring the philosophical moorings of current SRE discourse, there has been some suggestion that such engagement is irrelevant – despite it being a necessary and indeed inevitable part of the policy-making process. For choosing a 'good' policy approach towards SRE necessitates philosophical engagement around the moral issues at stake, and the challenge of reaching consensus on a moral framework for SRE, amongst such a diverse group of stakeholders, cannot be underestimated (Thomson 1997: 263–264). As a first step, I will begin to identify some of the key features of the normative frameworks that have shaped SRE policy discourse and decisions thus far. In light of this, I will present a case for a renewed exploration of the common values and virtues within RSE policy guidance moving forward.

Policy Development: A Shifting Moral Narrative

We begin our discussion on the moral narrative of policy development by observing that early commentators on sex education articulated a moral and spiritual understanding of sex and sexual behaviour, including the implications for individual and public wellbeing. Catherine Gasquoine Hartley, for example, in *Sex Education and National Health* acknowledged sex as something to be revered and 'most holy in the plan of life', and thus children should be educated accordingly (1920: 39). The essential purpose and meaning of sex was understood within a particular view of human nature and the public good, requiring a specific public morality to be taught: 'That we should leave our children to pick up their sexual information haphazard seems almost incredible. Can we allow them to learn about the most powerful, the most sacred, the most profound and vital of human functions from the gutter?' (1920: 20).

A few decades later, educationalists like Edward F. Griffith argued that no sex education should be given unless it was related to emotional and spiritual wellbeing: 'To develop man's intellectual abilities at the expense of the spiritual or the emotional is as misguided as to develop the emotions at the expense of the intellect' (1947a: 15). This understanding of sex education led to a distinction between 'sex instruction' and 'sex education', where the former is concerned solely with facts and science and the later with whole life learning and values (1947a: 15). As such, the nature of sex was intimately connected to one's spiritual self: 'Sex activity, whilst embracing our emotions and physical being, our instincts and our minds, can only fulfil its rightful purpose if its activity is acceptable to our spiritual nature' (1947b: 224).

This moral and spiritual understanding was evident in the content of earliest policy advice. *Sex Education in Schools and Youth Organisations: Education Pamphlet No. 119*, the first official document from the Board of Education on the subject, stated that the purpose of information and advice within sex education was to ensure that young people 'are not left in dangerous ignorance', nor left to 'acquire knowledge in ways which are likely to distort or degrade their outlook upon sex, and their sense of responsibility in regard to it' (Board of Education 1943: 4). In addition, the Board of Education recognized, from the outset of sex education policy, that the task of delivering wise instruction to young people was to be the corporate responsibility of 'all who enjoy the confidence of young people' (1943: 4).

Information was to be presented within a moral framework that attached a specific understanding to the nature and meaning of sex. Beyond the physiological instruction, advice was to be 'directed to the understanding and control of sexual impulse and emotion, leading on to the establishment of mutual understanding and respect between the sexes, and, as young manhood and womanhood is approached, to an adequate preparation for marriage' (1943: 4). The importance of self-control was not unique to the sexual impulse and emotion: 'All creative social effort demands self-control, and the exercise of conscience and discrimination in the realm of personal conduct and relationships' (1943: 5). Nevertheless, the challenge for educators would be to 'make such self-control and discrimination seem rational and inspiring' (Board of Education 1943: 5).

However one might judge these moral and spiritual directives though a contemporary lens, it is enough at this stage to note their explicit articulation in earliest policy discourse. Indeed, these moral directives were further reiterated by the Ministry for Education in 1963 in the Newsom Report: 'For our part we are agreed that boys and girls should be offered firm guidance on sexual morality based on chastity before marriage and fidelity within it' (1963: 54). Young people's sexual instincts were clearly to be shaped by certain virtues and values towards specific ends.

It was also evident that policy was shaped by a holistic understanding of the young person and their role and responsibility within society, and vice versa. In approaching health education, the Department of Education and Science (1968) focussed on much more than simply the prevention of disease or the reduction of harm:

> Our task is rather to make sure that bodily health plays its proper part in the whole education of responsible citizens. To discharge it successfully we need a clear understanding of the nature of our civilisation and its principles. We must also have regard for realities which go beyond the merely physical. Our roots lie deep in the Christian background of our civilisation and the things of the spirit cannot be passed over. (1968: vi)

In giving explicit regard to the moral and spiritual in policy discourse, we can observe that there was also a clear *telos* towards which a public sexual ethic was directed; in other words, schools had direction in terms of the norms and behaviours they were directing young people towards, and not just the ones they were instructing them against. Accompanying this, there was clear advice to schools on approaching the issue; while parents were affirmed as the primary educators, questions arising from children within the school setting concerning their own development were to be addressed in a considered and age-appropriate manner. Adolescents were also to be prepared for future life in community, another recognized aim of sex education:

> In learning to live a full life as an adult the adolescent must understand something of both personal development and social responsibility. It is the capacity for reconciling

> personal interests with social demands that leads to stability in relationships, to the appreciation of the other person's point of view and to the sacrifice of one's own interests, if need be, in the interests of the community. (Department of Education and Science 1968: 99)

As time went on, policy guidance on health education acknowledged that schools could no longer avoid their responsibilities in the area of sex education, particularly in view of the demands of a rapidly changing culture and the nature of the information being 'thrust' at children outside of school (Department of Education and Science 1977: 112). Indeed, even for those who heralded the 'sexual revolution' as a revolution of openness rather than behaviour, the challenge of equipping young people to make choices within this newly constituted sexual landscape could not be ignored (Rubin 1968a: 28; 1968b: 18).

The emerging sexual and moral norms continued to shape SRE policy discourse. Fundamental reforms surrounding its content and provision in the 1980s, including changes in its legal status, were 'driven by a clear moral and political agenda' (Thomson 1997: 261). As a result of this politicization, it was increasingly acknowledged that 'a value-less sex education programme cannot exist' (Reiss 1998: 10). There were clearly health concerns that were driving policy objectives, with the HIV and AIDS epidemic in the late 1980s reigniting the fear around the impact of sexual behaviour on the health of the nation; and as HIV and AIDS were emerging as a public health concern, sex education was becoming a 'political football' (Reiss 1998: 10).

Sex education first appeared on the statute books in England and Wales in Section 46 of the *Education (No 2) Act 1986*, making clear that where sex education was given, it was to be 'given in such a manner as to encourage those pupils to have due regard to moral considerations and the value of family life'. In comparison to earlier policy documents, the moral language had softened somewhat: rather than being given 'firm guidance', the pupils were instead to be encouraged to have 'due regard' for moral considerations. Further, in 1987 the Department of Education and Science published guidance for Local Education Authorities in *Sex Education at School: Circular No 11/87*, setting out in more detail the moral issues that required consideration. Young people were encouraged to adopt an objective and balanced approach to the diversity of attitudes and values in society. Alongside an understanding of the physical aspects of sexual behaviour, they were to be 'encouraged to consider the importance of self-restraint, dignity and respect for themselves and others and helped to recognise the physical, emotional and moral risks of casual and promiscuous sexual behaviour' (1987: 197). Recognizing the responsibility that both sexes had for sexual matters, an appreciation of the benefits of 'stable married and family life and the responsibilities of parenthood' was to be fostered (1987: 197).

Similar moral ideals and values were carried through into the *Sex and Relationship Education Guidance*, published by the Department for Education and Employment (DfEE) in 2000. The Guidance was produced for Head Teachers, Teachers and School Governors, taking into account the revised National Curriculum published in September 1999, the newly established Personal, Social, Health and Economic Education (PSHE) framework, and the 1999 Social Exclusion Report on teenage pregnancy. The objective of SRE was clearly stated: 'The objective of sex and relationship education is to help and support young people through their physical, emotional and moral development. A successful programme, firmly embedded in PSHE, will help young people learn to respect themselves and others and move with confidence from childhood through adolescence into adulthood' (2000: 3).

According to the Guidance, the three main elements of SRE are concerned with attitudes and values, personal and social skills, and knowledge and understanding. With regards to attitudes and values, the following priorities were listed: 'learning the importance of values and individual conscience and moral considerations; learning the value of family life, marriage, and stable and loving relationships for the nurture of children; learning the value of respect, love and care; exploring, considering and understanding moral dilemmas; and developing critical thinking as part of decision-making' (2000: 5).

It is important to note for our own discussion that the *Sex and Relationship Education Guidance* (DfEE 2000), including the incorporated attitudes and values, was not deemed relevant just for education policy, but its importance and relevance was also carried through into the Department of Health's policy guidance on sexual health improvement. This included an adapted wording of the above attitudes and values in their policy document, shaping a moral narrative in which teaching 'ensures that pupils are taught about the benefits of loving, healthy relationships and delaying sex, and also provides that pupils are aware of how to access confidential sexual health advice and support' (Department of Health 2013: 13).

Despite these articulated attitudes and values, Adrian Thatcher (2001: 234) notes that the SRE Guidance failed to recognize spiritual and moral development as a learning outcome of SRE, set within the framework of PSHE. This is a noted departure from earlier sex education policy content, and appears to be indicative of a more widespread concern over the neglect of the spiritual in education (see, for example, RSA 2014). In addition, along with a number of apparent 'contradictions and silences' (2001: 234), Thatcher highlights what he calls the 'empty generalizations' of many terms within the document, for example, 'moral framework' (2001: 236). Such terms, he contends, remained abstract concepts without content. A further example of the perceived moral deficiency of the document was its failure to give a moral reason – over and above prudential ones – why 'delaying sexual activity' might be a good thing: 'might there not be reasons to do with virtue, perhaps, or the acquisition of good character, or of chastity, even, which provide a relevant and recognizable moral vocabulary?' (2001: 235).

Of course, such a criticism presupposes that a moral reason is required. Various reasons may or may not be given for engaging in or abstaining from a particular activity; alongside prudential and moral reasons, there are aesthetic and religious ones (Carr 1998a: 168; see also Carr 2006). Nevertheless, if a characteristic of a sexually educated young person is someone who acquires certain skills, for example, the skill of responsible decision-making, where another's needs are taken into account as well as one's own, then such skills are inherently relational and arguably 'firmly grounded in moral values' (Halstead and Reiss 2003: 7–8).

It is at least apparent from young people's experience of SRE that it is the moral and spiritual content and guidance that they have judged to be inadequate. Indeed, the *Sex and Relationship Education Guidance* (DfEE 2000) acknowledged that young people often complain that there is a 'lack of any meaningful discussion about feelings, relationships and values' (2000: 11). In a survey carried out by the Sex Education Forum (SEF) in 2008, the results revealed that school-based SRE most frequently covered topics concerning puberty, and the biology of sex and reproduction. The topic least frequently taught concerned skills for coping with relationships. As one young person commented: 'I understand the science side pretty well but it seems a bit like a pencil – I know it's made from wood and soft graphite that gets broken off, but does that tell me how to write?' In addition, Brook, the UK's largest young people's sexual health charity, published similar findings in October 2011. In a study on SRE carried out amongst 2,000 14- to 18-year-olds, only 6 per cent reported receiving information in lessons that they felt they needed on relationships. Evidence would suggest, therefore, that the content of the current moral framework has not provided young people with the moral guidance that they have judged to be necessary in helping them navigate their relationships and the moral complexity of their environment, if indeed, this were a reasonable ask of any school-based subject.

Young people's experiences have been substantiated by findings from the government's inspection of school practice. The Ofsted Report on PSHE in English schools in 2012 highlighted that in secondary schools 'too much emphasis was placed on "the mechanics" of reproduction and too little on relationships, sexuality, the influence of pornography on students' understanding of healthy sexual relationships, dealing with emotions and staying safe' (Ofsted 2013: 6–7). Thus, responses to the Department of Education Consultation on PSHE in 2013 reiterated the importance of relationships education: 'It was suggested that pupils were being taught about the mechanics of sex without an understanding of relationship management, and that the latter was vital to ensure children and young people appreciated and respected themselves and their peers' (2013a: 4). The government reaffirmed that PSHE is expected to 'equip pupils with a sound understanding of risk and with the knowledge and skills necessary to make safe and informed decisions' (Department for Education 2013b). The perceived absence of moral and spiritual content and guidance is indicative of a shifting moral narrative in SRE discourse – one that has increasingly placed the onus on the young person to make their own 'informed' decisions according to their own self-scripted morality; the so-called 'consensus' position in SRE.

Seeking Moral 'Consensus' on SRE Policy

Arriving at the moral position of 'informed choice' has clearly been the culmination of a concerted and noteworthy effort to reach moral consensus on the 'right' policy approach to SRE. However, the process of doing so was initiated on a flawed premise: that moral consensus could be achieved by removing the philosophical moorings that give content and meaning to moral knowledge. Rachel Thomson, former chair of the Sex Education Forum (SEF), a leading advisory body on SRE policy and practice, suggested that consensus around a moral framework for SRE would be achieved by moving the discussion *away* from the 'abstract territory' of moral and religious philosophy and into consideration of the realities of young people's lives (1997: 267). In doing so, she proposed that we should simply face the future with optimism and trust that young people will emerge from this world of constant moral innovation, unscathed: 'To turn our faces from the past to the future will require an admission of uncertainty and the expression of trust' (1997: 268–269). This includes, suggests the sexual rights campaigner, Peter Tatchell, entrusting young people with the full range of information on sex and relationships: 'Most will respond to such candour by making sensible, responsible decisions. Those who do not would be reckless anyway, regardless of what they were taught or not taught' (2002: 70).

In a similar tone to Thomson and Tatchell, Simon Blake and Gill Frances suggest that if we regard SRE as an 'educational entitlement, not a social engineering initiative' (2001: 44), then our obligation is to ensure that we provide this entitlement. In doing so, we take a 'leap of faith' in believing that young people will be enabled to make informed decisions according to their own moral code (2001: 44). The only prerequisite to programme effectiveness, they suggest, is that they are able to enjoy their experience, while taking responsibility for themselves and their partner.

However, this apparent faith in young people's moral intuition is not an abandonment of moral philosophical engagement; instead, explicit moral judgements are simply being subverted in favour of a perceived 'neutral' discourse – one which seeks to promote rational, autonomous decision-making. This, Blake and Frances maintain, is the 'consensus' position with regards to SRE, where the educational focus is upon the 'acquisition of knowledge, the development of skills and the clarification of attitudes and values' (2001: 52). It was at least the position adopted within the 'Education Framework' of the Sex Education Forum, in which the 'three key elements to SRE' were articulated: 'acquiring information; developing skills; and exploring attitudes and values' (2005: 2).

Two key projects took place in the 1990s which shaped the moral narrative of this 'consensus' position. The first project, led by the Sex Education Forum, rejected the promotion of a single moral standpoint, instead reaching consensus on the fact that sex education should be 'relevant to all young people; respectful of the cultural and religious identities of the individual; understanding and accepting of diversity' (Thomson 1993: 4). The project encouraged rational engagement with shared values as part of the process of moral development, with the young person being encouraged to engage with, and being helped by the educator to understand, the implications of their own moral understandings (Thomson 1993: 9). At the same time the project recognized the part that religion might play in an individual's spiritual and moral development and the importance of religion as one aspect of an individual's identity, and, in particular, one factor in shaping a young person's sexual identity.

While recognition of the contribution that religion makes to moral and spiritual development should be self-evident, it is important to note that the Sex Education Forum's conclusions on the nature of this contribution paint a disjointed view of identity formation. In particular, it fails to appreciate the overarching influence a cohesive worldview, whether a religious or a secular one, can have in providing a moral framework that informs, shapes and directs all aspects of life, including sexuality. After all,

'all ethical reflection and action occurs in the context of a larger worldview' (Hollinger 2009: 43).

Mike Bottery identifies this as a problem of liberalism, in that it fails to appreciate the 'rootedness' of individuals within their cultural and religious communities, a strength of identity that often precedes their own sense of individuality (1998: 159). This is an important observation for educators and policy-makers in the future development of 'religious-appropriate' RSE curricula content; at least the assumption should not be made that a culturally defined understanding of sexuality can easily be 'foregrounded' (Shipley 2017: 171) as an identity category to be explored, without first affirming the pervading influence that religion can have in grounding identity and belonging.

The second project, which sought to achieve a shared moral understanding within SRE discourse, echoed the moral conclusions of the first. In *Sex Education, Values and Morality*, the Family Planning Association and Health Education Authority concluded that when it comes to developing a values framework for sex education programmes within a pluralist society, achieving consensus on attitudes, values and beliefs was not necessary. Indeed, as a general principle, the promotion of one particular lifestyle to young people was not considered good practice. Instead, in accepting and celebrating difference, and promoting a moral framework of equal opportunity and respect, it was recognized that 'values cannot be imposed, but children can be equipped with the skills needed to allow them to develop their own' (Family Planning Association 1994: 5).

This approach reflects a 'values clarification' theory of moral education, where the focus is on the 'process of valuing', and 'whatever values one obtains should work as effectively as possible to relate one to his world in a satisfying and intelligent way' (Harmin, Raths and Simon 1966: 28). This process of moral evaluation and discernment also echoes what Halstead and Reiss (2003: 61) identify as the three fundamental values within a liberal education: freedom, equality and rationality. In particular, as we have already noted, they point to the development of the rational mind of the young person – encouraging open, critical thinking – which cuts to the very heart of liberal education. Yet, while recognizing the significant role that this rationality plays in moral development, Halstead and Reiss caution against a narrow understanding of the young person 'that ignores the emotions and dispositions and a balanced sense of personhood' (2003: 65).

In effect, both projects emphasized the distinction between 'prescriptive' and 'enabling' values in sex education, promoting the latter as a way of developing a moral language that establishes consensus around the 'thou shalt', as opposed to the 'thou shalt not' of sexual behaviour (Thomson 1997: 265). Such an approach, it was argued, develops a moral framework that is inclusive rather than exclusive (Thomson 1993: 11), one in which young people should be given the freedom to explore and develop their own moral code (Blake and Francis 2001: 52). However, two immediate challenges arise in adopting this approach to policy discourse. The first is the impossibility of achieving a morally 'neutral' discourse.

The Impossibility of a Morally 'Neutral' Discourse

J. Mark Halstead and Michael Reiss, in *Values in Sex Education: From Principles to Practice*, propose two possible reasons why a morally neutral discourse within SRE might be viewed as preferable: first, 'the diversity that exists in contemporary society makes a consensus on values impossible, especially in a controversial domain like sexuality'; second, 'anything that gets in the way of the "safer-sex" message (such as moral guidance or advice) should be discarded as more of hindrance than a help' (2003: 8). Even where clarity is achieved through philosophical discourse, it may still 'illuminate complexities, sharpen dilemmas, undermine grounds for practical compromise and encourage further discussion and argument rather than decision' (McLaughlin 2005: 26). Therefore, seeking to move beyond philosophical discourse in the formulation of SRE policy may prove attractive in that it seemingly avoids conflict in decision-making. Yet even with a sympathetic hearing, these reasons still cannot achieve the illusion of moral neutrality. Indeed, attempting it is itself an expressed philosophical approach to moral education.

Instead, abandoning the philosophical roots of different approaches to SRE is not only to judge each one to be as morally tenable as the other – which itself is a philosophical commitment – but is to undermine the necessity of having a reason or defence for your policy position in the first place. As Carr points out, 'it is one thing to know quite well (in our bones) what is morally right, and another to understand why or how it is right' (2003b: 74). Moreover, seeking to move beyond the 'abstract territory' of philosophy in policy-making not only abandons the constructive and necessary task of philosophical inquiry, it also overlooks the philosophical presuppositions that are already implicitly embedded in education policy: 'Many educational policies contain (to a greater or lesser extent) assumptions, concepts, beliefs, values and commitments which, if not themselves of a directly philosophical kind, are apt for philosophical attention' (McLaughlin 2005: 19).

Thus, even for those who advocate a rights-based approach to SRE (see Ingham and Stone 2006: 194), appearing to adopt a position of entitlement rather than prescription, such philosophical judgements cannot be avoided. Philosophical discourse should not, therefore, be judged to simply exist within the realm of abstract ideas, with no relevance to reality, but it should instead be seen as a necessary and inevitable part of policy formulation, providing the foundations for a concrete vision of educational outcomes. This includes the philosophical and educational judgements being of a practical nature (McLaughlin 2005: 29), for practical morality is 'designed to produce certain types of persons, with specific virtues, mentalities, habits and skills directed to affect the world in a certain way' (Rorty 1999: 8).

Therefore, in dismissing any suggestion of neutrality, Halstead and Reiss instead assert that 'values permeate every aspect of sex education' (2003: 4), with values being defined as follows: 'Values are *principles and fundamental convictions which act as general guides to behaviour; enduring beliefs about what is worthwhile; ideals for which one strives; broad standards by which particular beliefs and actions are judged to be good, right, desirable or worthy of respect*' (2003: 5, italics in original). This permutation is in and of itself inevitable, for as they point out, 'sex education must in some way be educational, and education is an inescapably value-laden activity' (2003: 7).

As such, when it comes to exploring the nature, role and outworking of values in the moral framework of SRE, Halstead and Reiss rightly observe that disagreement over the aims and practices of sex education emerges when values come into conflict with one another. For there can be little disagreement over the biological facts of sex instruction, which in themselves are 'value-neutral'. These are arguably the easiest aspects of any sex education programme to learn (Collyer 1995: 29). Instead, it is in the presentation of the facts that an implicit moral framework emerges, presenting a particular vision of the moral self and human flourishing.

As we shall set out in Chapter 2, it is possible to observe the emergence of explicit and implicit value judgements from the outset of SRE policy discourse. For now it is sufficient to note that what the expressed philosophical commitment of Blake and Frances – as demonstrated in their views on programme effectiveness – at least highlights is both a predisposed moral position on teenage sexuality and a determined value judgement on the desired nature, aim and value of SRE. In addition, their expressed views are wrongly dismissive of the inevitable reality that every educational enterprise is an initiative in social engineering as it encourages or discourages certain choices or behaviours. This is true for the individual educator, where 'our private metaphysics and emotional prejudices remain private only so long as we are private citizens; once we take on the role of the educators, they come out into the open' (Wilson 1965: 99). It is also true for the state. One of the earliest critics of political liberalism, James Fitzjames Stephen, affirmed this to be the case: 'How is it possible for society to accept the position of an educator unless it has moral principles on which to educate? How, having accepted that position and having educated people up to a certain point, can it draw a line at which education ends and perfect moral indifference begins?' (1967 [1873]: 157). Therefore, whether it is acknowledged or not, 'school sex education is intended, for good or ill, to influence attitudes and behaviour' (Riches 1998: 36).

In light of this, and faced with the diversity of moral values that are vying for attention within SRE policy discourse, it would appear at least consistent with democratic aspirations to echo the sentiment of Graham Haydon in suggesting that engaging in philosophical discourse can lay the groundwork for 'more reasonable and informed discussion' on these values (1993: 17), giving public legitimacy to the process of moral inquiry. This involves a positive approach to the richness and diversity within the ethical environment (Haydon, 2004). At the very least, actively engaging in philosophical discourse within SRE policy formation will explore and articulate the nature, aims and value of SRE and enable adequate scrutiny of the different philosophical propositions and moral visions presented therein. This includes engagement with different religious worldviews, which leads us to the second challenge in merely accepting a perceived 'consensus' position within SRE discourse: the ongoing place of religion at the policy table.

The Place of Religion at the SRE Policy Table

In the interests of defending liberal principles, it is important to ensure that an implicit reason for the explicit rejection of the 'abstract' nature of moral and religious philosophy in the policy-making process is not on account of the desire of secularists to dismiss the prevailing influence of religion in the public square, particularly within education or on matters concerned with articulating a public sexual ethic. A. C. Grayling, for example, suggests our cultural confusion and preoccupation with sex is on account of the 'absurdly inflated' position that sex occupies on society's moral landscape. This is due, he suggests, to the prevalence of ancient law and customs, particularly associated with Christianity, with 'prohibitions, anxieties and what amounts to social rationing' exaggerating its importance (1997: 23). At the same time, he acknowledges the complexity of the issue, and the 'dramatic challenges' that have emerged as a result of 'sex-related dilemmas', pointing to teenage sex and pregnancy as one such challenge. In doing so, he recognizes that, 'despite the increased openness which has permitted objective research into human sexuality, there is still no widely accepted theory about it upon which personal decision or public policy-making can rely' (1997: 26). Therefore, while religion may be perceived to over-exaggerate the issue, addressing such 'sex-related' dilemmas cannot avoid the moral judgements that the secularist may seek to avoid. For even in the absence of explicit religious voices, the challenge of reaching moral consensus around appropriate and inappropriate sexual behaviour remains.

Alongside the vocal opposition to a religious sexual ethic, secularists seek to remove the influence of faith more widely from the arena of education. It is important to address, therefore, whether the current moral discourse around this policy issue – as, indeed, with any other issue of public policy – is open to the critique and contribution of religion. In view of the government's commitment to ensure that future Relationships Education and RSE is 'appropriate to the age of pupils and their religious background' (DoE 2017: 4), it is hard to imagine how this contribution can be overlooked or dismissed. Indeed, a renewed discussion around 'plurality' in SRE provision in light of the increased multicultural make-up of our communities has been raised as a key issue of 'serious concern' that needs to be addressed (Sundaram and Sauntson 2016: 2).

Engaging in political discourse will involve grappling with and seeking resolution to difficult moral questions, questions that invariably raise different understandings of the nature of reality and human flourishing. Importantly, it is worth reiterating that moral questions and propositions are not just the preserve of religious discourse. As Oliver O'Donovan points out, while it may be possible for a humanist to understand the nature of reality in 'natural' rather than 'supernatural' terms, it is not possible for them to leave unanswered the question, 'What is the chief and highest end of man?' (1994: 38). Therefore, framed within the liberal democratic policy process, it should be safe to assume that every expressed view undergoes the same level of intellectual and moral scrutiny, and that holding to a different standpoint is not automatically deemed intolerant. In addition, pursuing the liberal ideal does not assume or equate with moral indifference. It is worth reminding ourselves that J. S. Mill's vision of the liberal state did not include a society in which one should not actively engage in expressing opinions and judgement on the other's good (Crisp 1997: 187). Mill pointed instead to a freedom that should exist within liberal society to address the apparent 'folly' or 'depravation of taste' of the other without the need for, or threat of, any legal sanction (Mill 2006 [1859]: 77). According to Mill's vision of liberalism, the only thing that is unacceptable is coercion: 'We may cajole, entreat, exhort and otherwise try to persuade another person to act as we propose, and this does not reduce their liberty; it is coercion and coercion alone that we may not engage in' (Ryan 2006: xxviii).

Therefore, in a pluralistic context, where sources of morality are inevitably disputed, an account of morality grounded in anything other than social agreement 'is for most citizens of contemporary secular-liberal societies almost beyond comprehension' (Carr 2003b: 72). However, the assumption that a 'religious voice' is any less rational or any less constructive than the other voices in this process, and might therefore be more readily dismissed, is strongly contestable. As Nick Spencer suggests: 'All public engagement is, in a sense, faith-based engagement in as far as it is premised on conceptions of the good that are not necessarily shared or provable' (2011: 298). He continues: 'If we are to hope to reach any resolution or, less ambitiously, some satisfactory modus vivendi in our politics, we all need to be prepared, as it were, to show our moral workings' (2011: 298). Religious voices, alongside all other voices, should therefore be prepared for such openness and scrutiny. This should not result in the coercive imposition of any one position, including a religions one, but the careful consideration of all voices present, and the pursuit of constructive agreement.

Pursuing of the Common Good in SRE

In line with the pursuit of constructive agreement on public matters, Nigel Biggar suggests that a reasonable theological contribution to public discourse will 'not invoke divine commandments without taking care to explain these in terms of their service of human flourishing and the goods that comprise it' (2009: 167). This involves articulating an argument 'all the way from the top to the bottom, all the way from theological premise through moral principle to the careful analysis of cases' (2009: 172). At the very least, civic life is strengthened, suggests acclaimed political philosopher, Michael Sandel, when moral engagement allows the expression of differing moral and religious convictions: 'A politics of moral engagement is not only a more inspiring ideal than a politics of avoidance. It is also a more promising basis for a just society' (2010: 269).

Thus, in proceeding on the assumption that civic life is strengthened – not threatened or diminished – by religious convictions, two important and influential positions in contemporary policy discourse on education are thus directly challenged: first, the explicit and implicit position within SRE policy circles that engaging in moral discourse around the meaning and purpose of the subject is no longer a necessary precondition of policy formation; second, the expressed view that religion – outside of the RE classroom – has nothing constructive to contribute to the moral framework of education policy.

In response to the latter, Trevor Cooling contends that theological insight and education are not incompatible within a secular educational context and, indeed, that religious beliefs, rather than being viewed within education as an unwelcome problem, should be seen as a 'potential resource that contributes social capital through promoting the common good' (2010: 58). In doing so, he draws the important distinction between a secular and a secularist society: while the first welcomes the contribution made by religions in contributing towards a community framework of values, the second seeks to eradicate religious influence from the public square (Cooling 1994: 69). In effect, he argues for a 'transformationalist strategy' within education, which seeks to expound Christian belief within, and not apart from, a secular, pluralistic context, in a spirit of genuine partnership and in a way that 'honours both the needs of the context *and* our beliefs' (1994: 153). In clarifying his theological premise, he states: 'The theological rationale for the position that I have been putting forward is usually expressed in terms of "natural law", "common grace", or "the way of wisdom"' (Cooling 1994: 161).

The concept of common grace presents an 'important resource for addressing the contemporary issues of commonness and difference' (Mouw: 2001: 8). It is an approach to public theology that was developed in the work of Abraham Kuyper, who recognized that, while the church has a responsibility to maintain its own distinct character, it also has a responsibility towards the society in which it exists. As a result, education policy discourse should nurture respectful tolerance for the diversity of worldviews represented, fostering a 'deliberative' model of democracy, concerned with justice and the common good (See Wolterstorff 1999; DeMoor 2014).

Thus, in pursuit of the common good in SRE, there have been calls for the development of a larger set of 'common values', offering a means through which satisfactory agreement can be reached: 'A working framework of justifiable and defensible common values must be identified and articulated if effective programmes of sex education are to be produced in a multicultural society' (Halstead and Reiss 2003: 26). This inevitably involves the adoption of some concepts and the rejection of other, which may appear to compromise the guarantee of individual rights and liberties. However, in exploring the relation between community and rights, John Finnis notes: 'The pursuit of any form of human community in which human rights are protected by the imposition of duties will necessarily involve both selection of some and rejection of other conceptions of the common good, and considerable restrictions on the activities of everyone' (1994: 44–45).

In pursuing common ground and a community framework of values, there will inevitably be controversial issues on which it is impossible to achieve a unanimously agreed policy position; nevertheless, value judgements must still be made. For example, a significant value judgement within the 1987 Circular (No 11/87) on *Sex Education at School* was the expressed objection to any acceptance or promotion of homosexual behaviour: 'There is no place in any school in any circumstances for teaching which advocates homosexual behaviour, which presents it as the "norm", or which encourages homosexual experimentation by pupils' (197). At the same time, the Circular recognized that schools cannot avoid tackling controversial issues, and, therefore, should be prepared to give balanced and factual information, taking into account their own ethical and religious contexts.

Similarly, in light of the introduction of the Marriage (Same Sex Couples) Act 2013, the Equality and Human Rights Commission (2014) notes: 'No school, or individual teacher, is under a duty to support, promote or endorse marriage of same sex couples. Teaching should be based on facts and should enable pupils to develop an understanding of how the law applies to different relationships' (2). Marriage is now clearly an 'ideologically-contested' term (Sauntson and Sundaram 2017: 100), where different understandings must now be more clearly articulated and presented. Yet, difficult cases notwithstanding, David Hollenbach suggests that a respect for diversity does not inevitably result in the abandonment of shared goods. Instead, a vision of the common good in a pluralistic society presents the challenge of reaching 'an understanding of the goods that we can and must pursue together even though we do not agree about what is good in every aspect of life' (2002: 68).

Conclusion

Despite the opportunities to date for discussion and reflection on this wider set of 'common values', it is clear that dialogue has emerged largely out of, and thus, in support of a narrow liberal values framework. Where moral and spiritual content and outcomes were previously explicit in policy discourse, the attention and focus of the moral narrative has clearly shifted towards a perceived liberal neutrality and consensus.

Terence McLaughlin identified the crux of the difficulty in developing a shared approach to moral education in a pluralist society – its members do not share '"thick" or substantial views of human good' (2008: 52). Instead, shaped by the principles of liberalism, consensus is sought over 'basic or "public" values' (2008: 55). He suggests that such principles, including freedom of speech, justice and personal autonomy, are 'thin' because they 'do not presuppose some particular metaphysical theory of the self, or of the nature of human destiny' (2008: 55). Alasdair MacIntyre, in his acclaimed philosophical critique of the 'Enlightenment Project', noted similar: 'Liberal political societies are characteristically committed to denying any place for a determinate conception of the human good in their public discourse, let alone allowing that their common life should be grounded in such a conception' (2007: xii). At the heart of what he judges to be the failure of liberalism is the disconnection between concepts of morality on the one hand and shared conceptions of human nature on the other (2007: 52).

At the same time, McLaughlin's judgement rightly recognizes the challenges of moving beyond a 'thin' view of the good within a common school context to a more 'holistic' view of education which embraces the complexity of moral and spiritual development (2008: 56). In a society where there is little moral consensus, the conceptual and practical challenges in drawing up a necessary list of common values are indeed 'legion' (Carr 2003b: 71). Compounding this challenge is the fact that, due to unlimited pluralism and the pursuit of individual spiritual enlightenment, 'the spiritual as such is no longer intrinsically related to society' (Taylor 2007: 490).

Thus, despite efforts to reach consensus on values, there is a lack of consensus on the principles that should direct, in particular, the moral dimension of sex education (McLaughlin 1998: 188). In addition, we lack a language in which to speak easily about sex in schools (Jones 1989: 69). This is unsurprising in view of the plurality of worldviews in contemporary culture; indeed, it would be naïve to presume that a single and unified language could be found to accommodate divergent understandings of the meaning and significance of human sexuality.

However, when it comes to careful scrutiny of the philosophical concepts on the table, 'rationality should above all be concerned with what is true' (Trigg 2007: 36). Our discussion will ultimately engage with what Robin Barrow identifies as a debate of 'fundamental importance' within the philosophy of education: that which concerns moral truth and knowledge. This involves seeking for the truth by dismissing beliefs which appear to be unfounded (2010: 21–35). Therefore, faced with increasing moral diversity and complexity, what is inevitable in reasoning together within public moral discourse about the meaning and purpose of SRE is that we cannot avoid engaging in moral questions concerning the meaning and purpose of human sexuality. This is in view of the fact that 'it is in the meaning of sex that we find a framework by which we make sense of our sexuality as human beings' (Hollinger 2009: 13). However, when it comes to educating children and young people on the meaning and purpose of human sexuality, it remains to be seen whether our liberal democracy still accepts the tensions in worldview commitments that emerge, and has the capacity and the will to respect diversity while pursuing shared goods; or, equally, whether it has the courage to dismiss those beliefs that appear to be unfounded. This discussion will proceed on the basis that it does.

CHAPTER 2

Why Teach Morality and Sex? Pursuing a Liberal Ideal

> Is morality a matter of conforming to certain externally imposed rules, or a matter of autonomous decision-making, learning how to apply moral principles to particular situations, or a matter of being a certain kind of person?
>
> — J. MARK HALSTEAD (2010: 256)

> We should be as free in our sexual lives as it is alleged we should be in every other part of our life. And we should teach sex in a way that is consistent with that ideal.
>
> The onus is on the critic to show why it should not be thus.
>
> — DAVID ARCHARD (1998a: 448)

We have so far observed that the challenge of deciphering the normative ideals in the existing policy discourse surrounding SRE is a complex one. Doing so at least depends on the different parties in the policy-making process showing their moral workings – a part of the process which is neither straightforward nor explicitly required. Commenting, in general, on the political ideas in the policy-making process, Robert Leach points out that public policy 'proceeds on the basis of ideological assumptions, even though these may not be clearly articulated, or even consciously recognised' (1995: 14).

More specifically, when it comes to the formation and implementation of education policy, Paul Trowler highlights some normative questions that ensue when defining government involvement in education – questions which invariably engage with political and education values. These include: 'What has been identified as the "problem" that needs to be addressed here and what other interpretations are there? Who gains and who loses from this policy? What are the likely consequences, intended and unintended, of this policy for the education system and more broadly?' (2003: 173). In effect, the right policy cannot be chosen without reflecting on, and responding to, such value-laden questions, the answers to which will inevitably shape the normative ideals of SRE. In pursuing justice and the common good, therefore, it is the role of democratic discourse to engage with and critique alternative approaches to SRE in order to establish a position on the agreed 'good' of the subject – specifically, the desired outcomes of teaching the subject, or the end to which the subject is directed.

Amongst the most careful observers, policy discourse will begin to uncover a variance in worldview perspectives; such diversity is only exacerbated by the fact that 'within any given worldview, core commitments may vary widely' (Sire 2009: 23). This suggests that the moral and value judgements made in policy discourse and decision-making around SRE are probably more implicit and complex than first observed or assumed, and the moral workings of such judgements may even be unbeknownst to those who are articulating them. In the face of these challenges, gaining an understanding of the educational values of any society can be achieved by examining the broader framework of values within the society in question (Halstead 2005a: 111).

In light of this – and in beginning our exploration of the moral and values framework that has informed SRE policy in England – we take note of the overarching liberal metanarrative shaping the political landscape, which in turn informs the system of education. Thus, the moral ideals of liberalism will shape the aims, structure and content of education, as education in turn plays a central role in upholding the ideals of liberalism (see Levinson 1999). In our discussion, we are particularly interested in the implications of this for moral education; for I will argue that the philosophical values and principles that shape SRE are reflective of the wider dominant discourse surrounding moral education. Of course, there are few subjects in the school curriculum that do not raise moral questions, but Philip Meredith considers it a 'matter of degree whether the educational value of, for example, history versus sex education lies in the acquisition of "knowledge" rather than "personal development"' (1989: 42). Clearly, sex education acquires a central moral dimension as it is concerned with human relationships (Halstead and Reiss 2003: 3).

In observing SRE within the broader framework of moral education, we also affirm in our discussion that moral education is impacted by changes in moral customs and moral philosophy (Noddings and Slote 2003: 341). This is reflective of the fact that moral education, as 'an exercise in the transmission of culture', is '*always more a reflection of the social order than a mechanism by which the social order is transformed*' (Hunter 2000: 27, italics in original).

Alongside the moral philosophical approach in moral education, therefore, policy-makers are also responding to a cultural climate experiencing rapid moral change around moral customs pertaining particularly to sexual relationships. Indeed, as a policy issue, SRE has emerged within a Western culture in which sexual values, attitudes and behaviours have changed more in the second half of the twentieth century than they have done in the previous 500 years (Halstead and Reiss 2003: 17). This can generate an increased urgency in the debate over the content of SRE policy so that it is seen to keep up with cultural changes and respond appropriately to such changes. Indeed, this was reflected in the reasons given by the Secretary of State for setting the subject on a statutory footing – reasons which include addressing issues around online safety and protecting pupils from the 'growing risks associated with growing up in a digital world' (DfE 2017: 2).

This rapid change in the cultural climate can also be reflective of, and give rise to, increased demands from a diversity of moral perspectives on sex. This only adds to the complexity of policy discourse and the decision-making process; for in engaging in a debate around the formation of a sexual ethic for sex education, 'what is at stake are different fundamental evaluations of the meaning and purpose not only of sexuality in human life but of human life itself' (McLaughlin 2001: 229). Thus, a seismic shift in society's attitudes and values towards sex and relationships will consequently result in significant changes to relevant legal and policy frameworks, eventually reflected in curricular content. Such a shift, as we will come on to explore, has been evidenced in the UK and across the Western world.

Therefore, in addition to broader political and educational ideologies at work, particularly within moral education, this societal moral shift around an understanding of sex and relationships, and its implications for the moral framework of SRE, should not be underestimated. In turn, the challenge of reaching any kind of moral consensus is further intensified. As such, Clyde Chitty rightly observes that, when it comes to the education policy-making process and the social function of education and schooling, 'no one can pretend that the relationship between education and society is straightforward or uncontroversial' (2004: 15).

Why Educate for Morality?

The increased number of articles, books and conferences on moral and spiritual education highlights the socio-political interest and debate around this aspect of contemporary education (Carr 2003c: 213). Of course, this is not a debate that is unique to our time or context; from earliest Western philosophical accounts, the purpose and effectiveness of moral education came under scrutiny. Plato, for example, pointed out that knowledge of the good was at least dependent upon the direction of one's soul towards such an attainment; at the same time, there was no assurance of success: 'the entire program of moral education which the *Republic* sketches can offer no guarantee that we will not, in the end, prefer to remain wilfully ignorant' (Meilaender 1984: 74). However, this did not dissuade from the importance of imparting a moral vision or instructing moral conscience, and the political community played a role in doing so (Meilaender 1984: 97).

Identifying the motivation for teaching morality includes offering a foundational reason for doing so; in light of this, a strong defence is offered for the importance of moral philosophical engagement in the formulation and delivery of moral education. John Elias, for example, asserts: 'Moral philosophy is valuable in making educators aware that programs of moral education must be founded on some theory of justification or criteria of right or wrong. Unless such a theory is present in the system, what takes place is not education but either a form of conditioning, training or indoctrination or a mindless relativism' (1989: 62). In reality, this philosophical engagement is not only a necessary and inevitable part of moral education but, as we shall come on to examine, evident in the normative framework of health education (see, for example, Aspin and Williams 1981).

In exploring its philosophical moorings, it is evident that moral education is not just concerned with promoting independence and self-sufficiency, but has the dual function of benefitting both society and the individual, 'at once a necessary condition for social control and an indispensable means of self-realization' (Wren 2008: 11). Thus, a liberal account of education should not infer a 'neutral' account of moral decision-making or outcomes, or an account that is independent of the normative influence and judgement of society. Instead, when it comes to moral education, David Carr and Jan Steutel affirm that different conceptual approaches are 'nothing if not philosophical' (1999a: 3), for they implicitly and explicitly express different normative assumptions and commitments. At least when it comes to functioning within a school community, for example, it is impossible to avoid value judgements on good and bad behaviour; implicit values are inevitably embedded into the philosophy of the school, its teaching practice, and what is expected of its pupils (Wakeman 1984: 22–23).

Colin Wringe presents two kinds of moral motivation for engaging in moral education. First, a 'social utility view' responds to what society identifies as delinquent or irresponsible behaviour, employing various methods to deter young people from engaging in such behaviours. This view can act, he suggests, as a response to young people's licentious sexual behaviour. In contrast, a '"group values view" identifies and educates young people according to a system of beliefs, practices and relationships' (2000a: 39). He notes that in a pluralist, liberal society, a social utility approach may be deemed preferable as it does not necessarily seek to impose prescriptive values or beliefs on the young person (2000a: 40). Nevertheless, he acknowledges that a 'social utility view' is yet shaped by the preferences of the 'adult world'. In contrast, he observes that the group values view develops qualities that are judged valuable to the young person themselves (2000a: 40). However, he concludes that within the modern world 'neither approach is entirely satisfactory' (2000a: 42), acknowledging thus the challenge for educating in moral literacy: 'Learning to live morally in a world without absolutes, as perhaps our children must, is more difficult to conceive, and may require a measure of intellectual flexibility, which the younger generation will hopefully be able to attain more easily than ourselves' (2000a: 45).

In light of this judgement, he advances an alternative approach to moral education that appeals to the rationality of the young person and seeks to esteem the rewards of good behaviour in order to empower the young person to act well. Moral education, he argues, should help the young person gain an understanding of the moral complexities of an ever-changing world, in order to cope with these and, in turn, 'forge their own version of a satisfactory way of living together after our generation's practices and preconceptions have become inapplicable and passed into oblivion' (2000a: 48). Wringe himself recognizes the complexity that this presents for the practice of moral education and the 'various demands' on the moral life of the young person (2000b: 671); yet this approach accords with what he regards as the 'master-virtue' of moral education: 'independence and self-sufficiency' (1998: 235). It also echoes what Eamonn Callan and John White identify as the extrinsic goal of a liberal philosophy of education: presenting the young person with options for living, helping them to gain an understanding of themselves, and equipping them with the qualities of character and independence of thought to stand up for what they believe in (2003: 97). The liberal values of liberty and equality are thus upheld and grounded in the moral outworking of practical reason.

Furthermore, Mill's liberal theory of education championed the contribution that the emerging moral knowledge, independently chosen, would make to social utility (1867: 39). Great merit was placed on the possibilities of knowledge in the empirical sciences advancing society and increasing human happiness; the moral influence of the church, on the other hand, was regarded as a suppressive influence, stifling the possibilities of free inquiry (Anderson 2009: 358). This was consistent with what is noted to be the desire among early proponents of modern moral philosophy – to find a basis for moral knowledge, and derive concepts and principles that were independent of church authority (Rawls 2000: 8).

From its inception, therefore, the spirit of a liberal education was one which fostered the pursuit of individual moral inquiry and respected the freedom of the individual to determine and follow their own moral path.

This liberal ideal functions as a critique to what Carr points out to be the paternalistic nature of 'educational *traditionalism*' (2004: 16), which promotes the reception of knowledge and dispositions with uncritical conformity. Instead, the exercise and development of independent critical reasoning is a central motivation of moral education, and, indeed, a liberal education itself: 'forcing young people to do what they are told without understanding why and without choosing it for themselves is anti-educational' (Halstead 2011: 340).

Why Teach Sex? Emerging Aims and Values

Alongside our discussion on moral education, and in light of the shifting moral narrative surrounding the development of SRE policy, it is possible to develop categories and frameworks within which to understand the moral aims of SRE. J. Mark Halstead identifies three key value debates within sex education: '(1) the liberal values of a "responsible sexual behaviour" approach versus the conservative values of the "pro-abstinence" approach; (2) health-based values versus education-based values; and (3) determinate cultural or religious values versus personal freedom and choice' (1998: 235). While his value categories offer a helpful breakdown, it is at least apparent that they are not in themselves self-contained. For example, religious values are often associated with the 'pro-abstinence' approach, but this does not disqualify within programme content the encouragement of responsible sexual behaviour nor a recognition and respect for the dignity and freedom of the young person to choose their own course of action. Halstead further points to the outworking of six groups of values – socio-economic values, health-related values, values related to liberal education, children's values, cultural values and religious values (1998: 247). In view of the diversity and complexity of the values at stake, Michael Reiss observes that the aims and objectives of sex education are rarely analysed in any great detail (1993: 125). Instead, he claims, the notion of sex education in schools has simply been widened and thus the aims increased.

Nevertheless, Reiss does note that principled positions on school-based sex education are often simply classified according to the 'conservative/liberal' or 'religious/secular' divide (1998: 11). He later expands his categories, identifying five mutually inclusive philosophical frameworks for sex education: 'school sex education should not occur'; 'school sex education should promote physical health'; 'school sex education should promote personal autonomy'; 'school sex education should promote responsible sexual behaviour'; 'school sex education should take place within a religious framework' (2007: 554–558). A philosophical framework is so defined if 'it attempts to address in a sustained and coherent way questions of meaning and justification relating to its presuppositions and recommendations' (2007: 554).

Furthermore, David Archard points to three reasons that have been offered for why we should teach sex in school. His reasons highlight the interchangeability and limits of the categories offered by Halstead and Reiss. In reverse order, the third reason he gives is for 'evaluative reasons': young people should be enabled to 'make their own fully informed and reasoned choices in sexual matters, to understand the proper place of sex in their lives' (1998a: 437). This accords with Reiss's third philosophical framework concerned with promoting the personal autonomy of the young person. The second reason given for teaching sex in schools is for 'social reasons', with the aim of reducing the numbers of unwanted pregnancies and cases of sexually transmitted infections (STIs) (1998: 437). As we will explore in more detail in Chapter 3, this has been a significant motivating factor behind sex education in the UK and corresponds with the justifying principles of promoting physical health and responsible sexual behaviour. Finally, it is proposed that we should teach sex firstly for 'prudential reasons' in order that young people are free from guilt or embarrassment and enjoy pleasurable sexual experiences (1998: 437). Reiss points out that in teaching sex for this purpose, a distinction should be made between embarrassment and modesty, and warns that reducing 'guilt, embarrassment and anxiety about something may have the effect of condoning it' (1993: 129).

It is important to note that justification for this first reason cannot be found in the promotion of physical health, nor is it related directly to the promotion of autonomy or responsible sexual behaviour; as we shall come on to discuss, what the recommendation exposes is an underlying philosophical commitment concerned with the fundamental nature of sex. It is a commitment that doesn't fit neatly into Reiss's five philosophical categories. In effect, it most easily accords with a religious framework, due to its explicit belief about the meaning and purpose of sexual activity. Indeed, Archard recognizes the challenge of finding agreement on the form that sex education should take, and notes the inexhaustive categories of 'liberal' and 'religious' to denote the existing divisions in sexual morality (2003: 541).

More recent attempts at categorizing philosophical discourses within sex education have been much more expansive. Tiffany Jones's detailed literature review identifies twenty-seven possible discourses that could be used to categorize approaches to sex education, highlighting the fact that different approaches to sex education 'reflect differing underlying premises, views of human nature and assumptions about pedagogical processes' (2011: 371). She notes, in particular, that policies are mostly informed by one of two constructs of the child: 'the "romantic child" whose innocence must be protected, or the "knowing child" whose innocence is not tainted by the information seen as necessary for development' (2011: 371). As an outcome of her deliberations, she presents a 'sexuality education discourse exemplar' to aid in this process of policy analysis, categorizing the 'orientation' of sex education approaches into the following four categories: 'conservative, liberal, critical or postmodern' (2011: 371).

What Jones's detailed exemplar at least demonstrates for us is that even identifying and clarifying the various discourses is complex and therefore the ability to meet the demands of every underlying premise or pedagogical approach presents a significant challenge for SRE policy deliberation and decision-making. Nevertheless, we will proceed in our discussion by returning to what we identified in Chapter 1 as the current 'consensus' position within the moral discourse surrounding SRE – the promotion of rational, autonomous decision-making.

The Liberal Ideal of SRE

For the purpose of our proceeding discussion, a 'liberal' understanding of SRE policy will accord with the one exemplified by Archard in his discussion on how we should teach sex. Promoting a liberal approach to sex education, Archard argues, will involve providing young people with the maximum amount of information relevant to their sexual choices – with choice accorded a central role in the legitimation of sexual conduct – and defending a libertarian view of sexual morality which holds that 'anything sexually goes so long as it is in private, between consenting adults, and harms no-one else' (1998a: 448). Indeed, in line with his view of the liberal end of education – that of producing independent, autonomous citizens – he suggests that teaching about sex is no different from teaching about other subjects, nor is a person's sexual life exempt from the liberty principle: 'We should be as free in our sexual lives as it is alleged we should be in every other part of our life. And we should teach sex in a way that is consistent with that ideal. The onus is on the critic to show why it should not be thus' (1998: 448). This liberal ideal has been reflected in moral education discourse around sex education. In the first edition of the *Journal of Moral Education*, Alan Harris echoed this liberal position by suggesting that, while sex education cannot impose a 'particular attitude towards "sexual morality"', it must maximize freedom for the individual by providing 'the maximum possible degree of knowledge and understanding concerning sexual behaviour' (1971: 7).

Further to our discussion in Chapter 1 on the impossibility of achieving a morally neutral discourse, Archard (2000) argues that a value-neutral position on SRE is achieved when beneficial consequences are aimed at and recognized harms are avoided, i.e. the justification for the policy is neutral. He acknowledges, nevertheless, the difficulty with this position in that every approach to sex education will argue that their position will prove maximally beneficial and the other approaches will result in harm, leaving the dilemma for policy makers as to whether they should take account of all views on sexual morality (1998: 440). In response, he suggests that the liberal may adopt the approach that only accepts those views that are deemed 'reasonable'; however, as he points out, this does not resolve questions over behaviours which may be rationally defensible yet remain morally questionable (1998: 440). Nor, indeed, does it answer the question of who, or what, determines the criteria on which a particular behaviour might be deemed reasonable. Moreover, as soon as equality becomes an ultimate value, these questions become increasingly irrelevant. Julian Rivers (2006) warns against public moral discourse reverting to a position of 'liberal agnosticism', where a conception of the good or desired outcomes is sacrificed in pursuit of moral neutrality.

It is at least recognized within SRE Guidance that programme content should include knowledge of the law on sexual behaviour (DfEE 2000: 21); clearly unconstrained freedom is neither desirable nor possible and moral autonomy must at least be constrained by socially agreed norms of behaviour. However, beyond the moral boundaries defined by the law of consent, the moral imperative of a liberal approach to SRE is one that primarily places the onus on the young person to clarify their own moral values. This was evident in the 2010 Schools White Paper in which the Coalition Government defined the 'good' of sex education as follows:

> Children need high-quality sex and relationships education so they can make wise and informed choices. We will work with teachers, parents, faith groups and campaign groups, such as Stonewall to make sure sex and relationships education encompasses an understanding of the ways in which humans love each other and stresses the importance of respecting individual autonomy (2010: 46).

In light of this, the liberal metanarrative that is currently shaping the normative ethical framework of SRE, as espoused by Archard and Harris, presents the *telos* of education as the promotion of personal autonomy. Consequently, 'informed choice' has become the moral touchstone of SRE policy rhetoric.

However, where sexual autonomy is the desired moral end, fundamental questions over the ontological foundations of moral knowledge remain unanswered, and 'epistemological agnosticism' (Carr 2004: 27) is the result of values becoming subjective and relative. Thus, questions and concerns should invariably arise over whether the liberal ideal of enlightenment rationalism provides a coherent account of moral knowledge and moral truth – truth grounded in objective moral principles – with which to shape a robust moral framework for SRE and guide sexual behaviour. In line with these questions and concerns, Carr points to what for him are a few fundamental assumptions when it comes to exploring the nature of moral education: 'that the very possibility of moral education depends upon making sense of the idea of moral enquiry; that moral enquiry depends on making sense of moral knowledge; that moral knowledge is dependent upon the possibility of moral truth; and that this, in turn, requires a substantial account of the objectivity of moral values' (1998b: 114).

Conclusion

In this chapter we have more explicitly identified the liberal metanarrative that is shaping the dominant approach to both moral education and Sex and Relationships Education. In light of this, our discussion in the proceeding chapters will present a case for why we currently have an incoherent and inadequate public vision within which to shape future Relationships Education and Relationships and Sex Education policy. It is this post-Enlightenment account of education, one in which the aim of moral education is the 'deliberate development of rational moral autonomy' (Haydon 2003: 322), which we will argue presents a flawed anthropological and epistemological understanding of moral education and formation. Haydon, for one, points to the naivety of this rationalist metanarrative on at least two counts: first, it fails to engage with the expectation that a person should conform to public norms, and, secondly, it fails to account for an individual's sources of value (2003: 323–324). Also absent from a rationalist metanarrative is an adequate consideration of motivation and feelings and, consequently, little account of actual behaviour.

Thus, we assert that a moral discourse which is overtly focussed on promoting individual autonomy through the maximization of information and rational enquiry, presents a flawed anthropological understanding of the moral agent, and a 'less than human approach' (Glanzer and Ream 2009) to moral education. On this point, we echo J. K. A. Smith's pedagogical belief that 'education is not primarily a heady project concerned with providing information; rather, education is most fundamentally a matter of formation, a task of shaping and creating a certain kind of people' (2009: 26). A Christian philosophical anthropology, as such, points to the fact that our intentional, desiring and imagining nature takes precedent over our cognitive faculties, recognizing that our desires are constantly being shaped and directed by the dominant 'cultural liturgies' (2009: 71). Although Smith is particularly concerned with a critique directed at Christian education and worship, his anthropological presuppositions – his 'liturgical anthropology' (2013: 110) – can also be used to critique the policy and practice of education more broadly.

In particular, Smith critiques the reductionist picture of the human person as purely a rationalist, thinking, believing being, a picture which he suggests has been accommodated within Christian education. This echoes Nicholas Wolterstorff's critique of a Christian education which fails to appreciate the embodied, 'praxis-orientated', nature of the learner; instead Wolterstorff calls for the development of a 'new anthropology' which gives meaning to our reality as '*interactive* creatures' (2002: 82). Indeed, within the Christian worldview, it is difficult to conceive of the moral agent apart from their social reality: 'the solitary, thinking individual posited by Descartes finds no place in Christian theological anthropology. To be human is to be-in-relation' (Bridger 1995: 25). In acknowledging the embodied nature of the moral agent in community, therefore, it is essential to recognize the normative influence of public policy in shaping the social context and informing sexual practice: 'Just what kind of person is this habit or practice trying to produce, and to what end is such a practice aimed?' (Smith 2009: 83).

The attention Smith gives, not just to ideas and values, but to the influences of dominant cultural practices and institutions in shaping the learner echoes what for Glen Stassen and David Gushee is the importance for the character ethicist in understanding the 'master narrative' of society (2003: 76). Additionally, when it comes to moral education, in particular, character education, a view of the moral agent that is overtly focussed on their capacity for moral reasoning, is limited in scope and vision. As

McLaughlin and Halstead note: 'An education in character and virtue is concerned with the formation and shaping of persons in a wide-ranging way, and is based on the realisation that what is important in education (and specifically moral education) is the sort of person one is or becomes, and not merely the nature of the thinking one engages in' (1999: 134).

Beyond the vision of the moral agent in education, the liberal metanarrative also limits political moral engagement on the common good. Challenging the inadequacy of a government's 'aspiration to neutrality' in policy decisions (2010: 246), Sandel highlights instead three moral principles which he suggests are effectively adopted when seeking to choose the 'just' policy approach: welfare, freedom and virtue. The first approach he points to seeks to apply the 'greatest happiness' principle which underlies a utilitarian moral philosophy, seeking to maximize welfare for the greatest number. The second approach argues that a just policy is one which supports a libertarian position, respecting freedom of choice and individual rights. The third approach, which he himself advocates, appeals to the cultivation of civic virtue and a shared understanding of the common good (2010: 261).

In moving forward in our discussion I will adopt his first two approaches to offer a more detailed critique of the liberal metanarrative shaping SRE policy discourse: the 'welfare principle' as applied to public health and health education, and the 'freedom of choice' principle as applied to moral education. Based on the presumption that public education is at least to some extent concerned with the moral education of its citizens, and sex education is itself a moral-laden subject, we shall re-examine the current vision from the assumption that any re-examination is a worthwhile and necessary part of ensuring the robustness of the moral framework currently in place.

CHAPTER 3

Educating for Health: Promoting Welfare and Wellbeing

> The core of health promotion is not factual, but essentially prejudiced.
> — DAVID SEEDHOUSE (2004: 91)

> There is something odd about asking people to reason for themselves when there are no criteria for good and bad reasoning; and there is something dangerously misleading about the promotion of decision-making as if this can take place outside a moral form of life, a set of moral idioms, which are more or less adequate for the problems that young people are faced with.
> — RICHARD PRING (1987: 17)

We observed in Chapter 1 that sex education, from its policy inception in England, fell within the remit of health promotion, in particular, health education. This is unsurprising in light of the fact that significant changes in work patterns and life-styles invariably have consequences for health (Eisenberg 1987: 104). What we will continue to note is that it is impossible for the state to remain neutral on policy direction and practice when it comes to sexual behaviour; there are invariably certain behaviours that will be discouraged and, equally, those that will be promoted in line with a predetermined judgement of public welfare and wellbeing. Thus, the meaning of words matters, including an understanding of sexual 'health' and 'healthy lifestyle'.

Public policy norms concerning the value of 'health' have increasingly been shaped by international policy principles as set down by the World Health Organization (WHO). In particular, the WHO Ottawa Charter, and associated publications on health promotion, unveiled the ideological belief that 'health should be viewed holistically as a positive state; it is an essential commodity which people need in order to achieve the ultimate goal of a socially and economically productive life' (Tones and Tilford 1994: 4). Within this ideological framework, and in observing the normative justification for state action, public health ethics has shown itself to be 'predominantly a child of liberalism'. Accordingly, 'the language of policy justification that liberalism offers public health is primarily a language of rights, liberties, obligations, and autonomy on the contractarian and libertarian side; and a language of interests, utilities, preferences, and beneficence on the utilitarian or welfarist side' (Jennings 2007: 31).

This liberal metanarrative is carried through into the WHO definition, where empowerment is the moral touchstone: 'Health promotion is the process of enabling people to increase control over, and to improve, their health'.[1] An empowerment model of health promotion offers a resolution to the 'dilemma' of, on the one hand, the need to safeguard and protect the public's health while, on the other, respecting the freedom of the individual, including the freedom to choose an 'unhealthy' lifestyle (Tones 1997: 33). In light of this, a number of Reiss's principled positions for sex education come into play; sex education is seen to be responsible for synonymously promoting physical health, promoting personal autonomy, and promoting responsible sexual behaviour.

Health Education: Individual Empowerment and State 'Neutrality'?

Recent decades have witnessed a broadening of the scope of health education and the growing influence of the school as a setting for health promotion, with the developing concept of the 'health promoting school' (see Denman et al. 2002; Beattie 1996; Noble and Toft 2012; Rabie 2009). This

1 <http://www.who.int/healthpromotion/conferences/previous/ottawa/en/> accessed 25 August 2014.

is unsurprising as early international policy discussion on health education and, in particular, sex education recognized that creating a desire for health was the 'major task of the health educator, and its absence the major obstacle for the sex educator' (Rowntree 1971: 269). Thus, a close relationship between health promotion and health education emerged (Weare 2002; Tones and Tilford 1994), and the school was to play a central role in promoting health. Yet while the school provides a 'captive audience' for preventative health messages, teachers and educationalists have expressed concern over schools being used for medical rather than educational endeavours (Tones 1987: 8). Therefore, one of the challenges identified in achieving 'effective healthy schools practice' is that 'there is no clear agreement about what schools are for' (Noble and Toft 2012: 144). The implication in terms of meeting policy objectives is that success can only be assessed when a clearer understanding of the values and goals of both public health and health education are articulated.

More specifically, the health education curriculum in the UK is noted to lack the roots of a distinct pedagogy and to be 'hugely influenced by the moral and political climates of the day' (Harrison 2000: 3). In observing its increased profile in school, Jennifer Harrison notes three common approaches to health and sex education in UK schools: 'a disease-orientated approach', 'a focus on risk factors', and 'a health-orientated approach' (2000: 4–5). She remarks that many programmes are often a combination of the first two, which accord with a medical model of health that is largely preventative in nature. Yet a 'medical model' is understandably criticized for its 'relatively narrow and partial interpretation of human health and illness' (Tones 1987: 6).

Along with criticism directed at a medical model, concern has also been expressed at how the evolution of health education has uncritically embraced moral education (Pring 1987: 15). A conceptual understanding of health education widened beyond the initial scientific understanding of physical health, to include concerns which were 'increasingly of a social, "life-enhancing" and moral kind' (1987: 18). SRE is one such area of health education that is particularly open to such criticism. As noted in Chapter 1, earliest policy accounts acknowledged the intrinsic moral and spiritual questions at stake in educating young people on sexual matters.

While perhaps less explicit in current discourse, these moral judgements are made nonetheless. Thus, it is fair to suggest that health promotion is 'complicated enormously' when it moves beyond the remit of disease prevention (Cribb and Duncan 2002: 39); in doing so it at least raises the question over whether what is being exercised is in fact empowerment or control. For example, in addressing the issue of teenage pregnancy, Alan Cribb and Peter Duncan highlight the fact that the ethical dilemma for health promotion centres on whether policy and practice should be shaped solely to promote 'informed choice' and personal autonomy, or whether it should be directed towards the specific goal of reducing identified 'harm' (2002: 73). They note: 'Health promoters may take on the guise of neutrality, but this will only have the effect of obscuring the values they serve' (2002: 76).

In effect, health promoters are 'committed by their profession' to promoting certain attitudes, values and ways of living that are deemed better or worse (Downie et al. 1996: 171). These attitudes and values are inevitably shaped by an underlying vision of health and human flourishing. As such, it would be 'either extremely cynical or extraordinarily naïve' to suggest that health education should enable people to enjoy complete freedom of choice (Tones 1997: 36). Also, to draw a distinction between health education and health promotion is to deny any place for persuasion in health education, and demonstrates a 'dangerous naiveté' in putting faith in 'purely rationalistic and individualist methods of health education' (Campbell 1990: 22).

Instead, in clarifying the remit and scope of health promotion, a concern for the wider interests of society and a vision for public health do not and cannot go unnoted. Indeed, a public defence for sex education has been presented within an international public health framework on such grounds: 'Since it is in the interest of every society that its members are secure, have self-respect and take a responsible attitude to their sexual life, it is in the interest of every society to prepare its members for future sexual activity' (WHO 1984: 1). Similarly, Archard highlights one reason for teaching sex in schools is so that the state can ensure its future citizens learn about sex in the 'right way' (2003: 540). Once again, in articulating what this should look like, state neutrality is an impossible end. This raises distinct ethical challenges for health promotion, not least on account of the fact that judgements are being made about what constitutes 'better health' and about 'whether and how to intervene to promote it' (Jones and Cribb 2000: 95). It becomes apparent that governments seek to empower individuals towards a vision of public health, where health education – working in partnership with policy development – creates a 'healthy public policy' in which 'the healthy choice is the easy choice' (Tones 1997: 41).

As such, despite a perceived ambiguity over the theory and practice of health promotion (see, for example, McQueen 2010), its importance is undisputed: 'the concept of health promotion is rather like virtue: it means all things to all people – who are united only in their agreement that it is rather desirable' (Tones and Tilford 1994: 2). Moreover, where particular emphasis is placed on the 'implementation of evidence-based public health interventions' (Public Health England 2015: 4) as a means of determining sexual health policy and activity, when it comes to formulating health promotion, public health and health improvement policy, Andrew Tannahill (2008) warns that decisions based solely on 'evidence' will fail to give sufficient attention to the exploration of ethical principles in deciding the appropriate action. There are also warnings that a 'pre-eminent status' can be given to health in sex education discourse which 'can outweigh other important values including important ethical and moral concerns' (Blair and Monk 2009: 42). 'Healthism' has been coined to describe an approach where health is given an ultimate value, and the value that individuals actually apportion to it is overlooked (Ewles and Simnett 1992: 41). All of these factors add to the complexity that surrounds the moral framework of SRE policy.

In light of this complexity, extrapolating on the 'good' of SRE requires a closer examination and critique of the ethical recommendations that are explicitly and implicitly evident within the normative frameworks of health promotion and health education, in particular as they relate to young people's sexual health. For while it may appear that the state remains largely impartial on when and in what context young people have sex – taking into account, of course, parameters set down by the law and child protection guidance – it clearly does not remain impartial on how. This is on account of the perceived health risks or 'harms' that young people face. Public concern and intervention, therefore, are justified most frequently on the grounds of health protection (Jones and Cribb 2000: 101). Yet in light of the different possible approaches, and the influence of the social and cultural environment, 'it is vital for schools to be clear exactly what it is that sex education programmes are trying to achieve' (Harrison 2000: 6).

What will become apparent in our discussion in this chapter is that when it comes to policy decisions concerned with promoting health, the liberal position adopted by government is one that is not just informed by the ideals of individual empowerment, but also with the principle of beneficence and maximising the welfare of the population. As the WHO makes clear, in balancing sexual rights with the harms of sexual behaviour, there is invariably a distinction made between behaviours or 'expressions of sexuality' which lead to sexual health and wellbeing and those that put people at risk or make them more vulnerable to sexual and reproductive ill-health.[2] As such, the state inevitably makes judgements in line with its vision of health and wellbeing, in particular what is judged to achieve the greatest social utility: 'Good sexual health is important to individuals, but it is a key public health issue as well' (Department of Health 2013: 2). This necessitates a public value judgement on the place of sexual health in a vision of the common good, and 'highly important' collective goods involve having 'shared or common beliefs and values' (Beauchamp 1987: 72). This inevitably moves discussion beyond a medical vision of health to 'good life promotion', which is for some an 'illegitimate extension of health promotion' as it is dependent on opinion rather than objectivity (Seedhouse 2004: 108, 111).

2 WHO, 'Sexual and Reproductive Health: Gender and Human Rights – Defining Sexual Health' <http://www.who.int/reproductivehealth/topics/gender_rights/defining_sexual_health/en/index.html> accessed 10 November 2011.

A Public Vision of 'Sexual Health'

In expounding a public vision of health promotion, it is important to note the implicit value judgements that have shaped, in particular, a political vision of sexual health. Significantly, Eli Coleman (2010) charts the shaping of public health discourse with the ideas developed within the field of sexology. The discipline of sexology, defined as 'the scientific study of sexual desire and behaviour' (Irvine 2006: 1002), drew normative conclusions on human sexuality from behavioural observations, and translated those conclusions into policy recommendations. The moral imperative of these conclusions centred on promoting the self-actualisation of sexual preference, for the proponents of sexology identified a danger in associating any one normative understanding of sex as 'healthy'. Instead, through international policy strategies for sexual health promotion, they 'reaffirmed the concept of wellbeing and the absence of disease, dysfunction and infirmity' (Coleman 2010: 138).

Thus, despite the scientific remit of the study of sexuality, the understanding that emerged clearly moved beyond mere empirical observations to incorporate a moral understanding of sexual behaviour into sexual health policy. This is evident within the current WHO working definition of sexual health:

> a state of physical, emotional, mental and social well-being in relation to sexuality; it is not merely the absence of disease, dysfunction or infirmity. Sexual health requires a positive and respectful approach to sexuality and sexual relationships, as well as the possibility of having pleasurable and safe sexual experiences, free of coercion, discrimination and violence. For sexual health to be maintained, the sexual rights of all persons must be respected, protected and fulfilled.[3]

Socially constructed notions of 'sexual health', therefore, add to the moral complexity of policy discourse, for these two words clearly carry normative weight and meaning which extend beyond physical health outcomes.

3 < http://www.who.int/reproductivehealth/topics/sexual_health/sh_definitions/en/index.html> accessed 15 August 2014.

For example, in the government's advice on sexual health improvement, alongside sexual health services, 'relationships' are also viewed as part of the strategy: 'Sexual health covers the provision of advice and services around contraception, relationships, sexually transmitted infections (STIs) (including HIV) and abortion' (Department of Health 2013: 7). Invariably, there can be no morally neutral, evidenced-based, understanding of 'relationships'. Therefore, a public sexual ethic emerges, giving shape to the content of a sexual relationship. Furthermore, Roger Ingham and Nicole Stone, in their discussion on young people and SRE, suggest that, beyond the 'absence of unintended physical outcomes', the characteristics of 'sexually healthy society' include: 'positive psychological outcomes of sexual activity, high levels of mutuality and respect both in relation to partners and to the variety of sexual preferences and, although this is seldom discussed in policy and programmatic (or even academic) deliberations, some recognition of the role of pleasure' (2006: 193–194). Such an understanding of a 'sexually healthy society', in turn, informs an understanding of the form and content of Sex and Relationships Education.

As such, sexual health policy outcomes are not simply defined or driven by physical health outcomes, i.e. the absence of unwanted pregnancy or disease, but by a vision of wellbeing and human flourishing. At the same time, governments are reluctant to appear morally prescriptive. Although 'sexual health' includes the provision of advice and services around relationships, sexual relationships are noted to be 'essentially a private matter' and, as a consequence, 'people should have the freedom to make their own decisions about the types of relationships they want' (Department of Health 2013: 7). This highlights the complexity of evaluating public health interventions, particularly when people are free to act as they will, and also belies the underlying understanding of sexuality. It points to what for Oliver O'Donovan is the 'paradox' in the liberal goal of freedom of action: 'It follows that we conceive our freedom passively, as a freedom not to suffer, not to be imposed upon. It is the freedom of consumers, rather than participants' (1984: 9).

Where the government's liberal metanarrative prescribes the promotion of relational and sexual 'freedom' as intrinsic to their understanding of sexual health, this in turn impacts on, and shapes, the moral framework of SRE. Yet total independence and freedom is a false assumption, for it wrongly presupposes that it is possible to make autonomous choices independent from the inevitable shaping of a particular moral context; it is also based on the naïve premise that government can remain neutral on all sexual choices, even if only for the reasons of reducing 'unhealthy' outcomes of sexual behaviour. The value judgements around teenage sexual health, in particular teenage pregnancy, reiterate the fact that 'good life promotion' is an inevitable part of the policy-making process.

Teenage Sexual Health: What's the 'Problem'?

In charting the historical development of SRE, it is clear that a significant motivating factor behind the introduction of policy and practice has been a public response to the 'negative' social consequences of young people's sexual behaviour, in particular the occurrence of unplanned teenage pregnancy[4] and a year-on-year rise in cases of STIs (Davidson and Sauerteig 2009: 8). This is reflected in the indicators for improved outcomes within the government's 2013 *Framework for Sexual Health Improvement in England*, where two of the three prioritised indicators are concerned directly with teenage sexual health: 'under-18 conceptions' and 'chlamydia diagnoses (15–24-year-olds)' (Department of Health 2013: 7). These are the identified 'harms' of teenage sexual behaviour, the costs of which are taken into account in any utilitarian calculus of the right policy approach towards teenage sexual behaviour.

The moral prerogative of any policy initiative therefore is one of maximising welfare – a principled approach that is favoured within health promotion – where 'people should always act in ways which mean that benefits will outweigh disadvantages' (Jones and Cribb 2000: 98). In line

4 For those working in the field of public health, 'teenage pregnancy' refers to 'conceptions in young women under 20 which end in live birth or abortion' (Dennison and Hadley 2005: 136).

with this moral reasoning, a public-health-directed SRE programme will measure effectiveness by a fall in so-called 'risky' behaviours. This gives definition to the problem, so much so that it is suggested we should be concerned about young people exploring their sexuality on public health grounds, rather than necessarily on moral or religious ones (Ingham and Stone 2006: 193). Indeed, constructing young people's sexual behaviour within policy as inherently problematic is itself deemed problematic, for experimenting in various behaviours is viewed as a normal part of the transition to adulthood from which the majority of young people emerge 'no worse for wear' (Shucksmith 2004: 12). Thus, while teenage pregnancy and childbirth are an age-old phenomenon, they have increasingly been constructed as an issue of public concern in the West,[5] and when it comes to addressing this particular health 'problem', Britain has 'one of the more advanced and long-running initiatives of its kind in the developed world' (Arai 2009: 3).

As with tackling other health concerns, education has been seen to play a key role in tackling teenage sexual health problems; this accords with Archard's 'social reasons' for teaching sex in school. For example, where ignorance was viewed within New Labour's *Teenage Pregnancy: Report by the Social Exclusion Unit* as one of the root causes of the 'problem' of teenage pregnancy (Social Exclusion Unit 1999: 7), improved education was judged to be a key mode of prevention or damage limitation. Stopping teenage girls getting pregnant was, in fact, one of the earliest aims of sex education (Reiss 1993: 126). As such, teenage sexual health promotion became a central justification for the provision of SRE.

With its far-reaching and comprehensive programme and plan of action in tackling teenage pregnancy, New Labour believed their policy agenda was moving away from one of moral judgement to one of evidence-based practice: 'what had been portrayed as a moral problem was now (re)presented as a technical, or scientific, problem' (Stapleton 2010: 16).

5 UNICEF records teenage fertility rates under the category of risk taking behaviours. Out of the twenty-nine countries reported upon, the UK, behind Romania and the US, had the third highest rate of teenage births (above 29 per 1000) (UNICEF 2013: 26).

Once again, however, an evidenced-based approach to policy-making falsely pre-supposes the possibility of achieving a value-neutral stance on sexual behaviour within policy discourse. While it might be assumed that matters of health are devoid of value judgements – that the subject matter of health promotion 'just *is* a problem' (Seedhouse 2004: 80) – health 'problems' like teenage pregnancy are only problematic to the extent that they do not correspond with a vision of wellbeing, human flourishing and societal 'good'. Indeed, it is 'neither possible nor preferable to avoid ideological thinking in policy making' (Trowler 2003: 164).

Where a continued reduction of under-16 and under-18 conception rates remains a key priority in the government's ambitions for sexual health improvement, social and economic, as well as health reasons, are given to justify why teenage pregnancy remains problematic (Department of Health 2013: 37–38). Indeed, the economic and social fall-outs from teenage parenthood are identified as both a cause and a consequence of teenage pregnancy (Cunningham-Burley and MacIntyre 1993: 71). Thus, it would appear that socio-economic values have dominated political discourse in recent years, with the prevention of social exclusion becoming the focal point for government intervention (Social Exclusion Unit 1999: 4–5). Although not wanting to 'condone' young people engaging in underage sex, the 'clear and consistent message', which was to flow from New Labour's policy, was the emphasis on the socio-economic 'cost' of pregnancy and parenthood for teenagers (Social Exclusion Unit 1999: 5).[6] In line with this moral judgement, New Labour reframed the problem of teenage pregnancy, and teenage mothers 'moved from being deviants to being "dependents"' (Arai 2009: 131).

However, in attempting to move from moral judgement to evidence-based practice, a false dichotomy is created within health promotion between evidence and values. As David Seedhouse affirms, '*a judgement about a person's health necessarily depends upon evidence* and *the interpretation*

6 In 2004, the Health Development Agency reported that teenage pregnancy among under-18s costs the NHS alone an estimated £63 million a year (*Teenage Pregnancy: An Overview of the Research Evidence*, <http://www.nice.org.uk/niceMedia/documents/teenpreg_evidence_overview.pdf> accessed 13 March 2013.

of that evidence'; and while 'the evidence is not mute', it also 'never speaks entirely for itself' (2004: 89, italics in original). He concludes that 'different health promoters hold different sets of prejudices' and that 'in all cases it is political philosophy (however implicit) which fires health promotion' (2004: 91). Particular policy attention therefore continues to be directed towards the issue of teenage pregnancy, and the justification for which continues to be the potential social exclusion of the mother, with concern expressed over associated levels of poverty, low aspirations, poor educational outcomes and the impact on future employment opportunities (Department of Health 2013: 56).

Of course, the socio-economic fallout of teenage pregnancy is not the only issue of concern. Other issues might include 'underage sex, unintended pregnancy, unwanted pregnancy, sex outside of stable relationships, abortion, single parenthood, unwaged parenthood and unmarried motherhood' (Cribb and Duncan 2002: 67). Consequently, at the heart of the 'problem' of teenage pregnancy, suggest Cribb and Duncan, is an ill-defined moral judgement: 'There is nothing wrong with teenage pregnancy *per se*. It is an indirect label for a whole cluster of issues which require separate consideration' (2002: 67, italics in original). In fact, many of the issues that define teenage pregnancy as problematic are judged equally problematic for women of other ages (Cunningham-Burley and MacIntyre 1993: 65).

Indeed, it is perhaps pregnancy for other ages that should be judged more problematic. After all, many teenage mothers are not only biologically in their prime, but are 'better supported by kinship networks than their older, more affluent, contemporaries' (Stapleton 2010: 21). In light of this, concerns over young motherhood 'may have less to do with qualms about their welfare and more to do with sexual double standards' (Stapleton 2010: 21). This appears to reflect an ill-defined and incoherent public moral judgement on teenage sexual behaviour, and such observations highlight how confusion in defining the problem of teenage sexual behaviour can create ambiguity in the moral narrative that shapes policy outcomes and the content of what is taught in the classroom.

Determining the 'Right' Sexual Health Policy

In observing the liberal metanarrative shaping health education and sexual health promotion – where sexually moral behaviour is that which, according to Archard, 'harms no-one else' – the adequacy of a utilitarian calculus as a moral guide for individual and political action is found wanting. Specifically, in seeking to maximise happiness or pleasure, the full extent of the actual consequences, as opposed to just the expected ones for any sexual choice, are impossible to measure – both publicly and privately. This is illustrated by the results from *The National Survey of Sexual Attitudes and Lifestyles* which revealed that over half of women who had had sex before the age of 16 judged it in hindsight to have been too soon (Fields et al. 1994: 80).

Not only is it difficult for the individual to ascertain the consequences of their own actions, it is arguably impossible to measure the impact on all those affected; for how could such a 'measurement' fully assess the unintended short and long-term consequences of an act and how long would one have to wait to do so (Lennox 2004: 21). Even the most ardent proponents of sexual freedom argue that, in adopting an ethically responsible position, 'decisions are subjects of judgement and projection, and their outcomes are only slowly revealed' (Kirkendall 1976: 21). Indeed, there remains a long-standing critique directed against the adequacy of a utilitarian judgement on measuring the effects on all those concerned: 'Men are so closely connected together that it is quite impossible to say how far the influence of acts apparently of the most personal character may extend' (Fitzjames Stephen 1967 [1873], 145).

Nevertheless, in attempting to measure social utility, what we can observe and measure consequentially – at least in part and in the short term – are the physical health outcomes of current sexual norms in behaviour. These have resulted in significant 'harm', including unintended pregnancies, abortion, and an increase in cases of STIs. Limited progress was made during the lifetime of New Labour's Teenage Pregnancy Strategy; despite New Labour's ten-year goal to halve the number of conceptions among under-18s, the rate of under-18 conceptions in England between

1998 and 2008 fell by only 13 per cent (Teenage Pregnancy Independent Advisory Group, 2010). Recent figures show that teenage pregnancy rates have reached an all-time low, with the under-18 conception rate for 2014 in England and Wales recorded as the lowest since 1969.[7] Yet women aged 16 to 19 have the highest proportion of pregnancies that are unplanned (45 per cent) (Public Health England 2017: 22). Public Health England findings further report that young people aged 15 to 24 continue to experience the highest STI diagnosis rates (2017: 5), and when 'compared to people aged 25 to 59, STI diagnosis rates in under 25s are twice as high in men and seven times higher in women'.[8]

Despite health promotional messages targeting unprotected sex, these figures would suggest that the message or approach remains ineffective. Indeed, research shows that some young women, while being fully aware of the consequences of unplanned pregnancy, are choosing to reject the use of contraception and are continuing to have unprotected sex (Department for Health 2013: 33). Yet in line with the moral mantra of empowerment, the rejection of the 'healthy' decision is in fact a morally legitimate one. Perhaps such choices – including 'unsafe sex' and 'intercourse without contraception' – are more akin to 'bad habits' (Tatchell 2002: 64). Addressing these habits, suggests Tatchell, includes presenting safer sex as an 'attractive, sexy alternative', as well as encouraging kids to explore other means of sexual arousal (2002: 76). An increased openness about masturbation is another proposed way of achieving public health targets (Ingham 2014). Thus, it is not so much sexual behaviours themselves that raise moral questions, but the consequences of them in terms of achieving desired health outcomes.

In light of this moral calculus, Alan Soble warns that deciding what amounts to 'harm' in the public sphere has 'profound implications': 'a narrow notion of harm yields a permissive (sexual and nonsexual) ethics, providing little justification for using the criminal law to interfere with

7 <https://www.ons.gov.uk/peoplepopulationandcommunity/birthsdeathsandmarriages/conceptionandfertilityrates/bulletins/conceptionstatistics/2014> accessed 25 June 2017.

8 <https://www.brook.org.uk/press-releases/latest-sti-figures-show-young-people-remain-most-affected-group> accessed 25 June 2017.

behaviour; a broad notion of harm (which might include more offensiveness) implies the opposite' (2008: 102). As a result, he suggests that it is possible to argue on utilitarian grounds for the widespread use of contraception in order to reduce unwanted pregnancies, recognizing the difficulty in defining the 'good' and 'bad' consequences of making such a choice (2008: 103). Indeed, the moral justification for doing so, it could be argued, is particularly applicable to young people, in view of the perceived social and economic fallout of teenage pregnancy. In following through the logic, it is clear that a significant emphasis has been placed on improving outcomes through contraceptive provision and STI testing. It is estimated that for every £1 that is invested in contraception, the NHS will save £11, on top of savings made to welfare benefit costs, and figures from 2011 estimate that 'the provision of contraception saved the NHS £5.7 billion in healthcare costs that would have had to be paid if no contraception at all was provided' (Department of Health 2013: 39). It was also estimated that a quarter of funds transferred to local authorities in England in April 2013 for their public health responsibilities would be spent on sexual health services (Department of Health 2013: 39), evidencing the widespread emphasis on and provision of contraceptive services. Excellent sexual health practice, therefore, accords with providing young people with widespread and comprehensive contraceptive provision.[9]

Indeed, where harm is defined within narrow socio-economic parameters, it may be difficult to argue why long-acting reversible contraception (LARC) does not become a morally legitimate option for teenage girls, indeed all teenage girls. This is particularly the case in light of the fall in condom use among sexually active young people in England and the proven effectiveness of LARC methods over condoms in preventing pregnancy (Department of Health 2013: 10). Anecdotally, a columnist in *The Times* newspaper, commenting in 2012 on the six fold increase over the previous five years in the number of girls of 15 years and under who

9 See NICE (National Institute for Health and Care Excellence), 'Contraceptive Services with a Focus on Young People up to the Age of 25' <http://www.nice.org.uk/guidance/PH51/chapter/introduction-scope-and-purpose-of-this-guidance> accessed 1 July 2014.

had received the contraceptive implant from a school-based NHS clinic, admitted that 'contraceptive implants are an ugly measure, a flawed fix, that should rightly make society uncomfortable. But they are better than a lifetime of trouble for yet another vulnerable girl' (Turner 2012). A narrow definition of harm amounts to a permissive ethic. It should not be overlooked, of course, that the contraceptive implant offers the teenage girl zero protection from STIs, a serious consideration for any moral calculus in view of the STI rates among young women.

Moreover, in critiquing the liberal metanarrative shaping the policy discourse of health education, the danger exists that the concept of 'harm' is too narrowly defined and the negative consequences of sexual behaviour are reduced to unplanned pregnancy, abortion and STIs. Of course, this is not to downplay the significance of these outcomes. John Green, for example, points out that 'arguably no area of medicine brings in more psychological factors than sexually transmitted diseases' (2002: 21). Nevertheless, health promotional messages are in danger of being reduced to the avoidance of 'unprotected' sex, i.e. the failure to use contraception or to use it effectively (see, for example, Cates, Genuis and Steiner 2008). If the notion of harm associated with young people's sexual behaviour was broadened to include issues pertaining to their relational and emotional wellbeing, or, indeed, if evidence was to show damaging effects of LARC methods of contraception on young girls' developing bodies, we may well arrive at a different conclusion concerning their sexual behaviour.

Consequences of sexual behaviour invariably extend beyond the outcomes for physical health. To argue otherwise is to disconnect sex from a view of personhood, and reduce it to a mere biological function. Sexual activity at least occurs within, and contributes towards, our emotional wellbeing and development (Brandon 2009: 51), a view which corresponds with the WHO definition of sexual health. Indeed, sexual choices may also have adverse long-term implications for the quality of future relationships (Addo et al. 2012). Therefore, without at least an understanding of the psychological and emotional aspects of underage sex, including cognitive immaturity, the risks associated with teenage sex are only increased (Stuart-Smith 1996: 390–391).

In light of the limits of this liberal metanarrative, it is possible, of course, to point to other areas of public health policy in which the government has adopted a more paternalistic approach to lifestyle choices. For example, based on a calculation of 'harm' to the health of the individual and public at large, governments have introduced legislation around alcohol use and cigarette smoking, often by means of commercial regulation,[10] or regulating behaviour in the public space.[11] There have also been calls from the medical profession for the government to ban junk food adverts before the watershed and tax fizzy drinks, in order to tackle the national obesity crisis.[12] Such action is seen to encourage concern for the good of the wider population (Beauchamp 1987: 76). Of course, not all of these behaviours or policy judgements are morally equivalent. In contrast to discouraging tobacco use, for example, where it can be argued that the value that guides public policy is the uncontroversial and universal value of health (Verweij 2007: 195), the reasons that determine, for example, why teenage pregnancy or teenagers engaging in sexual activity is problematic, extend beyond the remit of physical health – both for the mother and the child – and are therefore much more complex.

An added ethical consideration relates to the content of the messages targeted specifically at young people on account of their 'unique vulnerabilities' (Michaud, Chandra-Mouli and Patton 2009: 1458). Age-specific concerns are taken seriously by the government, for example, when it comes to the dangers of underage alcohol consumption, with *The Government's Alcohol Strategy* (2012) noting the Chief Medical Officer's advice that young people under 15 should not drink alcohol at all: 'young people who start drinking alcohol at an early age drink more frequently and more than those

10 The Advertising Standards Authority (ASA) note that the UK has some of the strictest alcohol advertising standards in the world, with a particular focus on protecting young people, <http://www.asa.org.uk/News-resources/Hot-Topics/Alcohol.aspx> accessed 17 February 2013.

11 Chapter 1 of the *The Health Act 2006 (c.28)* introduced certain smoke-free premises, places and vehicles, <http://www.legislation.gov.uk/ukpga/2006/28/pdfs/ukpga_20060028_en.pdf> accessed 17 February 2013.

12 See, for example, Gallagher, J., 'Tax Fizzy Drinks and Ban Junk Food Ads, say doctors', <http://www.bbc.co.uk/news/health-21478314> accessed 17 February 2013.

who start drinking later; as a result, they are more likely to develop alcohol problems in adolescence and adulthood' (21).[13] In contrast, targeted sexual health messages more often than not focus on a population-wide message of harm reduction. As the Social Exclusion Unit's report acknowledged: 'The fact is that unprotected sex at any age is dangerous' (1999: 4). Therefore, where the policy emphasis is placed on responsible sexual practice, the concern is not for children engaging in adult behaviour, but on the need to 'reinforce responsible adult sexual behavior' (Pearce 1993: 47).

Thus, as we shall see in our proceeding discussion, determining the 'right' policy in addressing young people's sexual behaviour, and informing any cost-benefit analysis, is a socially constructed understanding of welfare, arising from a vision of human flourishing – a vision which is independent of utility itself. By adopting a value position that seeks to maximize utility, the state is, in effect, making a moral judgement on the common good (Sandel 2010: 261). In the case of teenage sexual health, it does so by granting recognition and value to a certain definition of young people's sexual behaviour over and above another and, indeed, over and above the achievement of social policy goals. As such, if SRE is instrumental to achieving the social goals of a healthy lifestyle – judged by Archard to be a 'neutral' justification for policy (2000: 23) – then the effectiveness of the chosen policy position should dictate policy direction.

Graham Haydon follows through on the logic of this consequentialist judgement: '*If* an approach that stresses informed choice is as a matter of fact the most effective in reducing teenage pregnancy (and there is a good deal of evidence supporting this), well and good so far as the policy perspective goes. By the same token, *if* an approach trying to enforce abstinence turned out to be more effective, that is the approach that – by a parallel argument – ought to be adopted' (Haydon 2010: 510). Of course, the enforcement of any behavioural choice would go against the grain of a liberal education; however, by rejecting outright even the possibility of abstinence-centred education, the underlying normative judgement on young people's sexual behaviour comes to the fore.

13 <http://www.homeoffice.gov.uk/publications/alcohol-drugs/alcohol/alcohol-strategy?view=Binary> accessed 18 February 2013.

The Ethic of Partiality in Sexual Health Education

The Health Development Agency (2001), in issuing guidance for professionals on effective interventions around teenage pregnancy, majored on securing personal values. It was acknowledged that young people come from a diversity of social and cultural backgrounds, and hold to different sets of attitudes, values and beliefs. Therefore, in line with equal opportunities, effective health and education interventions should be tailored to meet this infinite range of needs (2001: 1). Improved health service provision for young people also included an acceptance of young people's choices; practitioners were encouraged to adopt a 'non-judgemental, friendly and supportive' approach (2001: 4). The ultimate aim of the intervention was to ensure that the young person has the self-awareness and self-confidence to both 'take responsibility for their own health and share responsibility for other people's health' (2001: 2). Once again, state 'neutrality' was perceived to be achieved, where the core values of freedom and rationality are only contingent on the individual exercising tolerance and respect for others, securing the equal rights of all (Halstead and Reiss 2003: 59).

Nevertheless, the Health Development Agency (2001) explicitly rejected their own 'neutral' logic; in seeking to communicate a 'clear and consistent value message' with regards to young people and sexual relationships, they went as far as judging certain messages to be 'wrong', for example, 'do not have sex' (2001: 2). They defended their partial position by claiming that such a message 'excludes young people who are, or who have been, sexually active, has a limited life-span and could conflict with other interventions aiming to promote safer sexual behaviours' (2001: 2). Such a message, it would appear, promotes a prescriptive rather than an enabling value, a negative rather than a positive message. Instead, the Health Development Agency suggested that an inclusive message may be one such as 'it's OK to say no', reflecting the values of self-determination and respect for others. While such a message is commendable to the extent that it upholds the universal principles of freedom and respect, it highlights the weakness of a narrowly defined liberal approach to education, in that it gives no guidance on when or under what circumstances it would be right, or at least prudent, to say 'no'; it simply affirms that the young person has the freedom to do so. Conversely, when and under what circumstances might it be morally prudent to say 'yes'? As Taylor notes, within our contemporary ethic, 'choice' has become 'a prime value, irrespective of what it is a choice between, or in what domain' (2007: 478).

Critics of an abstinence approach to sex education claim that it is not informed by the expressed needs of children and young people, and therefore has as its starting point a particular values framework (Blake and Francis 2001: 9; Ingham and Stammers 2000). Instead, an apparent 'health' judgement presupposes an inevitability around young people engaging in sexual relationships, and thus makes a corresponding value judgement on the appropriate message. In effect, health discourse that does not view sex as 'intrinsically unhealthy' but only potentially 'unsafe' recognizes young people as embodied sexual agents. Thus, the provision of medical and legal information on how to avoid unplanned pregnancy, which young people have a 'right to know', is deemed 'morally neutral' (Alldred and David, 2007: 118, 110). Abstinence-only education, on the other hand, is judged to be discriminatory against children, even a form of 'childism' (Greslé-Favier 2013: 715).

Therefore, underlying the Health Development Agency's 'clear and consistent' value message is at least the presupposition that a sizeable majority of young people are, or wish to be, sexually active; conversely, not having sex is an undesirable, unnecessary or impossible goal. This value judgement reflects a certain attitude towards child sexuality, where a young person engaging in sexual activity is regarded as a normal and inevitable stage in their development (see, for example, Egan and Hawkes 2010). In line with this reasoning, the promotion of abstinence is viewed as an obstacle rather than an option in the promotion of 'safer' sexual behaviours. Indeed, it is judged unfair, if not impossible, to promote such behaviour change in young people who are already sexually active (Blake and Francis 2001: 44). Such a value judgement, however, has clearly moved well beyond an intervention focussed on disease prevention and dispels the aspiration of neutrality. Stanley Hauerwas suggests that it is the 'realist' that adopts the view that young people having sex is an inevitable reality. Believing that they are adopting an amoral position, or at the very least a non-moralistic position, he points out, however, that their position 'presupposes an ethical recommendation' – that the individual's sexual behaviour is a matter of individual preference and choice (1981: 178).

Even so, if preference and choice were indeed the only moral requisites to young people having sex, then it could equally be argued that 'wear a condom' is a negative, exclusive value message and similarly 'wrong'. It conflicts directly with, for example, the moral teaching of the Catholic Church. It also presupposes the inevitability of sexual experimentation, and consequently excludes those young people who are not, or who have not been, sexually active. It may also be seen to conflict with interventions that encourage young people to delay sexual activity for a future, monogamous relationship. Unavoidably, the normative judgement on young people's sexual behaviour, informed by a vision of human flourishing and societal good, once again comes to the fore.

This attempt at 'neutrality' extends to the classroom, where teachers are reluctant to pronounce moral judgements on young people's behaviour (Haydon 2010: 509). The effect of this is felt in the students' experience of SRE. The 2010 Ofsted report on PSHE in schools recorded that while students' knowledge on contraception and the biology of sex was good, they were less able to discuss issues pertaining to relationships, inhibited by teachers' lack of engagement and knowledge on the issues (Ofsted 2010: 14). Thus, while a strong association is being drawn between personal and social education and moral education on the one hand, the 'removal of explicit moral content' is observed on the other (Haydon 2010: 508–509). This invariably creates a climate of confusion for the educator. Traditionally, where teachers might have been regarded as failing to execute their jobs properly if they had not acted in a way that promoted and transmitted certain moral norms and values, this conception of teaching has largely changed Indeed, such an approach may be regarded by some as 'unprofessional', breaching a liberally motivated 'ethics of impartiality' when it comes to moral values and virtues (Carr 2003b: 68).

Nevertheless, in recognizing a public vision of sexual health that emanates from the top down, an ethic of partiality at the policy-making level is easily exposed. Health promotion is shaped by the moral principle of promoting social utility. In short, a reduction in unplanned pregnancies and cases of STIs – the identified 'harms' of teenage sexual behaviour – accords with the 'direct return' that most governments would expect from providing school-based sex education (Meredith 1989: 2); for in seeking to pursue a shared vision, concerns over teenage sexual behaviour and relationships and the emerging social problems may indeed prove to be another issue that tolerance alone cannot handle (Hollenbach 2002: 17). Yet underlying this liberal metanarrative lies an oft implicit moral judgement in policy discourse concerning a vision of health and human flourishing, which in turn influences the utilitarian calculus used within public health to maximise the welfare of the population. This is reflected in the moral content of the approach to health education adopted, which we will explore in more detail in Part II.

Conclusion

The vision of 'sexual health' in SRE is imbued with normative ideals that include, but go beyond, the prevention of underage conception and STIs. Indeed, it is a vision which is not contained by the perceived evidence-based approach to sexual health interventions, for it is worth noting that not all of the current evidence affirms the effectiveness of SRE in the first place. The Cochrane review of studies exploring the effectiveness of school based-interventions on sexual health outcomes, for example, with data from more than 55,000 young people worldwide, revealed that 'there is little evidence that educational curriculum-based programmes alone are effective in improving sexual and reproductive health outcomes for adolescents' (Mason-Jones et al. 2016). Yet such studies are unlikely to diminish the moral conviction within public health that 'statutory, high-quality relationship and sex education in secondary schools will equip young people with the skills to improve their sexual health and overall wellbeing' (Public Health England 2017: 2).

Our current liberal metanarrative framework is also limited and found wanting; for when it comes to discerning a public sexual morality based on social utility, alternatives have been floated, including a defence for a rule prohibiting premarital sex in view of the potential harms: 'now that antibiotic-resistant strains of venereal disease bacteria are increasing, and some diseases (herpes, AIDS) are caused by viruses against which we have little medical protection, the argument for a rule prohibiting premarital (and other) sex may still have some strength' (Odell 2006a: 199). This was an argument first articulated by Ronald Atkinson, who identified the potential for much harm in premarital sexual relationships (1965: 11). The fact that such a moral recommendation would prove unpalatable within the current liberal metanarrative demonstrates that a vision of wellbeing and welfare shapes the moral conclusions of any calculus. In determining the 'right' sexual health policy, our culture instead has placed a premium on securing sexual freedom, over and above the costs to public health, or, indeed, the relational 'harms' to the parties involved and the wider community – including the impact of sexual choices on an individual's character and on future relational stability (Brandon 2011).

Atkinson rightly recognized that utilitarian arguments are 'culture-bound', with the application of principles, therefore, vulnerable to social change, as, too, the notions of sexual practices that promote happiness (1965: 55). In light of this cultural shaping, and with the increased discourse around the inclusion of pleasure in SRE programmes, 'harm' could well be judged as denying young people access to information on how to make their sexual experiences more pleasurable. Also, in assessing the moral legitimacy of abortion provision, the greater harm may well be viewed as the 'potential hazard' of an unplanned pregnancy (Furedi 1996: 25), or its negative outcomes (Department of Health 2013: 34).

Nonetheless, while recognizing the limitations of the utilitarian calculus outside of an understanding of the existing social order, Atkinson sees little alternative to it as a moral framework for drawing up legislation within a morally pluralist democracy (1965: 59). As such, while the consequentialist principle in and of itself may be judged a useful measure in guiding public policy decisions – a means of finding an objective measure with which to maximise the outcomes for all affected (Beauchamp and Childress 2013: 361) – it cannot provide a definitive account of sexual morality, as it does not offer an adequate vision of the intrinsic good of sexual behaviour, nor provide a sound moral foundation on which to build a public sexual ethic.

Moving forward, where the liberal metanarrative in health education and promotion is found wanting, the increased emphasis on relationships within statutory RSE offers an opportunity for a richer moral language to be developed. In particular, in terms of cost-benefit analysis, it creates an ideal opportunity to address the largely unspoken cost of family breakdown in the UK, estimated in 2015 to be £49 billion.[14] In line with Sandel's just policy appeal to the common good, Jennings points to the need for civic virtue in public health: 'Public health must incorporate into its moral discourse concepts of the right and the good that pertain not to individuals in isolation but to selves-in-relationships; not atomistic bearers of interest, preference, and desire but social persons whose personal flourishing is inextricably linked to the flourishing of others' (2007: 37). Indeed, this understanding of civic virtue infused in a measurement of social utility could amount to a moral vision of public health that is not so much informed by falling conception and STI rates, but by an increase in committed, monogamous relationships, ideally marriage, and by the number of children growing up with both parents, thus increasing their wellbeing and life chances. This will call for a radical culture-shift in how sexual and relational wellbeing and flourishing is not only measured, but understood.

14 KLICE Comment, 'The Cost of Family Breakdown', <http://tyndalehouse.cmail20.com/t/ViewEmail/r/37761D1AA136541A2540EF23F30FEDED/D10E96B680E9E55C1C65CA3F48968C2E> accessed 13 July 2017; see also Relationships Foundation (2009), 'The Triple Test: Integrating Economic, Environmental and Social Policy', <http://www.relationshipsfoundation.org/wp-content/uploads/2014/02/Triple_Test.pdf> accessed 13 July 2017

CHAPTER 4

Educating for Morality: Informing Autonomous Choice

> The liberal education must help to create individuals who can make free, autonomous choices as to how they want to lead their lives. It should maximise the opportunities and capacities of individuals to exercise their own free choices. And if sex education is indeed a part of that general education then it should be shaped and informed by the same ideal.
>
> — DAVID ARCHARD (2010: 37)

> Sex educators want their students not only to know and to understand but also to feel, to care and to act (or not act) in various ways. Thus the influence of sex education extends to the emotions, motives, dispositions, virtues and other personal qualities of students.
>
> — TERENCE MCLAUGHLIN (2001: 221)

In continuing our discussion on the liberal metanarrative currently shaping SRE policy discourse, we turn our attention from health education to moral education, in particular, to the 'liberal' ideal espoused by Archard, an ideal which, he suggests, has three implications for sex education: 'First it means that young persons should be supplied with enough information to make informed, considered choices. Second it means that young persons should be taught to make their own choices. Third it means that choice should be accorded a central role in the legitimation of sexual conduct' (2000: 37). Only by educating according to these prerequisites, he argues, will we hold true to the ideals of a liberal education.

When it comes to assessing the moral quality of choices that emerge from this process of autonomous reasoning, or, indeed, the moral truth on which such choices are founded, the assumption is that such conclusions are determined by the young person themselves. There is a precondition, however, that the young person has the capacity to make 'considered choices about sex'; this is nevertheless an evolving precondition: 'There is no bright line here. The line may shift across time and education itself can play a role in shifting the line' (Archard 2000: 37).

As a precursor to our critique of this liberal ideal of 'informed choice', it is worth, of course, affirming that this critique is not directed against the capacity or freedom of the young person to make autonomous moral decisions. As Carr states: 'Moral behaviour is hardly deserving of the name if it is not in some sense autonomous rather than heteronomous; principled rather than unprincipled' (2008a: 100). Indeed, the capacity to choose is regarded as a central goal of a Christian approach to education. Aside from all the other things that education might entail for a young person, Brian Hill notes that 'if we have not equipped them with the tools of critical thought, and if we have not given them practice in making informed choices and accepting personal responsibility for them, then we will not have educated them' (1990: 44).

Instead, this critique is directed against the perceived agnosticism that currently exists concerning the ends of young people's choices and the flawed presuppositions on which the 'freedom of choice' principle is founded. In responding to this atmosphere of agnosticism, Halstead and Reiss point to certain qualities of character that are highly valued in our society, and, indeed, attitudes and behaviours which are deemed unacceptable. They also identify with the fact that many people believe children need help and moral guidance to make choices on their journey to maturity, particularly in the sexual domain (2003: 25). In addition, an 'informed choice' approach is in danger of assuming the possibility that moral identity formation can take place aloof from any concept of the good – a concept which is invariably shaped by particular cultural norms and values – and that objective moral principles can be derived from the process of moral reasoning. In effect, the current policy approach in England, which informs practice, is shaped by a moral framework that yields an incoherent and inadequate vision of moral education and human flourishing. As I will outline in this chapter, this is as a result of the public moral framework being shaped by an anthropological vision of the young person and a moral epistemology that is fundamentally flawed.

'Freedom of Choice': The Rational, Autonomous Agent

Contrary to the perception that an 'informed choice' approach to SRE is a 'neutral' one because the moral emphasis is on the young person's autonomous choice, it is important to recognize instead that this approach does not abandon the 'abstract' territory of moral philosophy, but grounds it in an approach to moral decision-making that accords with a Kantian understanding of self-authenticated choice. According to this moral philosophical position, our moral autonomy and freedom as rational agents accounts for our ability to uncover knowledge for ourselves without an appeal to a transcendent reality, nor an appeal to emotion, but in accordance with pure reason : 'A will which can be determined independent of sensuous impulses, and therefore through motives which are represented only by reason, is entitled *freewill* (arbitrium liberum), and everything which is bound up with this will, whether as ground or as consequence, is entitled *practical*' (Kant 1929 [1787]: 633).

Carr points to the use of Kant's deontological ethic as a means of deriving rationally determined moral rules and securing a moral basis for education and political and social theory (2003b: 175). A Kantian ethic, as such, rejects the maximizing welfare and happiness maxim within public moral reasoning, and adopts instead an approach that upholds the moral will of the individual: 'To act freely, according to Kant, is to act autonomously. And to act autonomously is to act according to a law I give myself – not according to the dictates of nature or social convention' (Sandel 2010: 109). A rejection of a utilitarian ethic is, Sandel points out, a rejection of the necessity of society to affirm one view of happiness over another (2010: 138). Where right is prior to the good, the subject capable of autonomous will is the basis of the moral law and the supreme principle of morality (Sandel 1982: 6).

The weighty influence of Kant's deontological ethic can be felt in modern discourse around moral education. In particular, in light of this 'freedom of choice' principle, the 'ethos of Informed Choice' within Personal and Social Education suggests that 'there is a conscious attempt not to "impose" values on the young' (Haydon 2010: 509). Instead, the role of the educator is to bring forth the rational presuppositions of freedom and the moral law which are already present in the child (Giesenger 2012: 783). In so doing, the role of education is to sharpen moral thinking and decision-making capacity (Moran 2009). Commenting on Kant's core text on education, *Lectures on Pedagogy*, Robert Louden notes: 'Kant understands both education and history as a development process involving the gradual realization of inherent human powers and capacities; the growth of freedom through rational control of instinct and desire' (2009: 284). The end goal of a Kantian education, he points out, is human perfection, where the moral actors behave consistently according to universalizable maxims (2009: 290).

In light of this, Carr suggests two ways in which a purely deontological ethic might need to be adjusted in order to make it palatable to modern liberals: 'first, it must be purged of its deeply metaphysical and non-empirical character; secondly, the more problematic egalitarian features of deontology may need modification or dilution in a more conspicuously liberal education' (Carr 2003a, 176). As such, where the moral objectivity of Kant's imperatives may prove problematic within a pluralist polity, Carr points to the theories which promote self-legislation, such as the cognitive development theory of Lawrence Kohlberg as more appealing to liberal educationalists: while morality is itself universal, the content is self-directed (Carr 2003b: 177).

Kohlberg's insights on moral development continue to receive popular acclaim (see, for example, Basinger et al. 2009). Rooted in the theories earlier developed by Jean Piaget in his seminal work *The Moral Judgment of the Child*, Kohlberg attempts to explore a theory of moral development that he believes moves beyond the polar positions of indoctrination and relativity and can be justified 'philosophically and psychologically' (Kohlberg 1981: 6). It is a theory which centres on the importance of cognitive development in achieving rational autonomy, and, as such, Kohlberg quantifies and articulates different stages of cognitive thinking in moral decision-making. In particular, in critiquing the 'bag of virtues' (1981: 9) approach, in which individuals are presented with a prescribed list of positive values to which they are expected to conform, he appeals to the combination of a 'psychological theory of development with a rational ethical philosophy of development' (1981: 50). Kohlberg's six developmental stages of moral reasoning culminate in the individual validating a socially agreed set of universal ethical principles, moving from a set of heteronomous principles to autonomous ones (Samuelson and Snarey 2008). Moral maturity is achieved by consistently holding to a rationally derived and self-legislated set of moral principles (Carr 2003b: 179).

While acknowledging the breadth of his thinking and influence, Carr suggests that Kohlberg's account of moral development is yet 'largely a mosaic of post-enlightenment ideas about moral *reason*' (1998b: 115, italics in original). This 'psychological regime', of which Kohlberg was a part, was a move away from a prescriptive morality to one that focussed on the competency of an individual to make autonomous moral choices (Hunter 2000: 81) Yet even those who continue to defend a cognitive-developmental approach to moral education concede to 'the impossibility of *proving* a philosophical "ought" through psychological inquiry' (Cummings and Richmond 2004: 202, italics in original). At the same time, this approach is not devoid of its own moral prescriptions. Richard S. Peters, for example, points to Kohlberg's own 'bag of virtues', principles which he identifies as constituting the basic content of morality, including justice, human welfare, respect for persons and society (1981: 177); and while Kohlberg's general theory appeals to principles like justice, it fails to account for why a child should come to care about applying this principle (Peters 1974: 330).

Despite these challenges, moral education has become concerned with the process of constructing moral values rather than imparting a prescribed set of moral truths. By creating a 'community of philosophical enquiry' in the classroom, values are open for creation and adaption (Robert Fisher 2000). In practice, therefore, developmental approaches towards morality 'share a common view that moral growth comes about through the child's progressive construction of ways of understanding the world, and not just an accommodation to the positions and practices of adults and society' (Nucci 2006: 663). In accordance with this process, an appropriate approach to sex education is viewed as 'one of communication, and not of indoctrination' (Wilson 1965: 106; David and Wise 1987).

In response, there are a number of points on which the 'freedom of choice' principle might be critiqued; we shall give particular attention to two – the idea that we can develop and exercise our morality independent of the norms and values of the surrounding culture, and that we can offer any defence for the moral objectivity of a self-legislated morality. As we shall expound on in Part II and Part III, we affirm Hauerwas's assertion that 'we do not create moral values, principles, virtues; rather they constitute a life for us to appropriate. The very idea that we choose what is valuable undermines our confidence in its worth' (1983: 3).

'Asocial' Individualism

To presume that a young person can shape their own moral identity, independent of an over-arching narrative and the social and moral values therein, is a central critique of this liberal metanarrative. Specifically, the 'asocial individualism' of liberalism is criticized for failing to take account of the community's role in shaping people's understanding of themselves and their values (Mulhall and Swift 1996: 13). Consequently, Sandel notes a fundamental problem with the 'deontological self': 'Where the self is unencumbered and essentially dispossessed, no person is left for *self*-reflection to reflect upon' (1982: 180, italics in original).

Therefore, while developing a young person – both in terms of their independence of thought, and moral reasoning and decision-making skills – may be rightly defended as a worthwhile and necessary endeavour of education, moral education that focusses exclusively on individual judgement and rational enquiry is found wanting. Indeed, Nucci (2006: 661) acknowledges that an understanding of moral development in education is moving towards an understanding of the social and context-specific nature of moral judgements (see, for example, Ball et al. 2014).

Thus, in recognizing moral autonomy as the ideal end towards which moral education is directed, self-legislated choices must yet be balanced with community consensus around a vision of wellbeing. In light of this, Fisher's proposed 'community of philosophical enquiry' in the classroom recognizes that such a process should develop values which are both personal and public, i.e. related to the interests of the individual and related to the interests of others (2000: 61, 62). Therefore, if a self-directed life is the ideal to be achieved, it is acknowledged that children must, at the very least, be brought up to understand that achieving this involves creating the conditions in which others can do the same: 'Can a concern for one's well-being be conceived in total abstraction from a concern with the well-being of other people?' (Callan and White 2003: 101). Consequently, moral decisions concerning sexual relationships cannot be viewed simply as a matter of self-regard, but must take into consideration the preferences and wishes of others through a process of 'informed consent' (Haydon 2010: 510). This has been carried through into policy discourse around young people's sexual health, where it is at least apparent that in challenging or affirming specific behaviours, or affirming societal norms and values, a liberal educator is already moving a young person beyond the pursuit of their own self-determined interest to have regard for the wellbeing of others.

Alasdair MacIntyre argues that in modern society, in the absence of an 'educated public' with 'some large degree of shared background beliefs and attitudes' (1987: 19) the dual purposes of shaping a young person for a social role or function, and teaching them to think for themselves and have independence of thought, are incompatible. He fails, however, to extrapolate on how education can reconfigure its aims in light of this reality. Carr (2003b: 177) points to John Rawls's *A Theory of Justice* as an attempt to bring a somewhat contractualist reinterpretation to Kant's universal principles, where a student sets aside their own concept of the good for the identified principles of justice and socially recognized primary goods – 'liberties, opportunities, income and wealth' (Nelson 2002: 199). Rawls presents the possibility of adopting an 'original position' of equality and fairness from which to derive just policy (1972: 12). This is noted to be the 'liberal egalitarian view' (Sandel 2010: 260).

Thus, the promotion of self-legislated morality is strongly critiqued within a communitarian approach to education and public policy. What results, it is argued, is the promotion of individual liberties at the expense of a commitment and identification with the goods of society and the community as a whole (Callan and White 2003: 104). The political and educational theory of John Dewey is noted to be a model of moral education that nurtures a communitarian commitment (Callan and White 2003: 104). In setting out his moral principles in education, Dewey identified the moral role of the school as one of service to the wider society: 'The educational system which does not recognize that this fact entails upon it an ethical responsibility is derelict and a defaulter' (Dewey 1975 [1909]: 7). It was the role and ethical responsibility of the school, he argued, to encourage and train the whole child for active participation in their network of social relationships, both within the school community and outside. Indeed, he went as far as to suggest that 'apart from participation in social life, the school has no moral end nor aim' (Dewey 1975 [1909]: 11).

In developing the individual within community, Dewey's assertion was that education was the primary means by which an individual's abilities were 'discovered and liberated' (Hook 2009: 491). However, Dewey's theory of education is critiqued for not giving adequate attention to the challenges of pluralism, which gave rise to the ideal of individual liberty in the first place (Callan and White 2003: 105). For in recognizing the plurality of community interests, moral education is presented with the challenge of preserving those liberal ideals which are shared by the political community at large, for example, freedom of speech, while at the same time embodying those ideals within a shared vision of the common good in society (Callan and White 2003: 107). In addition, in the absence of any objective criteria by which to reason over different moral choices, the state educator has no justification for recommending one choice over another, apart from that which is conceived by the state. This '*epistemological* or pragmatic progressivism' is evident in the philosophy of Dewey (Carr 2004: 19). For while Dewey may recognize the socializing function of the school, the moral knowledge which is imparted is socially conceived and constructed to serve this end, raising serious questions about the abandonment of any understanding of the objectivity of moral truth (Carr 2004: 19).

Ultimately, therefore, the emphasis within educational philosophy on the process of moral enquiry in deriving moral knowledge – whether individually conceived or socially constructed – leaves unresolved foundational questions on the objective nature of moral truth. Instead of starting from a transcendent understanding of morality, bringing external truth to bear on the process of moral inquiry, attention has shifted to self-scripted truth arising from within the process itself. Thus, if such an approach is adopted within moral education, Carr warns that 'we should at least be clear that modern liberal notions of individual entitlement and democratic consensus provide far from sure grounds for moral knowledge and truth' (2003b: 181).

This 'epistemological agnosticism' (Carr 2004: 27) in moral education is a warning that the 'informed choice' approach to SRE is in danger of gravitating towards a perceived relativist and subjectivist approach to moral truth with regards to sexual behaviour and relationships. Thus, where the moral impetus within SRE policy is on helping the young person to think morally and clarify their own values and attitudes, it is essential to question, and offer a moral defence, for the basis on which they do so; for 'the allegedly "impartial" goal of values clarification [...] appears to enshrine a deeply relativistic moral epistemology' (Carr and Steutel 1999a: 3). While encouraging young people to think through and understand their choices is an essential educational endeavour, deriving moral standards on sexual behaviour from the exercise of their autonomous will not only denies an objective moral order beyond the conclusions of individual reason, but denies the contextual framing that inevitably informs their choices. In addition, where advocates of a liberal approach to SRE acknowledge the decision making capacity of young people and the importance of moral enquiry, they falsely assume that 'accessing good information is key to making these decisions' (Blake and Francis 2000: 8).

The Falsity of Self-Legislated Morality

John Wilson, in *A New Introduction to Moral Education*, argued that in developing a new approach to moral education, we are no longer searching for a new basis on which to derive moral principles, but instead identifying those principles 'by which one judges between various moral codes and authorities' (1990: 26). When it comes to deciding on a moral code, he suggests 'we must be prepared to start from scratch' (1990: 28), for the authoritative foundations for moral education lie not in any prescribed belief or ideology, but in the value of education itself: 'Education has its own values, chiefly concerned with the pursuit of learning, truth and reason, and must not be contaminated by beliefs and values external to itself' (1990: 72).

Moral education is, accordingly, something you do rather than something that involves delivering a prescribed set of right answers. The liberal approach is therefore 'not ideological but logical or philosophical' (Wilson 1990: 62; see also Hirst 1967). This instigated a move within moral education away from the perceived 'authoritarian morality' of religion, arguing against any logical connection between the two (Downey and Kelly 1978: 6). Instead, within educational philosophical discourse in the UK, R. S. Peters and Paul Hirst led the way in advocating a philosophical approach focussed on the analysis of concepts, exposing their underlying presuppositions, including 'questions about the grounds of knowledge, belief, actions and activities' (Hirst and Peters 1970: 3; Peters 1970b; Hirst 1973). In line with this analytical movement, they acknowledged that these presuppositions were contingent in nature (Curren, Hagar and Robertson 2003: 187), and that justification of concepts remained unanswered without engaging in social and moral philosophy (Hirst and Peters 1970: 41).

Thus, providing rational justification for one's actions became a fundamental principle of a liberal education, where respect for truth 'depends on reasons and not on the word or will or any man, body, or book' (Peters 1970a: 55). The danger, of course, was that morality would turn into a subjective, relativistic enterprise and tolerance would become unchecked and unqualified. While Harris, for example, claims that the acquired knowledge through autonomous reasoning must be deemed '*worthwhile*' (1976: 21, italics in original), it is unclear on what or whose standards it should be judged so. Instead, where there remains no prescriptive 'facts' regarding the subject of morality, it is the role of the moral educator to help pupils '*think morally*' (1976: 30, italics in original).

Educating for rational autonomy should not, of course, infer the abandonment of all moral authority, including, as Callan and White (2003: 99) point out, those values which have previously shaped and directed the young person, in particular those passed on by parents and community. Instead, a liberal educator embraces a re-examination of them in light of the young person's own goals and aspirations. Also, educating for rational autonomy does not amount to mere indifference with regards to moral knowledge and outcomes. Wilson, for example, states that: 'It is hardly in dispute that education, at least to some degree, should be concerned with getting children to understand and act on "good reasons" as these apply in various spheres and departments of knowledge and life' (1977: 99). This amounts, therefore, to the emergence of a constructed vision of a 'morally educated person' (Sugarman, Williams and Wilson, 1967: 190); a vision which includes 'educating young people to realize the force of Kant's injunction to treat people always as ends and not as means' (Wilson 1977: 108).

Peters (1973: 144–145) defends a rational account of morality by distinguishing between form and content in moral education. He points to fundamental principles of morality which provide the 'form of our moral consciousness' but do not guarantee or dictate a uniform content. He notes that they provide 'general criteria of relevance for determining moral issues' rather than offering any definitive set of moral rules (1970a: 36) pointing as such to their 'logical necessity' and 'practical necessity' over their 'moral superiority' (1981: 180). Similarly, Hirst (1974: 46) pointed to 'rational' foundational principles of 'fairness, truth-telling, freedom, consideration of interests, and respect for persons', which he claims receive universal recognition, independent of any culture or religious belief; they are the principles that people consistently return to when justifying their actions.

Similarly, in developing a conceptual framework for moral education, Wilson suggests that we already know the '"rules of the game", we just don't adhere to them' (1990: 28). The justification for accepting any moral premise, therefore, is not on account of an external moral authority saying so, but because the individual themselves acknowledges that to do so is reasonable (Elias 1989: 57). Yet while elements of social training and natural sentiment may indeed lead us to behave in a 'moral' way, for example, respecting the property of others, it is the role of moral education, Carr argues, to bring 'meaning' and 'purpose' to our way of living, to demonstrate what is 'conducive to individual and social flourishing' (1999: 25).

In the spirit of liberal tolerance, Hirst's 'foundation planks' in effect become the categorical imperatives by which societal cohesion is maintained. As he suggests himself: 'Surely it is irrational for me to approve of my acting in a way that I do not also approve for anyone else in this or a similar situation' (1974: 45). This logic has been carried through into sexual moral judgements, for in a similar vein, Harris defends his sexual ethic by giving the example of a married man contemplating an affair with his secretary; the married man should only proceed, he argues, if he accepts that it would be morally justifiable for anyone in his situation to do the same (1976: 36). However, it remains unclear who or what mediates between a sexual behaviour that one person may seek to justify, yet another finds morally abhorrent. Additionally, Hirst concedes that the understanding of foundational principles can and will develop (1976: 49).

Thus, this progressive era in moral education did not embrace a relativist approach to morality per se, but instead put its faith in the innate ability of the individual to reason morally and to act accordingly (Hunter 2000: 61). In addition, it was not unconcerned with the training of character, but focussed on the development of autonomous characters with the ability to follow rationally prescribed rules (Peters 1974: 253). This witnessed to a 'new understanding of freedom and moral agency', and for the moral agent this meant that 'neutrality is the property he *ought* to perceive in the world, if he is to realize his potentiality as the free agent of dignity and rational control' (Taylor 1994: 20).

However, this perceived neutrality amounts to a flawed meta-ethical position. For in seeking to establish a rational basis for moral education, Müller points out that 'you cannot give children reasons, or encourage them to find out for themselves, before you have provided them with starting points of understanding and of searching' (Müller 1994: 222). He further warns that both parents and teachers will 'not find any lasting comfort in a subjectivist reinterpretation of the language of morals' (1994: 206).

In addition, there remains the practical challenge of making an unscripted morality intelligible to the learner (Haydon 1997: 84). The teaching of autonomy is noted in itself to be a challenge: 'Most conservative moralists set their moral sights too low, inviting blind obedience to authority; most liberal moralists set them too high, inviting disillusionment with morality' (Gutmann 1987: 61). Moreover, if the end goal of education is merely rationally determined moral decisions through the promotion of personal autonomy, why should students accept this 'illicit steering' or be required to conform to the views of their educators? In justifying an approach to morality that is determined by the autonomous will, is there room for its complete rejection in view of another principled way of living? If the liberal educator suggests that there is, this would evidence that autonomy is not a pre-requisite for wellbeing (Callan and White 2003: 99–100).

What results from this liberal metanarrative, argues MacIntyre (2007: 12), is an emotivist culture which lacks the criteria to determine whether moral judgements are true or false. For example, a worthwhile moral aim of SRE might be the promotion of responsible sexual behaviour, but defining what constitutes 'responsible sexual behaviour' within sex education material is invariably problematic (Reiss 1996: 101). As noted in Chapter 3, this is at least defined within sexual health promotion by an understanding of 'safer' sex. Yet, as we argued, this consequentialist approach to health promotion and health education provides a far from secure foundation on which to build a public sexual ethic. Furthermore, it is difficult to articulate – beyond the provision of information to meet sexual health targets – a coherent and adequate vision for 'teaching' the subject in the first place.

In effect, in adopting a theory of moral education where decisions over the values by which young people should live are reduced to individual choice, the philosophical exploration of values themselves, axiology, is effectively disregarded (Carr 1999: 31–32). In abandoning the process of axiology, a liberal approach to moral enquiry leaves important questions concerning moral knowledge and moral truth unresolved. This epistemological danger can equally exist for those seeking to develop a communitarian approach to moral education, as demonstrated in Dewey's approach (Haste 1996). Even with a Rawlsian concept of the good, the lack of independent sanction against which to assess one's wants and desires creates epistemological and moral difficulties (Sandel 1982: 165).

Thus, when morality becomes a human endeavour seeking human consensus, the ultimate difficulty arises in discerning 'who determines what counts as moral?' (Carr 2003b: 74). Perhaps it is simply a case of accepting that the relative, cognitive, structuralist approach to moral education – exemplified by Kohlberg – is the 'best we can hope for' (Van Haaften 1988: 32). Or maybe we should simply accept that the end goal of moral enquiry should never be certainties or absolutes, but instead we should concede that 'all inquiry – in ethics as well as physics, in politics as well as logic – is a matter of reweaving our webs of beliefs and desires in such a way as to give ourselves more happiness and richer and freer lives. All our judgements are experimental and fallible' (Rorty 2007: 188). When it comes to sex education, perhaps, as Thomson suggests, we should simply approach young people's sexual decision-making with optimism and trust.

Conclusion

In effect, as we noted in Chapter 3, an outcome of the current liberal metanarrative of SRE is that, while seeking to promote the freedom and moral autonomy of the young person, a moral judgement on what constitutes 'good information' is made, informed by value judgements that are beyond the dictates of a young person's autonomous will. This is evidenced in a 'values clarification' approach in the classroom, where choices are restricted in view of those activities that might result in 'serious danger' and where it is judged that 'the consequences of an unwise choice are not tolerable or that the alternatives can probably not be well enough understood to make a choice meaningful' (Harmin et al. 1966: 35).

In effect, within a 'values clarification' approach to moral education what is being judged and affirmed is not the decision-making capacity of the young person or the process of rational inquiry, but the source, validity and 'good' of the value-laden information received. Halstead and Reiss (2003: 25) point to fundamental liberal values which would be thwarted if neutrality was extended to all behaviours, for example, the outworking of the values of human rights, equality and respect for persons would be undermined by the tolerance of rape, child abuse or other forms of exploitation. As a result, there are inevitably sexual behaviours to which the prescriptive 'thou shalt not' and the prohibition on choice are already morally and legally assumed. This leads us to question what choices, if any, are currently restricted within SRE, in view of the fact that the consequences are judged to be intolerable or the choice cannot be regarded as meaningful. What we can say is such moral judgements around possible choices on offer are certainly not being made by the young person themselves.

For example, in exploring the possible content of SRE programmes, and the values that shape that content, Ingham and Stone stress the 'crucial importance of the values of mutuality and respect', while at the same time judging information that advocates sex within the moral context of marriage 'simply irrelevant and hopelessly idealistic' (2006: 202). Such a view is clearly not a moral conclusion arrived at through the rational, autonomous engagement of the young person, nor can one approach to sex education, i.e. abstinence-only-based programmes, be accused of being more 'moralistically based' than the other (2006: 204). Yet educators who present young people with an explicit moral reason for choosing one sexual and relational lifestyle over another, are dismissed for wrongly judging young people to be irrational and therefore in need of clear directives (Blake and Francis 2000: 8).

A serious concern arises, therefore, with the 'informed choice' framework for SRE in that sex educators are explicitly and implicitly making moral judgements on what they purport to be 'good' information; in addition, they are in danger of equating 'good information' with 'good' decisions directed towards 'good' ends – particularly when these are not clearly defined. Harris, for example, concludes that when it comes to the outcomes of moral education, 'there are no simple, uncontroversial rules about what sort of results are "good"' (1976: 37). All things being equal, he suggests, happiness may be regarded as a 'prime moral target', but not in all circumstances.

It would appear that the current liberal approach to moral education and SRE leaves teachers morally adrift. In reflecting on previous government guidance, Reiss (1993: 133) pointed out that many teachers felt ill-equipped to handle debates around sensitive issues such as abortion, homosexuality and masturbation, and were calling for more detailed instruction on how and what to teach. It is highly questionable, therefore, to assume that the moral framework of SRE is strengthened – or even at all adequate – when the exploration of attitudes and values becomes 'primarily a listening exercise' (Family Planning Association 1994: 19). On this approach, Paul

Vitz concludes: 'Very simply put, the contradictions and incoherence of values clarification demonstrate that it is a simpleminded, intellectually incompetent system' (1994: 83).

Indeed, in the absence of a moral vision concerning the 'ends' of different choices, the educator may be forgiven for claiming moral indifference to the outcomes of a young person's choice. As one school nurse reported: 'I don't consider I've failed if a girl gets pregnant as long as she's got pregnant because she knew where advice was and chose not to access it' (Alldred and David 2007: 111). At the same time, however, with what has been suggested to be the 'growing pathologisation of teenage motherhood' (Arai 2009: 142), the state has not and, arguably, cannot remain morally indifferent to the outcomes of young people's sexual behaviour. Instead, what emerges from the incoherence of an 'informed choice' approach to education is a social context in which, as sociologist Zygmunt Bauman observes, 'the entitlements of sexual partners have become the prime site of anxiety' (Bauman 2003: 51). Questions over the meaning and nature of sexual encounters give rise to such anxiety: 'What sort of commitment, if any, does the union of bodies entail?' (2003: 51).

Finally, and importantly, Carole Ulanowsky observes that a 'clarification/information' model of sex education does little to help young people deal with the challenges presented by a sex-saturated society: 'For the mature educator who develops and delivers sex education, this may be sufficient base on which to build *her* life, but it can leave young people morally adrift, to be blown any which way by their natural hedonism as by the unscrupulous forces of a sex-exploitive society' (1998: 22). She points out that many young people experience sexual intercourse earlier than perhaps desired, as 'they feel it is expected of them or because insufficient reasons have been provided as to why they shouldn't' (1998: 32). Where a liberal metanarrative will respond according to the principles of consent and the absence of harm, Halstead and Reiss (2003: 63) question whether it provides a sufficient moral basis for evaluating the appropriateness of sexual behaviour. In addition, instead of more information about sex, they suggest that young people's greatest need is support and guidance as they develop their sexual values and attitudes (2003: 50).

It is at least for the moment acknowledged that when it comes to SRE policy and practice, the promotion of enabling values does not disqualify the use of prescriptive values within individual school settings (Thomson 1997: 268). Yet when it comes to moral education, Carr points out that we are in danger of losing sight of the wider moral effect of education itself; where education 'actually concerns *personal* formation', he points out, 'it is hard to see how it can avoid the transmission of values, or of substantial views of the good life, that go beyond mere cultivation of attitudes or disinterested tolerance and respect for others' (2003b: 80). This echoes the embodied, interactive understanding of the learner, whose desires are being formed and shaped by the surrounding cultural narrative. It is therefore to the public moral narrative shaping our cultural understanding of sex and relationships that we must turn.

PART II

The Moral Narrative of Sex

CHAPTER 5

The Sexual Child and the Ethic of Sex

> There is, then, on the face of it, an intractable problem. All are agreed that there should be a sex education program. Sex should be taught in school. Yet there is widespread and ineliminable disagreement about what the content of that education should be, a disagreement which directly mirrors a substantive moral dispute about sex itself.
>
> — DAVID ARCHARD (2003: 543)

> But, while it is true that morality is not just about sex, it does not follow that sex is in fact a no-go area for morality. In other words, there is no reason to assume that, without a religious or faith foundation, there can be no ethical basis for sexual relationships.
>
> — BRENDA ALMOND (2006: 12)

Our discussion in Chapter 1 noted that government policy on SRE is extremely sensitive to changes in the socio-political climate – a climate ultimately shaped by the pervading public moral commitments of government and the surrounding culture at any given time. In light of this, a central tenet of the argument thus far is that the moral decision-making of the individual or, indeed, that of government policy-makers, does not happen in a moral vacuum. Instead, it is shaped by an existing moral narrative which determines a concept of the good and human flourishing. Culture and context matter for, as Sandel points out, the 'sociological objection' to liberalism is that 'try as we might we can never wholly escape the effects of our conditioning' (1982: 11).

It is essential, therefore, to explore the current moral vision that is shaping a cultural understanding of sex and relationships in SRE policy discourse – a vision which is informing answers to fundamental philosophical and ethical questions. For even where freedom and individual choice appear to drive moral discourse, neutrality is an impossible end: 'agnosticism about the significance of sex is no more neutral than agnosticism about the existence of God' (Gutmann 1987: 108). In view of this cultural conditioning, it is also a false premise to presume that 'evidence-informed' approaches to SRE are any more neutral in meaning and content than other approaches; they are, in effect, being shaped by a public vision of human sexuality and the goods associated with it – goods deemed necessary for human flourishing. Ann Blair and Daniel Monk suggest that the emerging tensions over sex education are primarily concerned with 'conflicting images of childhood and sexuality'; they observe that the law plays a 'critical role' in translating these conflicts and concerns into practical programmes (2009: 44–46). Thus, if teaching sexual literacy within education is just as important as teaching literacy in reading and writing (Tatchell 2002: 63), it is imperative that we understand the moral narrative that gives shape, meaning and content to the public script.

Changing concepts of sexuality have emerged, in particular, within the interwoven disciplines of sexology and psychology. These have been informed by, and in turn have shaped, philosophical discourse around the emerging moral narrative on sex (Soble 2006b). In light of these, the changing perceptions within the intellectual community around the concepts of childhood and sexuality, notably evident at the turn of the twentieth century, have been credited with significantly impacting the ideology of sex education across Europe; in particular, Sigmund Freud, Havelock Ellis and Albert Moll are recognized as critical contributors to this new knowledge base (Sauerteig and Davidson 2009: 2). Hollinger adds to this list Margaret Sanger, the founder of Planned Parenthood, and notes: 'Each not only wanted to provide information for a society that was largely ignorant of sexuality, but wished to push the populace in new directions in sexual attitudes and behaviour, based on naturalistic assumptions' (2009: 52). As noted in our discussion in Chapter 3 on a public vision for sexual health, the secular humanistic worldview of sexology rallied for an expansion in the boundaries of human sexuality, freed from the prohibitions and restrictions imposed by a transcendent law (see, for example, Kirkendall 1976). The emerging science of sex offered 'new touchstones for the classification of sexual behaviour, which did not, overtly at least, draw upon a moral framework' (Egan and Hawkes 2010: 75).

Within psychology, a new revolutionary understanding of child sexuality was defined largely by the psychoanalytic concept that a child's sexual feelings were to be seen as an integral part of their overall development; Freud's theories of infantile sexuality played a critical role in shaping this idea (Sauerteig and Davidson 2009: 2). His psychoanalytical conclusions on sexuality were as follows:

> (a) Sexual life does not begin only at puberty, but starts with clear manifestations soon after birth. (b) It is necessary to distinguish sharply between the concepts of 'sexual' and 'genital'. The former is the wider concept and includes many activities that have nothing to do with genitals. (c) Sexual life comprises the function of obtaining pleasure from zones of the body – a function which is subsequently brought into the service of that of reproduction. The two functions often fail to coincide completely. (Freud 1949: 10–11)

It is questionable whether this emerging psychological discourse advocated for the dismantling of moral boundaries for the sexual child and the unrestrained pursuit of sexual pleasure. In *Civilization and Its Discontents*, Freud, while not denying the sexual life of the child, contended that: 'A cultural community is perfectly justified, psychologically, in starting by proscribing manifestations of the sexual life of children, for there would be no prospect of curbing the sexual lusts of adults if the ground had not been prepared for it in childhood' (Freud 1985b [1930]: 294). However, in their account of the sexual child in modernity, Egan and Hawkes lament the fact that Freud's sexual child epitomized the prevalence of Foucauldian social expectations and control: 'it simultaneously identifies the existence of a lively and complex sexual subjectivity only to neutralize this potential behind a thick veil of normalization' (2010: 149).

Indeed, earlier influential voices in this emerging discourse around child sexuality also noted with dismay the subversion of this sexual agency. American psychologist, G. Stanley Hall, for example, in his pioneering work on adolescent psychology, concluded that the 'development of the sex function is normally perhaps the greatest of all stimuli to mental growth' (1914: 108). He went on, thus, to argue that it was one of the 'cardinal sins against youth to repress healthy thoughts of sex at the proper age' (1914: 109). Furthermore, Bertrand Russell, writing at a time when it was illegal to share knowledge about sex with children, argued that allowing children to remain ignorant about sexual matters was both intellectually damaging and caused 'very grave moral damage' (2009 [1929]: 64). This perceived ignorance was based on the assumption that parents lied to their children on sexual matters. Yet his views appear to be, in large part, shaped by the emerging presuppositions about childhood development and sexuality, in addition to a self-confessed 'attempt to build up a new sexual morality' (2009: 58).

In light of these psychoanalytical and philosophical conclusions on child sexuality, Lutz Sauerteig and Roger Davidson – in charting the historical development of sex education in Europe – note a shift in the moral overtone of discussions around sexual behaviour to be an outcome of these intellectual endeavours: 'Thus, what had formerly been perceived as a function of immorality and/or pathological behaviour, was, in the twentieth century, explained as phases in a child's "normal" development' (2009: 2). Sauerteig and Davidson observe that another marked outcome of this emerging psychology of child sexuality was an increased recognition of the expertise of the professional over the competence of the parents in addressing issues of sex education. In addition, while the moral influence of the church in many countries across Europe in the late nineteenth century waned, the stature and moral influence of medical and educational experts grew (2009: 7).

Thus, at an international policy level we can observe an emerging 'consensus' position on this public vision for 'sexuality education'. The *UNESCO International Technical Guidance on Sexuality Education* (2009) –'one of the most downloaded documents from the UNESCO website' (Yankah and Aggleton 2017: 65) – affirms a key idea concerning how the concept of sexuality is understood: 'human beings are born with the capacity to enjoy their sexuality throughout life' (UNESCO 2009: 26). Thus, this international policy Guidance, targeted at global education and health authorities, seeks to challenge the 'politics of silence' around children and young people's sexuality and the denial of young people as sexual beings (Yankah and Aggleton 2017: 56).

Yet, despite this 'consensus' position, what we can also trace within contemporary sex education discourse are calls for a re-thinking and affirmation of the sexual agency and sexual subjectivity of the young person independent of political norms and values. In particular, a post-structuralist feminist discourse critiques the political nature of language and its development as a product of the value systems and meanings at work within any particular social context. According to proponents such as Louisa Allen, sexuality education should be re-imagined by placing the needs and desires of young people at the centre of programme effectiveness, rather than any constructed agenda or adult-determined measure of programme effectiveness (Allen 2011: 2; Allen 2005).

Such an approach challenges, for example, the construct of paternalistic concerns around the 'sexualisation' of childhood. The Home Office (2010) 'Sexualisation of Young People Review' framed its definition of sexualization within an understanding of a child's learning and development: 'Sexualisation is the imposition of adult sexuality on to children and young people before they are capable of dealing with it, mentally, emotionally or physically' (Papadopoulos 2010: 6). From this definition, it appears that concern over premature exposure or 'sexualisation' is not so much an explicit challenge to the information or behaviour associated with 'adult sexuality' per se but to the ability of the child to understand and process the content, as well as to negotiate appropriate responses. It accords with the 'romantic' and 'knowing' construct of the child which Jones associates with 'a conservative orientation to education' (2011: 381) – an orientation which aims to protect the purity and innocence of the child through censoring, controlling and framing the information they receive. This left policy open to the accusation that the notion of sexualization was 'vague and obscure' – it appeared that it was not so much 'sexualisation' that was the problem but 'premature sexualisation' or 'hyper-sexualisation' (Smith and Attwood 2011: 329).

In contrast, the promotion of the sexual agency of the child and young person advocates an orientation to education which can be seen to affirm a 'commitment to breaking down the taboo associated with young people's sexual knowledge and behaviour, and to re-orientating policy and public health practice with a greater appreciation and understanding of sexualized culture and young people as sexual consumers – something that, to date, we know very little about' (Bale 2011: 311). Indeed, the promotion of the sexual agency of the young person is, for Allen, an issue of 'social/ sexual justice' (2011: 181). This accords with the view of those who have denounced the negative influence of a protectionist law on a young person's knowledge and experience of sexual matters: 'The notion that sex *per se* is harmful to the young has been chiselled into extensive social and legal structures designed to insulate minors from sexual knowledge and experience' (Rubin 2007 [1984]: 151, italics in original).

However, affirming children as 'socially viable sexual subjects' (Egan and Hawkes 2010: 153) should not divert attention away from engaging with, and critiquing, the public moral narrative around relationships and sex that inevitably conditions their sexual choices. Nor, indeed, should it overlook the continued role of parents as primary educators, or the attitudes and values that a public education system will desire for its young people to appropriate. To do so would be to presume that every alternative sexual choice or behaviour is morally equivalent and tenable; where 'most of our sex codes must now compete in the open market-place of ideas' (Rubin 1968: 110), they must do so with careful and critical moral scrutiny.

The Philosophy of Sex and Love

Alongside, and integral to, the changing understanding and concepts associated with childhood and sexuality, is an evident 'moral zeitgeist' within contemporary philosophical discourse on sex. This is particularly evident in an emerging philosophical genre specifically concerned with the 'concepts, propositions, and arguments' affiliated to sex and love (Soble 2006b: 784). The foundation of 'The Society for the Philosophy of Sex and Love'[1] in

1 <http://www.philosophyofsexandlove.org> accessed 9 November 2014. See also A. Soble (ed.) (1997), *Sex, Love, and Friendship: Studies of the Society for the Philosophy of Sex and Love, 1977–1992*, Amsterdam: Rodopi, for a collation of sixty contributions to this philosophical discourse over the first fifteen years of the society.

1977 was a significant indicator of the growth in this philosophical genre. Alan Soble, its founder and the editor of the formidable two-volume *Sex from Plato to Paglia: A Philosophical Encyclopedia*, has played a significant role in this renewed philosophical discourse, prompting fundamental questions to be asked about the meaning and purpose of sex. Indeed, David Archard, whose philosophical position on SRE stands at the heart our critique, sat on the Advisory Board for the *Philosophical Encyclopaedia* and points to the philosophical analysis of Alan Soble and Igor Primoratz in his own discussion on sex education (Archard 2003: 547). Therefore, while it is beyond the remit of our discussion to offer a comprehensive review of this philosophical genre, we will give particular attention to some of the insights and conclusions that have emerged which are relevant to our own discussion.

For a start, Soble offers a detailed and engaging analysis of the conceptual notions associated with sex, including sexual desire, sexual activity and sexual pleasure. This is done in order to answer what, for him, are the first elementary questions of analytical philosophy: what these concepts are (2008: 47). He identifies two further sorts of conceptual questions: 'What are the logical links among all these central notions?' and 'Must this be so? Must the analysis of this particular sexual concept rest or depend on the analysis of some other sexual concept, or could we analyse it independently of that other concept?' (2006b: 785). Such an understanding, he suggests, is particularly important to any discussion on sexual ethics – as indeed it is for sex education – for as he notes, if we don't know what a sexual act is, we will not know what to engage in or avoid (Soble 2006a: 15).

Emerging philosophies of sex have thus attempted to analyse sex on its own terms, free from cultural and moral 'baggage' which might somehow cloud judgement. This has been done, however, with the acknowledgement that it is impossible to escape the conditioning that culture provides: 'The effects of knowledge, social expectations, and norms on our sexual pleasure (or our retroactive judgements about what we experienced) implies that the culture is surely an important influence on our sexuality' (Soble 2008: 67). Thus, concepts such as sexual desire are not simply analysed on their own terms, but are done so in light of 'multiple layers of social meaning' (Jacobsen 2006: 222).

What is evident from this philosophical endeavour is that, despite offering a detailed and useful, yet a self-confessed inconclusive and insufficient exposition of these concepts (2006a: 23), underlying this philosophical endeavour are presuppositions about sexual desire, sexual activity and sexual pleasure that will set the moral tone for the discussion and shape political action. These are framed, in particular, by the belief that contemporary culture is emerging out of the antisexual tradition of the past – a moral judgement which affirms MacIntyre's conclusions that concepts, actions and beliefs cannot be separated: 'Every action is the bearer and expression of more or less theory-laden beliefs and concepts; every piece of theorizing and every expression of belief is a political and moral action' (2007: 61).

Responding to an 'Antisexual Tradition'

Igor Primoratz, in *Ethics and Sex*, points to the mid-sixties as the time when the philosophy of sex came 'into its own' (1999: 7), partly explained, he suggests, by the many cultural and social factors contributing to the so-called sexual revolution. What was of marked significance in this era, he claims, was the fact that, where previously only the basic concepts of morals, politics and law were analysed, increasingly the norms and values that shaped them were coming under critical scrutiny (see also Primoratz 1997). Primoratz offers a selected and critical overview of the philosophers who, in his view, have historically contributed towards our understanding of sex within the West, suggesting that surprisingly only in recent times have professional philosophers engaged a 'stronger *and* sustained' interest in the subject of sex (1999: 3). This, he believes, is explained in part by the 'strong metaphysical tradition' of Western philosophy that tended to extol the function of the soul and treat the body, which included sexuality, as a necessary evil. Where supreme value was placed on the life of rationality, freedom and inner peace, this could only be achieved by subduing the natural passions, including the sexual appetite (1999: 4). Soble, in addition, identifies Western philosophy's concept of sexuality as being equated from the outset with animal appetites, positioning it 'on the disreputable side of the fence between mind and flesh' (2008: 23). This concept of sexuality was shaped by the worldview of asceticism which, emerging within the Platonic tradition, influenced early and medieval Christianity.

In light of these observations of this 'antisexual' historical narrative, it would yet appear to be a boldly distorted claim to suggest that the foundations and history of Western thought had nothing of value to say on the matter of sex or sexual morality, even if what it did have to say is judged to be in some way incoherent and negative towards the body and sexuality. Stammers, for example, observes that in Plato's thinking there was the understanding that *eros* should be directed towards a transcendent moral good (2007a: 19). Similarly, Dale Kuehne, in his evaluation of the understanding of sex within early Western civilization – what he refers to as the 'tWorld' (traditional world) – comes to a similar conclusion: 'For Plato and the tWorld, sexuality was a drive and appetite that had a function and purpose, but if not harnessed and channeled appropriately, it would enslave us' (2009: 41).

It is important, therefore, at the very least, to acknowledge that the purpose of these earliest philosophical endeavours into the metaphysics of sex was to understand sexual activity in accordance with the form it took, in addition to the place it occupied within the wider purposes of human nature and activity. This invariably involved apportioning a moral significance to its content and context. Even for influential philosopher and social theorist, Michael Foucault – who viewed sexuality as a socially constructed discourse, determined and shaped by the 'regime of power-knowledge-pleasure' (1978 [1976]: 11), with no inherent meaning – the importance of ethical considerations around sexual behaviour within Western thought did not go unnoted. In his account of Greek sexual practices, he observes the challenge in satisfactorily categorizing the many acts and practices that would in some way have been regarded as 'sexual', while at the same time recognizing the ethical considerations attached to these behaviours: 'The manner in which this kind of pleasure was enjoyed was considered by them to be an ethical problem' (1986 [1984]: 36). As he remarks: 'For classical Greek thought, this force was potentially excessive by nature, and the moral question was how to confront this force, how to control it and regulate its economy in a suitable way' (1986 [1984]: 50).

The Romans follow the Greeks in Primoratz's 'antisexual tradition', as do the influence of the early Christian philosophers – in particular Augustine and Aquinas – whose contributions only added to this tradition the religious command, 'Be fruitful and multiply!' (1999: 5). They did so by developing 'theories of sexuality which confined sex to heterosexual genital intercourse within monogamous marriage' (1999: 5). Further, the moral philosophies of the Enlightenment – those proposed, for example, by Hume and Kant – fared no better in progressing a more positive view of sex, continuing instead to uphold the moral view of sex within the context of monogamous marriage (1999: 6).

While all of these traditions are worthy of critical moral scrutiny, it would seem to be a flawed philosophical endeavour, if, like Primoratz, one simply progresses an analysis of them by dismissing centuries of rich philosophical thought on account of it being 'antisexual'. Such a charge arguably exposes the imposition of a subjective and pre-determined moral understanding of sex onto the philosophical task. In contrast to this 'antisex' rhetoric pitched against Western philosophical tradition, Stammers concludes that what we can ascertain from the overwhelming view of philosophers throughout the ages is that sexual goodness does exist. This is mostly derived, he suggests, from an awareness of the transcendent meaning of sex, a specific understanding of its function, or the longstanding recognition of the union which frames and results from the sexual act (2007a: 88–92).

This 'antisexual' rhetoric has nevertheless carried through into sex education discourse. Harris, for example, in exploring the meaning of sex education, argued that 'it is high time we adopted a wholly positive approach to sex education, instead of grudgingly throwing a few titbits of information in an atmosphere of moral gloom' (1971: 10). A positive approach to sex education infers a less restrictive or prescriptive attitude towards sexual morality, which seemingly is judged to be a hangover from the falsity of previously conceived ideas: 'At present, the situation of sex education is rather like that of astronomy in the time of Galileo: hedged around with taboos and superstitions, and conducted by a process of tight-lipped indoctrination' (1971: 10). Tatchell, in addition, asserts that: 'Sex is portrayed overwhelmingly in a negative light, with far too much emphasis on the dangers rather than the pleasures – creating needless fears and anxieties' (2002: 64; see also Hirst 2013; Lamb et al. 2013).

However, adopting a 'wholly positive approach' to sex education does not equate with adopting a definitively moral or, indeed, an immoral one. Instead, moral parameters must still define the shape and limits of sexual behaviour. For while Tatchell would seek to differentiate between a moral framework and a moralistic one – where seemingly inclusive, rather than exclusive, judgements are made on sexual behaviours and lifestyles (2002: 65) –public moral discourse is not, and never has been, wholly inclusive; sexual behaviours will inevitably fall on either the right or wrong side of a socially constructed scale of moral respectability. According to Tatchell, immoral behaviour includes 'coercive and unsafe sex, domineering and violent relationships' (2002: 65); 'disordered relationships' are judged to be those that are just 'plain dull', placing particular moral weight on a subjective level of individual satisfaction and fulfilment (2002: 63). These 'positive' and 'inclusive' judgements are inherently moralistic.

What is Sex? A Conceptual Account

A further exploration of key findings from the emerging philosophy of sex and love reveals that a previously held moral knowledge, which accorded value and meaning to sexual behaviour within an identified relational matrix, is being largely replaced by a newly scripted liberal metanarrative. In adopting an analytical approach to his philosophical enquiry, Soble seeks to offer an account of what a sexual act is (2006a). In doing so, he suggests that contact with, or use of, a sexual body part may not be necessary for an act to be described as sexual; for example, hands can be used in a sexual way and flirting could be categorized as a sexual act (2008: 50). In addition, acts that have the potential to be procreative or that serve as a precursor to coitus cannot sufficiently define a sexual act, for such a category excludes the practice of, for example, solitary masturbation (2008: 51). While he argues that pleasure may be used as a measure of the quality of the sexual act, Soble recognizes that while some sexual acts generate no pleasure, this does not negate the sexual nature of the act (2008: 52). Primoratz responds to this by suggesting that if an action does result in some experience of arousal and pleasure in the sexual parts of the body, it should be described as sexual (1999: 46). Yet Soble concedes that his analysis of the concept of sex is inclusive.

Alan Goldman further recognizes the balance that needs to be struck between questions that are both conceptual and normative, and argues that what we need is a 'reflective equilibrium' between the two (1977: 267). This is achieved, he suggests, by thinking about 'plain sex': 'Because sexual activity, like other natural functions such as eating or exercising, has become imbedded in layers of cultural, moral, and superstitious superstructures, it is hard to conceive it in its simplest terms' (1977: 267). He is critical of what he describes as the 'means-end analysis', where, in his view, an unnecessary end goal is attributed to sexual activity (1977: 268). These include the end goals of reproduction, love, communication and interpersonal awareness. The simplest analysis of sex, according to Goldman, is that 'sexual desire is desire for contact with another person's body and for the pleasure which such contact produces; sexual activity is activity which tends to fulfil such desire for the agent' (1977: 268).

Goldman argues that such a definition enables us to bypass the process of analysing specific sexual activities in order to account for their sexual nature, recognizing instead that the desire for contact with another person's body is a sufficient 'minimal criterion' to qualify a normal desire as sexual (1977: 269). However, despite his dismissal of the 'means-end analysis', it appears that his own analysis has itself attributed an external goal and purpose to sexual activity. For while he claims that the goal of sexual desire is simply to achieve the physical contact, without aiming for something that the physical contact might express, the external goal and purpose is expressly one of pleasure.

For Primoratz, Goldman's '"down-to-earth" approach to sex is truly refreshing' (1999: 43). However, in his view, his 'minimal criterion' does not go far enough in giving a plain description of sex as it maintains the interpersonal understanding of sexual activity, and thus excludes the practice of masturbation. In rejecting the idea that such an activity may be regarded as a substitute or deviation for contact with another person's body, he therefore argues for the adoption of a 'plainer' view of sex: 'Sexual activity can then be defined as activity that tends to fulfil sexual desire, while sexual desire is sufficiently defined as the desire for certain bodily pleasure, period' (1999: 46). However, such a view is problematic for Soble for if there is no desire for the sexual act, for example, in the case of a prostitute, that does not refute the sexual nature of the act (2006a: 23).

Notwithstanding the evolving nature of this philosophical discourse and the thought-proving questions it raises, not least for public moral discourse – for example, 'Do all sexual acts merit equal moral value?' and 'Are there some acts that are judged to be of greater moral value than others, and if so, on what grounds?' – what is problematic with such analysis is that in its attempts to strip sexual behaviour of any inherent moral significance, it is in effect shaping a new moral narrative that is informing our public sexual ethic. We will explore this in more detail in Chapter 6, but for now it is worth noting that, while every sexual ethic is worthy of moral scrutiny, the danger exists in modern discourse that the richness of philosophical and theological insights – and corresponding normative judgements – around sexuality are dismissed solely on account of their perceived negativity and restriction on sexual behaviour. In light of this danger, we will investigate further how the deconstructing of norms and values around sexual behaviour has been particularly pronounced when it comes to the normative link between sex and procreation and sex and love.

Sex and Procreation

In giving an account of his understanding and evaluation of sex, Primoratz identifies the historic and ongoing normative link between sex and procreation – and subsequent to identifying it, he rejects it. His rejection is informed, in particular, by what he regards as the 'extremely restrictive sexual ethic' of Augustine and Aquinas, which understood sex in terms of its procreative end within marriage (1999: 12). Augustine's own experience, Primoratz suggests, accounted for this restrictive ethic – an experience which attested to the controlling power of sexual arousal over reason and will.

Of course, these earlier accounts of a Christian sexual ethic have not gone unscrutinised within the Christian tradition itself. Indeed, Hollinger affirms that with Augustine we find a 'very complex and nuanced theology of sex' (2009: 48). While sexual abstinence was the preferred state (O'Daly 1999: 401), and 'holy' virginity esteemed as 'the more perfect gift' (Augustine 1955 [401]: 143), Augustine at the same time did not reject the purposes and good of marriage. Instead, he defended matrimony on the grounds that it not only allowed for the procreation of children, but also for the 'companionship between the two sexes' (Augustine 1955 [401]: 12). Similarly, Aquinas's judgement on the value of marital intercourse was not solely limited to procreation, but he recognized the actions which contributed to the good of marital *fides* (fidelity) (Finnis 1998: 145).

In noting this normative link between sex and procreation, Primoratz also draws attention to what he regards as the internal inconsistencies of, in particular, a Catholic sexual ethic. For example, if the practice and intention of limiting sexual intercourse to 'safe days' is to avoid conception, why then is contraceptive intercourse condemned (1999: 15)? Soble echoes this criticism: 'One might argue that if God designed heterosexual coitus for procreation, restricting coitus to those times of the month when fertilization is unlikely to occur is unnatural and immoral' (2008: 91). In defence of the logical consistency of Catholic practice, Elizabeth Anscombe argued in her papers 'You can have Sex without Children' (1981) and 'Contraception and Chastity' (1972) that a distinction could be drawn between acts that are intrinsically generative and intrinsically nongenerative in their intention.

Yet, beyond what might be judged to be moral complexities and internal inconsistencies of practice, what appears to be particularly objectionable to this new genre of philosophical exploration on sex and love are the normative conclusions by philosophers like Anscombe about the nature of sex and the purpose of marriage: 'Anscombe does not *argue* for the proposition that nonmarital sex is morally impermissible. She *assumes* it' (Burgess-Jackson 2006: 55). In addition, objections to a normative link between sex and procreation are made on account of the fact that it is relevant only to those who choose to uphold it: 'merely *a* sexual ideal, not *the* ethics of sex' (Primoratz 1999: 20).

It remains unclear, however, why an emerging normative conclusion on the nature and value of sex should be considered any more definitive than a 'restrictive' ethic that recognizes the 'good' of the procreative potential of sexual activity. At the very least, the elementary biological truth that intercourse is a reproductive activity cannot be regarded as a trivial matter (Pruss 2011: 25), and the potential of the reproductive function of heterosexual intercourse marks it out as a distinctive type of sexual activity. Even if the 'human good' of the child may be excluded from sexual activity, we cannot 'pretend that sex has nothing to do with this human good' (Gormally 2011: 37). Instead, where reproduction is an obvious outcome of human sexual capacity, having a child can be regarded as a 'common good', relevant to all (Gormally 2011: 30), and while 'affirming the centrality of procreation' within a Christian sexual ethic, sexual activity is also viewed as contributing more broadly to the good of marriage and the good of society (Porter 1999: 221).

In addition to this point, it is important to note that the normative link between sex and procreation is not limited to a Catholic sexual ethic. Hollinger's evangelical ethic, for example, affirms that sex, by its very nature, is procreative. He supplements this affirmation with the caveat that he finds 'no biblical or logical justification for contending that an inherently procreative act cannot employ stewardship in attempting to prevent conception', providing the methods employed are ethical (2009: 105).

Alongside rejecting a normative link between sex and procreation, contemporary philosophical discourse – as exemplified by Primoratz and Soble – appears to also fundamentally reject a normative understanding of sex within the context of monogamous marriage. For example, in reaction to Peter Geach's judgement that sex outside of marriage is poisonous (1977: 147), Primoratz responds by suggesting that people have 'come to hate sex in marriage and regard it as just as poisonous as sex outside it' (2001: 204–205). Soble also suggests that sex within marriage will provide decreasing amounts of pleasure as the novelty of sexual encounter diminishes; therefore, 'spouses experiencing passion outside the marriage, after it has died in the marriage, may be a viable option' (2008: 198). However, this is to make a value judgement on the quality of sex, rather than the relational nature and context of marriage or its moral good or end as an institution and context for a sexual relationship.

As noted with the 'antisexual' rhetoric earlier, the normative disjuncture being drawn between sex, procreation and marriage can also be reflected in SRE policy discourse. For example, the relational values and norms, evidenced in the *Sex and Relationship Education Guidance* (DFEE 2000), advised that young people should learn the 'value of family life, marriage, and stable and loving relationships for the nurture of children' (2000: 5). However, at the same time, the Guidance also recognized there are 'strong and mutually supportive relationships outside marriage' (2000: 4), seemingly putting marriage and non-marriage on an equal footing (Thatcher 2001: 234). Moreover, in view of recent changes in the public definition of marriage in Great Britain, Rivers warns that the re-definition of marriage will sever the 'presumptive connections' which currently exist within society between marriage, childbearing and kinship (2012a: 4).

Sex and Love

Halstead and Reiss (2003: 51) suggest that children and young people's biggest need within sex education is not more information, but support and guidance in developing their sexual attitudes and values; this includes, they suggest – as part of educating the emotions – reflecting on the nature of love, including 'sexual love, intimacy and desire' (see also Halstead 2005b). Yet, alongside the dissolution of the normative link between sex and procreation, it is possible to evidence the dissolution of the normative link between sex and love – at least a sexual love that is permanent and exclusive.

For example, while an aspect of the attitudes and values content of SRE includes 'learning the value of respect, love and care' (DfEE 2000: 4), it is not clear in the Guidance whether these values are moral requirements or even ideals in a sexual relationship. At least among a number of our identified philosophers, the normative link between sex and love is being rejected. Soble, for example, points out that the many reasons people give for getting married, having sex or loving someone are so disparate that, for him, this 'reinforces the idea that the three are not essentially linked'

(2008: 206). However, once again, subjective observation and reflection is being translated into normative conclusions.

In contrast, Roger Scruton's analysis on the place of love within sexual relationships explores different philosophical questions and arrives at very different conclusions. In offering insight beyond a mere conceptual analysis of sexual desire, Scruton explores instead the purpose or end of sexual desire; in his view, this amounts to the channelling of our animal urges towards 'an interpersonal aim, and an interpersonal fulfilment' (2006: 289). He recognizes the capacity for erotic love to be a virtue, and, unlike Goldman, apportions 'incomparable value' to this exchange of love (2006: 337). Contrary to Soble, he regards sexual desire as 'inherently "nuptial"'; the end goal of sexual desire is love: 'Love is the fulfilment of desire, and therefore love is its *telos*' (339).

However, particular objection is taken to Scruton's case for the inherent 'individualizing intentionality' of sexual desire, with Primoratz accusing him of being not only out of touch with common cultural experiences, but incorrect in his assessment: 'The phenomenon of unfocused sexual desire, sexual hunger not directed at anyone in particular but felt as hunger and desire none the less, would seem to present an obvious counterexample to Scruton's central thesis' (1999: 27). Although it would equally point to the god-like danger that C. S. Lewis apportioned to *eros* (2002a [1960]: 135). In addition, Primoratz questions Scruton's understanding and use of the term 'interpersonal', recognizing that while humans are on the whole 'interested in sexual access to other humans, rather than physical objects, or animals, or inflatable dolls', the other may simply be '*a* person' rather than '*the* total, unique person he or she is' (1999: 29, 30, italics in original). To emphasize the irreplaceable desire for the other is, according to Soble, to defy experiential knowledge (2008: 172). Experience would show, he claims, that one desire is often replaced with another. In view of this, when it comes to love, we should forget the '"forever" thesis' (2008: 129).

In identifying with this 'uphill struggle' of combining sex with love, Primoratz draws on Goldman's assessment of the 'internal tension' between the two (1999: 31). Goldman concludes that while sex, as a form of recreation and a necessary 'outlet' for desire, is pleasurable and thus enjoyable, it does not contribute towards the 'lasting kind of value which enhances one's whole life' (1977: 283). Love, on the other hand, occupies a superior standing: 'By contrast, love typically develops over a long term relation; while its pleasures may be less intense and physical, they are of more cumulative value' (1977: 283). As Primoratz concludes, 'there is casual sex, but love is never casual' (1999: 31). He draws his conclusions on the basis that sex, stripped of any inherent moral significance, should be enjoyed on its own terms, whether in a loving relationship or in a casual encounter. His argument appears simply to rest on the presumption that when it comes to sex and love 'the combination does not seem to be an obvious and necessary one' (1999: 31). The only moral precondition is that informed and freely given consent is given and the person is apportioned due respect.

However, what appears particularly objectionable to Scruton's understanding of a normative link between sex and love is the implied obligation for sexual exclusivity and permanence. Indeed, such a 'restriction' is judged by Grayling to be both an 'unnatural' and 'unkind' arrangement: 'By linking sexuality with the domestic emotions and the social institution of monogamous marriage – along with expectations of mutual lifelong romance, which infidelity is believed to destroy – the settled domestic relationships become a trade-off: if you desire to form and preserve such a relationship, you must cramp or deny your normal sexual expression' (1997: 28). Recognizing that the power and roaming tendency of sexual desire 'poses a threat (moral or prudential) to love', Soble accepts that love will inevitably suffer, and multiple sexual relations may not, in themselves, be inherently immoral (2008: 195). Similarly, in his account of what constitutes virtuous sexual behaviour, Raja Halwani concludes that promiscuity, sex work and open marriages, conducted in accordance with the virtues, can equally lead to a flourishing life (2003: 170).

Thus, with a marked expansion in its use, Bauman suggests that the 'love' word no longer possesses the promise and intentionality that it once did. Standards, he asserts, have been lowered: 'One night stands are talked about under the code name of "making love"' (2003: 5). Pitirim Sorokin also notes that within our 'contractual sensate society', an increasing desire and appetite for sensory values has triumphed over our contractual duties and relationships (1992: 160). In view of this, there is a danger that the meaning and importance attached to sexual love places disproportionate value on *eros* in comparison to other understandings of love. Bertrand Russell, for example, described romantic love as 'the source of the most intense delights that life has to offer' (2009 [1929]: 46). He commended the weight of its value for human happiness: 'In the relation of a man and woman who love each other with passion and imagination and tenderness, there is something of inestimable value, to be ignorant of which is a great misfortune to any human being' (2009: 46). However, the value he placed on love was rooted in an 'ethical egoism' and conditional on the freedom and spontaneity from which it sprung, with the end being the happiness and pleasure that it generated for the individual (Hollinger 2009: 25–26). In light of his utilitarian calculus, Russell's ethical framework defended practices which included pre-marital sex and adultery (Odell 2006b). As a result of this overemphasis on *eros*, there is evidence of a normative disjuncture between sex and a sexual love that reflects permanent and faithful presence. The findings of an MTV survey in 2008, for example, revealed that, of the 1,000 young people questioned, 40 per cent believed that one-night stands are 'no big deal', and one third of young people believed it is acceptable for someone to have had as many as ten sexual partners by the age of 21 (Beckford and Jamieson 2008).

At the same time, Halstead and Reiss note that love is the missing dimension of sex education. While recognizing the difficulty in articulating and discussing in a classroom context, they observe that sex and love are two concepts that are closely interconnected and mutually complement one another, pointing out that 'the lessons of history, many people's experience and formal research all suggest overwhelmingly that the combination of sex and love is both enriching and elevating' (2003: 130). This requires an exploration of the relational nature and context of sexual relationships that allows for human flourishing, which further requires an understanding of how our human nature is related to our sexuality, and how love is understood within the narrative that we inhabit.

Helmut Thielicke, in his theological account of the nature of human sexuality, asserts that the biological is 'given character by the personhood of the human being' (1964: 20). Thus, meaning is apportioned to the totality of the person, not just their sexual functions to the 'thinking, feeling, and willing' aspects of their personhood (1964: 20). Sex understood as the 'interchangeability of function-bearers', he concludes, has implications for the individual self: 'Wherever sexual chaos, i.e., exchange of partners at will, prevails, we are confronted with a crisis, a breakdown of personal *being*, of personhood' (Thielicke 1964: 23–24).

Conclusion

In exploring the moral narrative that gives content and meaning to the public sexual ethic shaping SRE policy and practice, we have observed in this chapter the philosophical presuppositions that are informing the current moral vision. It is a moral vision which increasingly promotes the sexual subjectivity of the child, while at the same time strips sexual activity of any inherent significance and meaning. With different conclusions being drawn over the nature of love and the nature of sex, what we are left with are disparate value judgements over the intrinsic association between the two. Primoratz, for example, while critiquing Scruton's moral assumptions on the interpersonal nature of sex, does recognize that his vision of human sexual experience may well be regarded as an 'ideal', i.e., 'richer, more fulfilling, more worthwhile than casual sex' (1999: 30). He concedes, however, that ideals are at the same time only ideas and 'cannot be legislated for universal guidance; they cannot generate moral prohibitions and cannot ground condemnation of those who choose to do otherwise' (1999: 30).

Yet, if Scruton's 'ideal' of sexual relations cannot amount to a normative precondition, it prompts the question as to why the ideal of free and informed consent and respect for persons requires universal moral acceptance? While Scruton is warned against presupposing certain norms rather than norms being generated through the descriptive task (Primoratz 1999: 28), it appears that his critics have brought their own normative presuppositions to the philosophical task: 'Mutual free and informed consent, in the absence of third-party harm, guarantees that sexual acts are moral. No law of God supplements this principle of proper relations among humans' (Soble 2008: 91). This echoes Archard's moral vision on how we should teach sex, and would appear to be the moral touchstone within a secular humanist worldview understanding of sexual morality – one which is increasingly a given, requiring little to no justification. It is taken to be the unquestioned and unchallengeable rule of ethics that 'all moral thinking must lie under the government of the Harm Principle' (Grayling 2010: 326).

However, it is unclear why this ethical 'ideal' should hold any more credence than any other within a socially constructed normative framework, including those that shaped the supposed 'antisexual' tradition of the past. Indeed, as identified in our discussion on health education in Chapter 3, the harm calculus is itself socially conditioned and offers far from conclusive moral guidance. Halwani, for example, tightens the moral boundaries of free and informed consent in the absence of third party harm by suggesting that casual sex may still be wrong, even if fully consensual, in view of the consequences, for example, unplanned pregnancy and STIs; though he identifies these as 'an "external" reason for its wrongness' (2006: 138).

In the meantime, the development of future guidance around Relationships and Sex Education will require a renewed discussion on whether there are common moral ideals that will form the ethic of sex. Even if sexual ideals are deemed to have moral significance, they may amount to simply moral ideals rather than definitive rules on behaviour (Primoratz 1999: 171). Nevertheless, I will continue to argue that an increased emphasis on the sexual subjectivity of children and young people requires a richer moral framework within which to understand the appropriate expression of their sexual nature. That will require an acceptance that there is something inherently moral about sex – an assumption that cannot be drawn from contemporary philosophical discourse and its underlying naturalist presuppositions.

CHAPTER 6

A Naturalist 'Principle of Pleasure'

> Enjoy your own sex life (so long as it damages nobody else) and leave others to enjoy theirs in private whatever their inclinations, which are none of your business.
>
> — RICHARD DAWKINS (2006: 300)

> If we do not bring to the examination of our instincts a knowledge of their comparative dignity we could never learn it from them. And that knowledge cannot itself be instinctive: the judge cannot be one of the parties judged; or, if he is, the decision is worthless and there is no ground for placing the preservation of the species above self-preservation or sexual appetite.
>
> — C. S. LEWIS (2002c [1947]: 710)

The purpose of exploring the emerging 'moral zeitgeist' with regards to our understanding of the meaning and purpose of sex is to identify the moral conclusions that are being drawn within the current liberal metanarrative on sexual morality and the impact on SRE discourse. By glimpsing the work of key contributors like Soble and Primoratz, who have explicitly engaged in developing an analytical account of sex and love, it is possible to note the deconstruction of sex from identified normative ends, notably procreation and love. Indeed, as we further our discussion in this chapter, I will observe in particular that contemporary philosophical discourse entertains the view that sex has no intrinsic moral significance. Thus, a question is raised for SRE discourse, the answer to which is essential in developing an adequate moral framework: Does sex raise any particular moral issues for young people that are intrinsic to the nature of the activity itself?

The acclaimed moral philosopher, Peter Singer, is clear that it does not. In *Practical Ethics*, he states: 'So the first thing ethics is not, is a set of prohibitions particularly concerned about sex. Sex raises no special moral issues at all' (1979: 2). He defends his position as follows: 'Decisions about sex may involve considerations of honesty, concern for others, prudence and so on, but there is nothing special about sex in this respect, for the same could be said of decisions about driving a car. (In fact the moral issues raised by driving a car, both from an environmental and from a safety point of view, are much more serious than those raised by having sex.)' (1979: 2). Singer's sexual ethic is coloured by the belief that discussions on ethics and morality are generally too closely influenced by the 'sexually-obsessed morality of conservative Christianity' (1997: 19) – a belief that reflects the 'antisexual' rhetoric in current philosophical discourse.

Goldman adopts the same analogy of driving a car when talking about decisions concerning sex, noting that 'immoral' conduct on the road is judged so because it places others in danger 'a circumstance which, when avoidable, is to be condemned in any context' (1977: 281). While no one could deny the moral significance of decisions made behind the wheel of a car, Geach responds by suggesting that 'car driving is not the manifestation of a fundamental human inclination, in the way that sexual activity is' (1994: 181). If we were to compile a list of things essential for a 'well-ordered human being', she adds, sexuality would inevitably be on the list, whereas the ability to drive a car may invariably be absent (1994:181). Her conclusion, of course, presupposes that there is a need to order the human passions and that there is conceivably a right ordering when it comes to sexual matters, invariably founded on a belief about the fundamental nature and purpose of human sexuality.

When it comes to the morality of individual sexual practices, John Harris echoes the views of Singer and Goldman in concluding: 'There is no reason to suppose that there is such a thing as sexual morality in the sense of a morality which provides grounds for moral judgments about sexual desires or practices which cannot be shown to be immoral in any of the ways which would make such practices immoral if they involved no sexual elements at all' (1985: 190). While it is apparent that Harris, Singer and Goldman do not seek to eradicate the application of moral principles to sexual behaviour, they at the same time do not recognize an intrinsic association between the two. Instead, they seek to 'demolish the very tenacious idea that there is something good, or at least morally respectable, about things or practices or even inclinations that can be thought of as being, in some sense, natural' (Harris 1985: 175). Of course, such a statement needs to be qualified with a clearer articulation of how 'natural' is understood; at least for Harris, it infers that there is nothing intrinsically right or wrong about any sexual practice – that they may all be considered natural.

Taking the discussion over the intrinsic morality of sex into the realm of sex education, Jones acknowledges that there are 'special features of sex that impose special obligations' (1989: 63). Drawing on the comparison of a person performing surgery on another, he suggests that a special obligation of care is required for both acts in view of the vulnerability of the other and the potential for damage. However, the same moral logic could again be applied to driving a car or flying a plane; there is equally a special obligation of care needed due to the vulnerability of the other and the potential for damage.

Primoratz deduces that sex is 'morally neutral'; the same moral rules and principles that apply to sexual behaviour equally apply to non-sexual behaviour: 'In sex, just as in non-sexual matters, we can hurt, harm, coerce, deceive, or exploit others, or default on our promises and commitments – and we are morally required not to do so' (1999: 173). Also for Goldman, his analysis of 'plain sex' achieves moral neutrality: 'To the question of what morality might be implied by my analysis, the answer is that there are no moral implications whatever' (1977: 271). That is to say, there are, in his view, no moral requirements that are intrinsic to sex: 'We can speak of a sexual ethic as we can speak of a business ethic, without implying that business in itself is either moral or immoral or that special rules are required to judge business practices which are not derived from rules that apply elsewhere as well' (1977: 271).

Thus, Primoratz concludes: 'Rape is not wrong as *sexual* battery, but as sexual *battery*' (1999: 174). Goldman arrives at the same conclusion: 'the immorality of rape derives from its being an extreme violation of a person's body, of the right not to be humiliated, and of the general moral prohibition against using other persons against their will, not from the fact that it is a sexual act' (1977: 281). Halwani, however, raises objection to this position, believing that it is wrong because of the sexual nature of the violation. In his view, such an act demonstrates intemperance, a vice specific to sexual behaviour and feelings, which does not contribute to human flourishing (2003: 172).

The comparison and equivalence being drawn between sexual activity and other activities would seem to further highlight the current disjuncture in our understanding of the aims, purposes and moral end of sexual desire and activity. The comparisons fail at least to give full weight to the social framing that inevitably accompanies any sexual union, in addition to the nature and power of the motivating factors, including that of sexual desire. Out of all the human desires, it is sexual desire, concludes Bauman, that strives for togetherness and union, and 'renders any human being, however accomplished and in other respects self-sufficient, incomplete and wanting – unless united with another' (2003: 38).

The Moral Value of Pleasure

In liberating sexual activity from any pervading and intrinsic moral significance, it is possible, as Goldman does, to arrive at the following conclusion: 'Sex affords us a paradigm of pleasure, but not a cornerstone of value' (1977: 283). The aim, purpose and 'good' of sex is a paradigm of pleasure, and as interpreted within the arena of sexual rights and liberty, pleasure has gained in value and significance, particularly evident among proponents of sexology: 'We assert that physical pleasure within the context of meaningful human relationships is essential, both as a moral value and for its contribution to wholesome social relationships' (Kirkendall 1976: 17). As Primoratz concludes, pleasure is definitive to the nature of sex: 'What else could it be? What else remains when we put aside its biological aspect and its romantic and expressive potential?' (1999: 41).

Yet in the face of a perceived amoral position on sex, the emergence of pleasure as a moral value for guiding sexual activity is notably problematic, not least in light of the fact that pleasures are highly subjective; within human experience there are clearly many different types of pleasures. As a result, even the earliest proponents of utilitarianism had difficulty in measuring the comparative value of pleasures: 'But which pleasure, which happiness ought to guide me?' (MacIntyre 2007: 64). While Bentham did not make a distinction between the quantity and the quality of pleasure (Odell 2006a: 195), Mill viewed the pleasure of the mind superior to the pleasure of the body: 'Human beings have faculties more elevated than the animal appetites, and when once made conscious of them, do not regard anything as happiness which does not include their gratification' (2004 [1871]: 279).

Thus, within a utilitarian moral framework, the value of pleasure amounts to more than mere sensuous self-indulgence, but it is also accorded an intrinsic value (Crisp 1997: 32–33). The intrinsic value corresponds to the intrinsic nature of the human being: 'It is better to be a human dissatisfied than a pig satisfied; better to be Socrates dissatisfied than a fool satisfied' (Mill, 2004 [1871]: 281). As Sandel notes, with such a statement Mill moves outside of his own moral framework, identifying a measure of human dignity that is not derived from our desires: 'The higher pleasures are not higher *because* we prefer them; we prefer them because we recognize them as higher' (2010: 56).

In effect, where pleasure emerges as a 'good' end, if not the end of sexual activity, this is to apportion pleasure an incorrect value, for the 'value of pleasure is measured by the value of the activity or experience in which one takes pleasure' (Gormally 2011: 31). As pleasure remains a purely subjective experience and judgement – making it impossible to place a moral value on the other person's sexual preference and behaviour – it also raises important questions around the moral limits a state can impose on sexual diversity. According to Bentham, the welfare value of a pleasure or a pain should be determined, among other factors, according to its duration and intensity (2004 [1824]: 86). Thus, acts such as rape, paedophilia and incest, Odell suggests, could be judged immoral on account of the measure of harm done to the victim, outweighing the pleasure experienced by the perpetrator (2006a: 197). However, the same calculus applied to practices such as incest, bestiality and necrophilia may invariably give rise to a different moral conclusion. Of course, there are fundamental judgements on human dignity and wellbeing that are factored into value judgements on such sexual behaviours, as demonstrated in the Sexual Offences Act 2003 discussed in Chapter 7, but these clearly lie outside of a consequentialist moral framework. Thus, the inadequacy of narrowing an understanding of secular morality to harm and fairness comes to the fore. To do so, observes Jonathan Haidt, is to miss the Sanctity Foundation within the moral matrix: 'Whether or not God exists, people feel that some things, actions, and people are noble, pure, and elevated; others are base, polluted, and degraded' (2012: 174).

In expounding the purposes of sex within a Christian worldview, Dennis Hollinger presents a biblical understanding of pleasure that is 'expected and honoured in sex' (2009: 113). In addition to scriptural revelation, he notes that 'through reason and human experience a person can know that pleasure in physical intimacy must be set in a context and have some limits' (2009: 114). The implications for a moral understanding of sex thus follow: 'A morally legitimate sexual act is an act of pleasure. But it is never pleasure alone, isolated from other commitments and other moral goods. In martial sex we experience pleasure that is physical but also emotional and spiritual, for true pleasure is far more than a tingling of nerve endings' (2009: 114). The difficulty, of course, with this understanding, configured within 'religious discourse', is that it is viewed as exclusive and a denial of the sexual agency of the young person and their legitimate right to seek sexual pleasure (Allen 2014: 179).

Yet O'Donovan points to the danger of this pleasure discourse being detached from any intrinsic moral end: 'the more we detach erotic relationship from its natural ends, the more the element of play predominates, and with it the exploration of ingenuity and device within the erotic realm' (1984: 20). Within the realm of pleasurable sex – 'plain sex' – the boundaries of ingenuity become blurred and the purpose of the activity unclear. Indeed, it would appear that in arriving at a conclusion that subjective pleasure is the end of sexual behaviour, the inference is that all sexual acts, stripped of any objective meaning, are given equal value, for there is no criterion from which to argue otherwise. As Scruton notes, 'a world without values is one in which all activity has an ending, but no activity has an end' (Scruton 2006: 335).

Accordingly, a secular humanist worldview admits to offering no clear answer to the question of the 'natural place' of sex within human purpose (Grayling 1997: 24). This creates great difficulty in defining those sexual acts that are inherently right or wrong. Even sexual practices, according to Harris, which may be regarded as 'obscene and disgusting' (1985: 177) are not for this, or any other reason, immoral: 'There is nothing wrong with sex of any kind including fetishism, bestiality, necrophilia, buggery, incest, paedophilia and the variety approved by the missionaries' (1985: 191). It is the 'general immorality' of acts that involve 'violation, injury exploitation and so on' that are objectionable and the sexual attitudes that express love and respect for others that are 'morally preferable' (1985: 191).

While Harris's morality is grounded in consequentialist principles, we should note that those values that fall within the scope of 'general morality' do so on a non-consequentialist basis. What he wishes to establish is an ethic that could be universally applicable. Similarly, Singer states that ethics requires us to 'go beyond "I" and "you" to the universal law, the universalisable judgement, the standpoint of the impartial spectator or ideal observer, or whatever we chose to call it' (1979: 11). Singer's preference utilitarianism involves taking into account the interests and preferences of not only those closest to us, but indeed our enemies, as we decide what we ought to do. However, such an approach, by his own admission, can provide perhaps a persuasive but not a conclusive ethic.

'Discourse of Desire' in SRE

The concepts of pleasure and desire are receiving greater attention in discourse on sex education, 'increasingly accepted as a "good" within sexuality research' (Allen, Quinlivan and Rasmussen 2014: 3). In *Sex and Relationships Education (SRE) for the 21st Century*, published in 2014 by Brook, the PSHE Association and the Sex Education Forum, the supplementary advice notes that SRE should be delivered by people trained and confident in talking about issues which include pleasure, and sex should be taught as a 'normal and pleasurable fact of life' (Brook, PSHE Association and Sex Education Forum 2014: 5). Sex education programme content, in particular, has come under criticism for its failure to engage with a 'discourse of desire' (Measor, Miller and Tiffin 2000: 125; see also Fine 1988). This is argued to be an essential element in responding to young people's need for information and seen as providing 'counter discourse to education based on fear and pathology' (Allen and Carmody 2012: 462). Young people, accordingly, need space to articulate and express their desires, where pleasure becomes a construct of the individual's sexual preference. As Primoratz suggests, the value and end of sex becomes simply 'the desire for certain bodily pleasure, period' (1999: 46). Sex education programmes are thus in danger of being judged inadequate if they fail to engage with various means of arousing sexual pleasure: 'Pupils wanted information about ways of interacting sexually that could be exciting and even satisfying, but which stopped short of intercourse' (Measor, Miller and Tiffin 2000: 128).

Of course, critically scrutinizing the increasing prominence of pleasure in SRE discourse is not to deny its importance, nor to cover the good of pleasure associated with sexual experience under a veil of embarrassment or shame; the purpose of examining this discourse of desire in SRE is to question instead the moral status apportioned to pleasure, foreseeing the challenges that will invariably arise when seeking to use pleasure as a gauge for assessing the moral legitimacy of sexual behaviour, isolated from other moral goods. As Stammers (2007b) observes, 'sexual pleasure is powerful and easily obtainable', and without a good reason to refrain from sexual activity, 'young people will understandably engage in it'. He argues that if we are to effect any change in sexual behaviours – behaviours, for example, that impact on sexual health outcomes – we must question the role that pleasure plays in colouring our moral understanding of sex, for 'neither abstinence nor condom-use are likely behaviours in the absence of even a rudimentary moral understanding of sex'. As he suggests, the first denies any sexual pleasure while the second reduces it, at least for men.

Moreover, in associating sexual desire with the realization of individual identity, the logical question arises as to why, in the name of liberal equality, should the Curriculum not be expanded to include teaching on all sexual practices that have the potential to maximize individual sexual satisfaction and pleasure, for example, auto-eroticism or fetishism (Carr 1998a: 175)? After all, if, as Tatchell notes, 'there is no "one-size-fits-all" when it comes to sex and love' (2002: 68), and education is about 'dispelling ignorance and imparting knowledge' (2002: 69), then the obvious place to end up is exactly where he does: 'Sex education has an obligation to give all the facts and tell the whole truth about every kind of sex and relationship' (2002: 69). Similar conclusions are evident in the question and answer section of the *Respect Yourself* website, an information resource for young people from the age of 13 produced by Warwickshire County Council along with Public Health Warwickshire. In responding to a question concerning the normality of having sexual fantasies over dolphins, the following answer was given: 'Sex and normal don't really go together. People get turned on by some very weird things and this is perfectly normal. As long as you are not hurting anyone else then it is ok. Although, sex with animals is illegal (fantasising is not)'.[1]

Yet, while pleasure is advocated as the 'good' of sex, it is also regarded as inherently meaningless; in contrast to desire, 'pleasure is only related to itself, it does not represent anything and therefore cannot be counterfeit. Pleasure is free of use, almost devoid of meaning' (Allen and Carmody 2012: 463). Reflecting on 'ethical sex', on the other hand, requires 'consideration of the interrelationship between desire, acts and pleasure and their impact on others' (Carmody 2009: 89). However, in the absence of a clearly defined notion of human flourishing and its association with our sexual nature, it is difficult to decipher what amounts to harm or the impact on others. Indeed, where sexual activity itself is regarded as a necessary precondition to human flourishing, in the absence of a sufficient moral

1 'Respect Yourself: Your Questions', <http://www.respectyourself.info/your-questions/#> accessed 26 February 2012. Concern over this website was raised by the Family Education Trust. In highlighting what they judged to be explicit and inappropriate information, they received reassurance from the government health minister that she did not find the content troubling, instead placing priority on the need to provide young people with easily accessible information on relationships and sex (Family Education Trust, 'Controversial "Sexual Health" Website for Teens receives Support from Health Minister', *Bulletin*, Issue 150, March 2013, 6).

understanding of sex, we may end up simply concurring with Thomas Nagel's conclusion, and teaching others to do the same: 'Even if perverted sex is to that extent not so good as it might be, bad sex is generally better than none at all' (1969: 17).

Discerning 'Natural' Moral Knowledge

In light of the judgement that sexual acts carry no intrinsic moral significance, it is left to the exercise and boundaries of the liberty principle to provide a sufficient means of determining sexually moral behaviour, as evidenced in Archard's moral conclusions on how we should teach sex: 'anything sexually goes so long as it is in private, between consenting adults, and harms no-one else' (1998a: 448). Thus, in view of the utilitarian ethic shaping policy discourse around SRE, and shaping the moral framework in which sexual behaviour is understood, it is necessary to draw attention to what is argued to be the fundamental epistemological flaw of utilitarian thinking – the hedonistic assumption that something is good in itself, based solely on the premise that we are pleased with it, or that it is desired (Mill 2004 [1871]: 278). Accordingly, a sexual act is judged, not in view of a particular inherent moral quality, but in light of the consequences of the act. In seeking to derive ethical conclusions from natural properties, it is the flexibility that utilitarianism affords to the moral agent that understandably appeals to its followers. As J. C. C. Smart and Bernard Williams suggest, 'with its empirical attitude to questions of means and ends it is congenial to the scientific temper and it has flexibility to deal with a changing world' (1973: 73). A principal attraction is that it does not require an appeal to a transcendent source of moral authority (see, for example, Rachels 2003: 93).

In light of this, where moral principles are reduced to human constructs, naturalism is the worldview in which moral knowledge is grounded. Born out of the emergence of Enlightenment reason, it persists today, suggests Sire for two reasons: 'First, it gives the impression of being honest and objective. One is asked to accept only what appears to be based on facts and on the assured scientific investigation of scholarship. Second, to a vast number of people it appears to be coherent' (2009: 92). However, questions concerned with naturalism's coherency and objectivity continue to be challenged, and even without arguing a case for the existence of God, it is possible to argue for the untenable nature of moral claims that arise out of an evolutionary naturalistic worldview: 'theists can, where naturalists cannot, offer a framework on which our moral beliefs may be presumed to be warranted' (Linville 2009a: 392; see also Linville 2009b).

G. E. Moore, for example, notably argued that Mill's ethical theory primarily falls down on account of the so-called 'naturalistic fallacy', i.e. the 'failure to distinguish clearly that unique and indefinable quality which we mean by good' (1966: 59). Mill's attempt to equate 'good' with 'desired' failed to recognize the very clear differentiation between 'desired' and 'desirable', i.e. ought to be desired or deserves to be desired. In Mill's defence, Crisp points out that he did not claim that goodness could be equated with desired, but recognized instead the obvious deviation of many people's desires (1997: 74–75) Nevertheless, in appealing to people's experience as a source of knowledge, he did argue that desire offers the only evidence for the goodness of something. He could only, in effect, offer a defence of his theory based on empirical observation, the acceptance of which would be left in the hands of the observer: 'But if this doctrine be true, the principle of utility is proved. Whether it is so, or not, must now be left to the consideration of the thoughtful reader' (Mill 2004 [1871]: 314).

It is worth noting that Moore expanded on a hedonistic understanding of utility to include values such as 'beauty, knowledge, health, success, understanding, enjoyment, and deep personal relationships' – values which contribute to wellbeing (Beauchamp and Childress 2013: 355). Yet it would appear that he fared no better in giving an objective account of the good. For while advocating the 'non-natural' property of good – the 'intuitions' that are incapable of being proved or disproved – he drew his own conclusions on the things that are 'ideal' or goods or ends in themselves and the 'truths' of moral philosophy: 'that personal affections and aesthetics enjoyments include *all* the greatest, and by far the greatest, goods we can imagine' (Moore 1966: 189, italics in original; see also MacIntyre 2007: 15). Yet in critiquing the ongoing appeal to intuition in moral philosophy,

MacIntyre notes 'that the introduction of the word "intuition" by a moral philosopher is always a signal that something has gone badly wrong with an argument' (MacIntyre 2007: 69).

Of course, the attention given by Moore to the problem of deriving 'good' from nature was not unique; there is a longstanding critique against ethical naturalism, exemplified in the Enlightenment philosophy of David Hume, which argues that there is no rational basis for deriving an ethical 'ought' from nature, and that to do so is not only a failure to recognize that nature gives conflicting signals, but it is to commit an essential category mistake (1975 [1740]: 469–470). Hume acknowledged that 'observations of nature are first-order activities, whereas value judgments are second-order, that is, they do not belong to the same category' (Lennox 2011: 101). Hume himself offered neither a meta-ethical nor a meta-physical account of moral reality (Linville 2009a: 415). Thus, while evolutionary naturalists give an account of our cognitive faculties in deriving moral reason, Linville suggests that it 'inspires no more confidence than that displayed by Hume' (2009a: 417).

Thus, a secular worldview cannot account for the human capacity for moral reasoning and the ability to discern moral knowledge in the first place (see, for example, Ritchie 2012). While an evolutionary naturalist adopts the premise that moral beliefs are developed as a bi-product of natural selection, Linville notes that they must further ask 'whether there is a reason to suppose that the *belief-producing mechanisms* of our moral beliefs are *truth-aimed*?' (2009a: 404). Indeed, why should human reason be trusted to determine a workable ethic if, in staying true to an evolutionary naturalistic worldview, humanity's rational faculties are a consequence of irrational blind chance? It follows that, in its attempt to offer a coherent worldview, naturalism ends up being 'logically self-defeating' (Samples 2007: 212).

Those who continue to argue that moral truth can be derived from nature, science, or through human observation come up against the same epistemological hurdle – they cannot justify the objective foundations of their moral knowledge or moral reasoning. More recent attempts include Sam Harris's claim that morality is simply an underdeveloped branch of science: 'Once we see that a concern for well-being (defined as deeply and as inclusively as possible) is the only intelligible basis for morality and values, we will see that there *must* be a science of morality' (2010: 28). However, by starting with the assumption that concern for wellbeing is in and of itself 'good', he is already presupposing a moral conviction which has not been derived from science. In addition, he suggests that our conceptions of wellbeing are evolving; yet while we may be able to use science to maximize human wellbeing, as in the sphere of medicine, we cannot use science to determine why we should. Also, while it may seem apparent why we would naturally choose to promote our own happiness, it is not so obvious, on the basis of our own desires, why we would want to or, indeed, be required to promote the happiness of the other.

According to Singer, living an unethical life is not immoral or irrational per se, it is simply unwise. In his attempt to find a good reason why we ought to choose an ethical life, he resorts to an appeal to some observable element in human nature which engenders feelings of goodwill towards the other. Instead of introspective reflection, one is motivated to get out into the world and do something worthwhile: 'As yet, I offer no philosophical justification for taking this apparently objectivist stance. For the moment, it is enough that, in practice, it seems to work' (1997: 246). It is conscientious members of society, he concludes, who will tend to promote that which a society regards as valuable, where values are decided by the majority. Singer's theory is problematic not least by the fact that it is based on the assumption that we naturally seek what is morally good (Hollinger 2009: 29). Richard Dawkins, in detracting from his evolutionary premise that our actions are simply a product of the mindless outworking of our genes, similarly argues for the ability of modern man to rebel against his genes in favour of altruistic behaviour, but fails to explain on what basis we either have the ability or the inclination to do so (Lennox 2011: 111).

Again, such a philosophical conclusion has already been tried and found wanting. Henry Sidgwick appealed to the same element of goodwill within late nineteenth-century English society to justify his utilitarian position, in what he referred to as the 'Morality of Common Sense' (1889: 37). Such an observation, he concluded, should aid and control the moral philosopher in his 'theoretical construction of the Science of the Right' (1889: 37). However, no reason is offered as to why an individual should be morally obliged to behave in accordance with this spirit of goodwill.

Thus, while an appeal to a life that transcends self and promotes the happiness and goodwill of the other may indeed be regarded as a noble one, a justification for doing so, based on Singer's observation that 'it seems to work', demonstrates, at best, a dangerously shaky philosophical commitment and, at worst, a defence for its complete rejection. Indeed, it is unclear how society is to identify a conscientious member on naturalist grounds, if, according to physical determinism, it is illogical to judge any action as blameworthy or praiseworthy (Samples 2007: 211).

It follows that a naturalistic worldview, without any sound intellectual defence of our capacity for moral knowledge, also provides us with no definitive moral obligation to behave in a certain manner, thus destroying the very possibility of absolute moral values. As Lewis reiterated: 'From propositions about fact alone no *practical* conclusion can ever be drawn' for one is 'trying to get a conclusion in the imperative mood out of premises in the indicative mood: and though he continues trying to all eternity he cannot succeed, for the thing is impossible' (2002c [1947]: 707). As a consequence, Douglas Groothuis warns that naturalism is a prime source of our culture's 'truth decay', and contains within it 'the philosophical seeds of its own destruction' (2000: 43). He points to nihilism as the end result of postmodern presuppositions: 'When everything is deconstructed, no original remains' (169). Indeed, nihilism is arguably not a postmodern construct but one that was already evident in Enlightenment thinking: for 'if the sphere of reason is wholly unfettered, no knowledge can rest upon an unquestioned foundation, because even the most firmly held notions can only be regarded as valid "in principle" or "until further notice"' (Giddens 1990: 48–49). Thus, in seeking to derive objective moral knowledge from reason or desire we can observe the insurmountable challenges in creating a robust moral framework for future Relationships and Sex Education programmes from a naturalistic worldview premise. This challenge is only compounded when we note that the conclusions of 'objective' public research into sexual behaviour arise from a naturalistic worldview premise.

Teaching 'Natural' Sexual Behaviour

As noted in Chapter 5, the discipline of sexology has been influential in shaping a moral understanding of sex. Alfred Kinsey, a leading proponent of this burgeoning movement, was instrumental in instigating a scientific, ground-breaking study of sexual behaviours: 'No theory, no philosophy, no body of theology, no political expediency, no wishful thinking, can provide a satisfactory substitute for the observation of material objects and of the way in which they behave' (Gebhard et al. 1953: 9). It was claimed that the purpose of the research was not to draw authoritative moral conclusions, but simply to provide an empirical account of patterns of sexual behaviour and to understand humans as sexual beings: 'This is first of all a report on what people do, which raises no questions of what they should do, or what kinds of people do it' (Kinsey, Martin and Pomeroy 1948: 7).[2] The importance of such empirical observations continues to be lauded: 'Understanding human sexuality is a necessary step for understanding the links between human nature and intimate relationships. Thanks in part to Alfred Kinsey scientists are a lot closer to achieving this goal today than in 1938' (Fletcher et al. 2013: 258).

However, research into sexual behaviour is not as 'neutral' as it may appear, with implicit and explicit moral judgements accompanying empirical observations. The first British National Survey of Sexual Attitudes and Lifestyle (NATSAL), for example, instigated as a response to the lack of empirical evidence on sexual behaviour in Britain, noted the traditional conventions that 'still colour our moral judgement' (Field et al. 1994: 230). The report inferred that sexual morality should instead be a matter of social construction in order to accommodate social convention, encouraging the modification of health advice to accommodate current sexual preferences. In so doing, it was suggested that health educators should use the survey results to 'harness those attitudes most likely to support sexually healthy

2 The Kinsey Institute, founded in 1947, continues to work towards 'advancing sexual health and knowledge worldwide', <http://www.kinseyinstitute.org/about/index.html> accessed 12 November 2014.

behaviour' (1994: 232). In justifying the adaption of moral messages to suit the social climate, the report argued that it would seem futile to encourage 'monogamy and sexual restraint on a population heavily committed to polygamy and sexual licence' (1994: 231). Indeed, such a position reflects the belief of Archard that sex education should 'work with, and not against the grain of the social realities in which young people find themselves' (2000: 13).

However, the danger of equating custom with morality should not be overlooked. O'Donovan warns that it is 'thoughtless people' who 'fail to distinguish custom (like eating bacon at breakfast) from their moral obligation (like protecting their children from danger)' (2010: 6). He continues: 'But it is the first word of moral consciousness, a word as old as civilisation itself, to warn us against such thoughtlessness. A reflective culture finds its final justification of human acts outside local tradition or custom, however sacred' (2010: 6). Thus, if a public sexual ethic is to aspire to universal moral principles, it cannot simply adapt to the sexual and social mores of the day.

Finally, in returning our discussion more directly to contemporary philosophical discourse on sex and love, Primoratz points, in particular, to the naturalistic philosophy of Schopenhauer and Nietzsche as an impetus for a new understanding of sexuality (1999: 6). Again, the end result of such a philosophical commitment for a public sexual ethic should not be underestimated. Friedrich Nietzsche – described as '*the* moral philosopher of the present age' (MacIntyre 2007: 114, italics in original) – called for a 'Revaluation of all values!', accompanied by a reassertion and awakening of animal instinct (Nietzsche 1968 [1895]: 199). In condemning all forms of 'Anti-natural' morality, he formulated his own principle: 'All naturalism in morality, that is all *healthy* morality, is dominated by an instinct of life' (1968 [1889]: 55).

In light of this, he argued that the harnessing of sexual impulse and passion should be condemned as a suppression of life itself. Wininger notes that 'Nietzsche's entire philosophy, from start to finish, is an indictment of those who fear the erotic' (2006: 712). Yet while his reader may be 'teased by his metaphorical promises' about sex, he fails in his writings to present a vision for a new sexuality (2006: 713). Schopenhauer also outworked his scientific and naturalistic credentials in his psychology of sex: 'Unlike many previous philosophers (essentially Platonic and Christian), Schopenhauer refused to distinguish between a higher psychological or spiritual ideal of love and a lower physical state of sexual desire' (Richey 2006: 969).

Thus, a moral understanding of sex – evident within contemporary philosophical discourse – which reduces the nature and end of sex to the individual pursuit of pleasure, can be seen as a consequence of reducing our sexual behaviour to a naturalistic understanding of reality: 'Humans are then functionally reduced to their material impulses that ultimately seek pleasure, happiness, or their own interests' (Hollinger 2009: 29). In addition, it follows, as an inevitable consequence of the underlying naturalist commitment, that no sexual practice is objectionable or preferable, as might be suggested, for there can be no appeal to an objective account of intrinsic worth or value; within a naturalistic worldview there are, in effect, no grounds on which to make such an appeal. According to Grayling's 'Secular Bible', 'no human law or folly can change the river of life, that must flow in its power from the beginning always onwards, 30. And seek every path to its future, accepting no obstacle or hindrance. 31. For its own monarch is nature, its one guide nature's hand, its one aim fulfilment of nature's great imperative' (2011: 8).

Where utilitarianism seeks to ground its moral principles in the unguided, mindless forces of nature, it runs into insurmountable difficulty. As Lennox concludes: 'How can something that is ultimately mindless and impersonal, and therefore amoral, impose any sense of *morality* upon us whatever?' (2004: 25, italics in original). Accordingly, when it comes to sex, why should the 'unwanted infliction of pain, suffering, harm, injury, and so on' (Harris 1985: 189), that are somehow beyond the natural, fall within Harris's sexual moral framework? Of course, there are few who would disagree with Harris's identified moral duties towards the other; however, the ethical imperative for such duty cannot be derived from nature. In light of this, Anscombe seemed justified in concluding: 'It is a necessary feature of consequentialism that it is a shallow philosophy' (1983: 36). Indeed, she raised objections to drawing moral standards from society at all, believing that 'one cannot be impressed by this idea if one reflects what the "norms" of a society can be like' (1983: 37).

Conclusion

In this chapter we have given particular attention to the moral proposition that there is nothing inherently moral about sex. The moral value of a sexual act is instead determined by the value that the individual moral agent places on it, framed within a libertarian political philosophy. This results in the moral conclusion, espoused by Archard, that 'anything sexually goes so long as it is in private, between consenting adults, and harms no-one else' (1998a: 448). In effect, sexual morality becomes a matter of social construction and perceived consensus, with moral knowledge derived from the natural rather than the transcendent.

In light of this, we have argued that naturalism faces insurmountable difficulty in providing a robust foundation from which to derive moral principles and shape a moral framework for sexual behaviour. For if, as Grayling suggests, 'the propagation of beings is the greatest object of nature' (2011: 8), why should even a humanly constructed moral law stand in its way? Furthermore, if all actions are determined by the mindless forces of nature, what reasons can be given for encouraging young people to think morally about their sexual behaviour, including a careful examination of the intentions, purpose and meaning apportioned to their sexual desires and choices? The answer cannot be instinctive, devoid of a transcendent appeal to moral authority, for if it is, then it, by its nature, holds no objective value.

In effect, a naturalistic worldview confers no inherent moral dignity on sexual behaviour. As Hollinger points out, Singer's own ethic remains open to the possibility of sexual contact with animals on the condition that no harm is done to the animal (Singer 2001). This sexual practice, according to Harris, is not inherently morally objectionable: 'If we assume, for example, that the animals either enjoy themselves or do not find sex more repulsive than other human contact that they have, the only thing wrong with bestiality would be any harmful effects on the human agent' (1985: 179). Such a conclusion, Hollinger notes, 'reminds us that there really is no intrinsic meaning in the naturalistic worldview, and hence no inherent moral limits to natural impulses' (2009: 56).

While it may seem that sexual practices such as bestiality are outside the bounds of our current understanding of social norms – as our following discussion on the law on sexual offences will demonstrate – it may come as a surprise to note that their intrinsic 'wrongness' is not always publicly pronounced. In responding to the question of whether it is illegal to have sex with an animal that is dead, the answer given to young people on the *Respect Yourself* website stated: 'People can and do fantasise about very weird and wonderful things however bestiality – sex with animals (dead or alive) is illegal. Animals cannot consent (agree) to sex and it is wrong to ever force anyone or anything to have sex'.[3] The moral assumption from the answer given is that sex with an animal, dead or alive, is illegal, not because there is something intrinsically immoral about the act, but because the animal is unable to consent. Indeed, there is nothing in the answer to suggest that such an action might have a harmful effect on the human agent, which, within Harris's ethic, is the only moral caveat.

In view of the confusion that exists around our moral understanding of sex and the possible implications for current social and relational order, we must turn our attention to examine what it is that presently dictates the public moral boundaries of our sexual behaviour – the law. As Robert Louden points out, the absence of 'agreement regarding human purposes and moral ideals seems to drive us (partly out of lack of alternatives) to a more legalistic form of morality' (1997: 215). Thus, we will continue our discussion on the moral narrative of sex and relationships by exploring the moral vision in our current legal framework.

3 'Respect Yourself: Your Questions', < http://www.respectyourself.info/your-questions/#> accessed 26 February 2012.

CHAPTER 7

Love, Law and Consent

> How sexual consent should be discussed with young people is the subject of current policy debates and contestations in the UK and elsewhere.
>
> — VANITA SUNDARAM AND HELEN SAUNTSON (2016: 5)

> What people do with each other sexually is not a matter for themselves only: it has implications for their families, other families and society as a whole.
>
> — JONATHAN BURNSIDE (2011: 386–387)

As we noted from the outset, the state's role in the sexual lives of its citizens cuts to the heart of the debate around the parameters of individual liberty – a major reason why the implementation of statutory Relationships and Sex Education remains a controversial policy decision. Ronald Dworkin, in outworking his liberal theory of law, argued that government needs 'compelling justification to regulate reproductive or sexual acts' (2011: 376). Each person, he contended, must live an authentic life, a life which maintains ethical independence and ensures that they alone have personal control over, and responsibility for, their own body. Furthermore, the legal philosopher H. L. A. Hart warned that the frustrations of sexual desires in the face of punishment 'may create misery of a quite special degree' (1963: 22). His judgement is shaped by a presupposed value judgement on the role and importance of sex in the life of the individual: 'suppression of sexual impulses generally is something which affects the development or balance of the individual's emotional life, happiness and personality' (1963: 22). This value judgement has also shaped conclusions within philosophical discourse on the relationship between sex and the law: 'A society composed of miserable, off-balance citizens is not one the law should help create or maintain' (Gruen 2006: 584).

In light of this libertarian utopia, Taylor notes nevertheless that realizing this 'ethic of authenticity', at the expense of wider society, is unworkable: 'It is clear that to have any kind of liveable society some choices have to be restricted, some authorities have to be respected, and some individual responsibility has to be assumed. The issue should always be which choices, authorities and responsibilities' (2007: 479). The exception with which Dworkin qualifies his ethical maxim concerns cases of deliberate harm (2011: 288); this leaves the state to arbitrate within moral discourse as to as to how 'harm' is defined and measured, which in turn shapes our public understanding of sexually immoral or offensive behaviour.

As already discussed in Chapter 3, the meaning and exercise of the 'harm principle' is socially conditioned in accordance with a vision of human good and flourishing and therefore 'it is difficult to establish a precise formulation of liberal principles concerning harm and offense' (Adeney 2006: 600). Along with this, a concept of the human good is, for theorists like Dworkin, 'systematically unsettlable' within the public sphere (MacIntyre 2007: 119). Therefore, as we have argued from the outset, morally neutral law and policy is unachievable; law and policy-makers inevitably execute moral leadership in their decision making (McIlroy 2009: 101; McIlroy 2012). In so doing, a clear challenge is presented to the legislature in making value judgements on what constitutes the sexual and relational good in society in the face of increasing moral plurality and uncertainty over the meaning and purpose of sexual behaviour. In the spirit of legal positivism, it is the responsibility of the government to 'create morally valuable opportunities, and to eliminate repugnant ones' (Raz 1986: 417).

The Legal Limits of Sexual Behaviour

Notwithstanding the evolution of the policy framework on SRE, the law on sexual behaviour maintains at least a twofold ongoing responsibility within the public structure of liberal governance: to secure and protect individual rights and freedoms, and agree and uphold legislatively and judicially defined moral parameters on sexual behaviour and diversity. It arguably acts as the final arbiter on public sexual morality, with particular attention given to the law as public educator (see, for example, Burge-Hendrix 2007). The moral weight of the law also contributes to the formation of civic virtue: 'Society has at its disposal two great instruments by which vice may be prevented and virtue promoted-namely, the law and public opinion; and the law is either criminal or civil' (Fitzjames Stephen 1967 [1873]: 150). Therefore, in the absence of what is judged to be an 'extremely poor' standard of public debate on moral questions (McIlroy 2012: 159), it is evident that the law plays an increasingly central role in setting the parameters of what society judges to be the limits of sexual autonomy, in particular the criminal law, described by Fitzjames Stephen as 'by far the most powerful and by far the roughest engine which society can use for any purpose' (1967 [1873]: 151).

That said, when it comes to young people engaging in sexual behaviour, the heavy hand of the law is not to be viewed as a deterrent in accessing, in particular, sexual health services, nor as an obstacle to young people exercising their own autonomy. For example, the *Respect Yourself* website, endorsed by Public Health Warwickshire, notes that the legal age of consent is 'not there to stop underage teens from having sex together, it's there for protection, to prevent paedophiles'. In effect, 'the only person who can tell you you're ready – is you – not your partner, not your folks not your friends and ultimately not a policeman'.[1] The role of the law is one of protection and not of punishment.

1 'Respect Yourself: Sex and the Law', <http://www.respectyourself.info/sex/sex-and-the-law/> accessed 26 February 2013.

In particular, what continues to define and shape the moral parameters of young people's sexual behaviour is a legally defined understanding and application of the principle of consent – argued to be 'the touchstone of morally permissible sex' (Primoratz 2001: 201). Yet, neither the understanding nor the application of this principle is straightforward or without complication; difficulty arises in both trying to achieve a satisfactory definition of consent, as well as a sufficient means of assessing its validity. Lori Gruen points out that when it comes to the legal parameters of sexual behaviour, there are two laws that she believes even the most ardent liberal would find acceptable: 'laws that prohibit sexual activity between an adult and a child, and laws that prohibit sexual assault, rape, or non-consensual sex' (2006: 584). As she concedes herself, however, even these laws are not free from controversy, for they require an understanding of who qualifies as a child and what constitutes the presence or absence of consent.

Children and Legal Consent

Consent has become an essential normative concept shaping the moral framework of SRE and surrounding discourse, as exemplified in Archard's liberal approach. It is also evidenced within government policy where, for example, in the Department of Health's ambition for sexual health improvement in England, the moral prerequisite for any sexual contact is consent (2013: 14). The recent supplementary guidance for SRE emphasized the lack of knowledge and understanding that young people currently have around consent and the basic legal facts, emphasizing that teaching about consent was 'central to learning about healthy, equal and safe relationships and choices' (Brook et al. 2014: 9). In light of this, and in view of our earlier discussions, the morality of a sexual act is measured – not so much by the nature of the act itself – but in terms of who engages in it (Fischer 2011: 39).

Thus, when it comes to moral judgements that are currently being made on the legality of children and young people engaging in sexual behaviour, such judgements appear to rest on the perceived vulnerability of the child, largely founded on the welfare principle: 'Those who are still in a state to require being taken care of by others, must be protected against their own actions as well as against external injury' (Mill 2006 [1859]: 16). The parameters of this principle are currently shaped by an assessment of the limits of the young person's emotional development and decision-making capacities. In his discussion on the concept of consent, Alan Wertheimer notes: 'Even if B's consent is given completely willingly and even if there is no deception, B's token of consent is morally transformative only if she has the requisite emotional and cognitive capacities' (2003: 215; Wertheimer 2006). However, this might, as Archard suggests, be a 'shifting line' of capacity (2000: 37), and therefore not age-dependent.

In view of the increased discourse around promoting young people's 'sexual subjectivity', it is necessary to understand and assess the rationale behind current legal limits on children and young people's sexual behaviour, in order not only to identify the meaning and purpose of the moral commitments that they seek to uphold, but to assess the philosophical rigour of these commitments. For whatever the perceived advancement in the understanding and competence of children and young people, the core sentiment of Mill's concern for their care and protection remains as a valid challenge to the application of liberalism; in particular, the need to identify where the legal limits should be drawn to secure protection of the young person and the welfare of society against the potential 'harms' of sexual behaviour, whatever they are judged to be. For while advocating for the rights of the child in sexual decision-making, it is also Archard's view that social relationships and the social context should play a role in determining the age of consent (1998b: 129).

Similarly, Matthew Waites, in tracing the historical meaning and application of consent, notes that recent developments in the sociological understanding of childhood and youth have had 'profound implications' for the legal limits of young people's sexual behaviour (Waites 2005: 13). First, questions have arisen over assessing capacity according to age; he suggests that 'judgements of who is capable to give meaningful consent to a sexual act depends upon the kind of competence in "consenting" which one might regard as relevant' (2005: 21). These have historically included the ability to act freely and rationally and, as he points out, are also assessed on the basis of achieving the knowledge and emotional skills to handle situations, which he believes can to some extent be taught (2005: 21). However, he acknowledges the arguments of those who suggest that social context must also be taken into account in assessing capacity, extending the possibility of competence to younger children (2005: 22). Thus, age does not always provide a fixed measure for assessing capacity to give consent. Wertheimer – while appreciating it as a 'useful *proxy*' – sees no reason why age need be a necessary indicator of competence, pointing instead to an assessment of an individual's mental capacity to consent (2003: 217, italics in original). Therefore, in assessing the competence of young people to give sexual consent, Waites sets out what, in his view, are key questions for public debate: 'How do children/young people experience sex? Can children/young people give "consent" to sex? Do children/young people need protection from sex? And is the law an effective means to protect them?' (2005: 24).

The Legal Framework: Sexual Offences Act 2003

The law on sexual behaviour in England and Wales has undergone parliamentary scrutiny in the past decades, culminating in the enactment of the Sexual Offences Act 2003. The Home Office, in the conclusions of their review, acknowledged sexual relationships to be the 'most intimate and private part of life' while at the same time recognizing the role of the criminal law in dealing with those relationships which are deemed 'non-consensual, inappropriate or wrong' (Sexual Offences Review Group 2000: iv). A central theme of the review was the protective role that the criminal law should play in preventing the abuse of children. The contours of this protection are defined by the moral mantra of preventing harm; a sexual offence is committed, according to the Act, where a sexual activity takes place without reasonable belief that the other person has consented. The Act states: 'Whether a belief is reasonable is to be determined having regard to all the circumstances, including any steps A has taken to ascertain whether B consents' (Sexual Offences Act 2003 (c.42): 2). 'Consent' is defined as follows: 'a person consents if he agrees by choice, and has the freedom and capacity to make that choice' (39).

In determining capacity, the Act specifically recognizes vulnerable groups deserving of particular protection, including persons with a mental disorder, and children; and when it comes to an assessment of the limits of capacity and the legal protection that should be afforded to children, the law draws a fixed line by stating that children under the age of 13 do not have the capacity to consent to any form of sexual activity (Home Office 2004: 8). In such cases, the defendant's claims of consent will prove irrelevant. In addition, an offence is committed against a child under 16 if the defendant did not reasonably believe that the child was 16 or over (Sexual Offences Act 2003 (c.42): 4).

In exploring the rationale for age of consent laws, Waites suggests that 'the distinction between *risk* and *harm* is a crucial starting point' (2005: 30, italics in original). This echoes Wertheimer's view that it is 'easier to evaluate the expected benefits and harms of youthful sexual relationships and then reason backward to the competence to consent' (2003: 220). In identifying the harms within this calculation, Waites concedes that, while no directly harmful consequences may occur – as is legally presumed in the case of a consenting adult – the increased vulnerability of young people is to be taken into account, due to their 'structurally disadvantaged position within the social hierarchy'; this suggests that there is a risk of harm arising from young people engaging in sexual behaviour on account of the unequal power dynamics which exist within the structure of adult-child relations (2005: 30–31). Indeed, protecting young people from this power dynamic extends beyond articulating an age of consent; a sexual relationship between an 18-year-old pupil and a 23-year-old teacher, for example, is deemed harmful on account of the social boundary of trust that is breached.

As noted already, while the Act rightly seeks to protect those who are vulnerable to abuse, it appears there is a limit to which the legal parameters are allowed to infringe on the moral autonomy of the young person – as evidenced in their right to consent to sexual health services. The Department of Health (2004), in response to the age limitations set down in the Sexual Offences Act 2003, made it clear that the legislation did not affect the duty of care and confidentiality that a health professional owes to a 'Gillick competent' young person under 16 in the provision of reproductive services. In light of this advice – and where the duty of confidentiality to under-16s is promoted across health professional guidance – conflict and confusion inevitably arises as to what an appropriate response to underage sex should be. Indeed, there are warnings and evidence to suggest that the normalization of underage sex is exposing children and young people to increased risk of sexual exploitation (Wells 2017).

Waites, for one, highlights a problem with this inconsistency in the state's response to young people's sexual behaviour: 'The difference in the state's role between the two scenarios (legal prohibition of sexual activity v. provision of sexual health services) demonstrates that different principles are being applied, and raises the question of whether these are appropriate and well-founded' (Waites 2005: 31). This continues to be a matter of legal and ethical debate at a national and international level (see, for example, Heywood 2008; Loughrey 2008; Bridgeman 2006). In light of this moral incoherence, we cannot underestimate the continuing 'gatekeeping' role that those within healthcare play in making competence judgements (Beauchamp and Childress 2013: 111), particularly in view of the fact that Public Health England has reinforced the age of consent as a means of protecting young people, not punishing them or denying them access to services (Department of Health 2013: 14). We also cannot underestimate the challenge of doing so within the current moral narrative.

Furthermore, in responding to those who call for the de-criminalization of young people's sexual behaviour, Waites argues that having an age of consent enforces social norms on what is deemed appropriate and inappropriate behaviour, conveying a moral message to young people and wider society, and protecting the collective interests and welfare of young people (2005: 225). Setting out his own position, he proposes a reduction in the age of consent from 16 to 14, with a two-year 'age-span provision' – a maximum of two years age difference between the partners' birthdays – in order to give legitimacy to young people engaging in sexual behaviour with their peers (2005: 239). In defence of his proposal, he states:

> What is abundantly clear is that the current age of consent is unsatisfactory and needs rethinking. In contemporary Britain, favouring an age of consent of 16 applying to

> all sexual behaviour implies faith in a wistful fantasy that young people will abstain. There is a need instead to admit the limited direct impact that law has on young people's sexual behaviour, and to confront the realities of their situations and experiences. (2005: 241)

We can assume that such a proposal, based on Waites's own argument, would convey to young people and wider society a message around the moral legitimacy of young people engaging in sexual behaviour at an earlier age. This is in line with affirming the sexual agency of the young person to determine when they are 'ready' to engage in sexual activity. However, what is not clear is how such a move corresponds with a rationale for protecting young people from the risk of harm, without of course naively assuming that unequal power relations occur only at the level of 'adult' to 'child' and not 'peer' to 'peer'. A 78 per cent rise in allegations of children committing sexual offences against other children in England and Wales over the past four years (2013–2016) would strongly indicate this is a false and dangerous presumption to make. Indeed, in light is these findings, the children's charity Barnardo's has reportedly warned that child-on-child sexual abuse may become the UK's next major child protection issue.[2]

Once again, the application of the harm principle, without a richer moral understanding of the meaning and appropriate context for sex, proves inadequate in providing a robust moral framework for SRE. As Guy Brandon suggests, the application of consent by itself leads to a 'narrow and unrealistic assessment of who is affected, whether in positive or negative ways. Consent needs to be a starting point, not the end point' (2009: 51). In addition, broader moral questions concerning the value and worth that society places on the engagement of young people in sexual behaviour, including the meaning and purpose apportioned to it, extends beyond the concept of consent. These questions must be brought within the scope of a more comprehensive public debate on the issue, particularly in view of the

2 'Claims of child-on-child sexual offences soar in England and Wales', <https://www.theguardian.com/uk-news/2017/feb/03/claims-child-sexual-offences-soar-england-and-wales-police-barnardos> accessed 13 July 2017.

fact that relationships will be centre stage in the development and delivery of future Relationships and Sex Education programmes.

Beyond Consent: The Legal Limits of Sexual Diversity

In addition to addressing non-consensual sexual activity, the Sexual Offences Act 2003 also identifies sexual behaviours that are judged 'inappropriate or wrong'; these include exposure, voyeurism, bestiality, necrophilia and incest (2003: 36). Although Harris and others, as noted in Chapter 6, would conclude that such acts are not intrinsically immoral, there continues to be a role for the criminal law in upholding a moral boundary on sexual diversity. Thus, in addition to the prevention of harm to others through non-consensual activity, it is evident that what Feinberg identifies as legal paternalism – the role of the law in prohibiting the individual causing themselves harm, and legal moralism – the role of the law in prohibiting conduct which is judged inherently immoral, still operate within the existing system of criminal law (1984: 12).

In light of this, questions should invariably arise over the application of the liberal principle of equality. For where equality is identified as a core theme of the sexual offences legislation, Jonathan Burnside questions why equal regard for individual sexual preference should extend only to heterosexual and homosexual behaviour, and not extend to other sexual practices. In response, he notes that the principle of equality is positioned within a normative framework: 'The Act's vision of equality is necessarily founded on a series of moral distinctions' (2011: 383). A question mark, therefore, arises over whether a future revision of sexual offences legislation may further dilute our current moral distinctions; or, indeed, with any future revision, whether the reverse might also be possible.

In his discussion on objects, events or acts that a society deems abominable, Jeffrey Stout suggests that such judgements are made on account of the perceived threat they pose to the 'established cosmological or social order' (1990: 149). Thus, acts are deemed abominable if they breach one's social role within the socially legitimated purposes accorded to sexual activity (1990: 154). For example, Stout suggests that bestiality calls into questions one's social identity, with particular moral significance placed in breaching the line between human and non-human (1990: 152). Renewed public moral discourse around the meaning and purpose currently attached to sexual activity becomes even more apparent, for if Gruen is correct in her assumptions, legal moralists will only endorse the prohibition of behaviours which the public condemns (2006: 587). Thus, where sexual morality becomes a product of social construction, Nancy Fischer admits that 'we should keep in mind that sexual practices that might be considered as being within the confines of acceptable moral behaviour today could be constructed to be morally corrupt in the future' (2011: 39).

Indeed, on the basis of our current moral narrative around sex, and the naturalistic worldview on which it is founded, a future shift in the moral classification of sexual behaviours which are presently judged immoral and, therefore, illegal, is certainly not inevitable but is logically possible. Primoratz, for example, suggests that if the immorality and illegality of paedophilia rests solely on the fact that harm is done to the child then, in his view, the 'issues of its moral and legal standing are far from settled and await further philosophical and empirical investigation' (2006: 761). He argues that there is inconclusive evidence either way in terms of the harm inflicted on the child, and the current legal prohibition of such sexual behaviour would instead appear simply to be the 'most prudent and morally appropriate choice' (2006: 761). Indeed, there are those who have already argued that any classification of sexual acts, on account of their morality, is akin to racism (Rubin 2007: 161).

If in the future there was sufficient evidence to suggest that the harm (as notionally defined at the time) done to the child was not as severe as currently judged, would the moral quality of this sexual act change? Historical and anthropological accounts of child abuse note after all that the understanding of child abuse is determined by the relevant cultural context (Montgomery 2007). Also, in light of the influence of sexology in shaping a public moral understanding of sex, it should not go unnoted that Kinsey and other leading sexologists argued that 'there are as yet insufficient data either in our own or in other studies, for reaching general conclusions on the significance of sexual contact between children and adults' (Gebhard et al. 1953: 120). On observing those children that were 'upset or frightened by their contacts with adults', Kinsey and his colleagues suggested that, 'if a child were not culturally conditioned, it is doubtful if it would be disturbed by sexual approaches of the sort which had usually been involved in these histories' (1953: 121).

Of course, these 'empirical' observations were intended to give only an account of what people do sexually, not what they should do. Yet if no objective moral understanding is brought to bear on this type of sexual encounter, the danger exists that a social climate is created where such behaviour is deemed socially permissible and does not breach Stout's cosmological or social order. Without an objective account of sexual morality, we have no basis on which to refute the assertion of Havelock Ellis that 'every age or land has its own morality' (1931: 369), and that in another age or another context, the sexual behaviours that are currently judged 'inappropriate or wrong', may be deemed morally legitimate. In view of even the logical possibility of creating such a moral order, we should be wary of a world in which, as Grayling advocates, we are masters of our own destiny (1997: 23).

Conclusion

Jacqueline Laing, in exploring the connection between law and justice, claims that if we want to maintain the notion that certain activities are 'timelessly unjust', then we cannot view morality and law – 'i.e. that which binds the human conscience' – as simply a human construct. Judging on the basis of human experience and historical precedent, she concludes: 'Both morality and law, properly understood, had better be more than that' (2012: 132). Thus, in examining the role that criminal law plays in regulating sexual behaviour, its deficiency as the sole arbiter of public sexual morality and its limits in fostering civic virtue should not go unnoted. Instead, 'a civil society that referees the minimal rules necessary to uphold civil life and facilitates respect for and the right to diversity needs to be supplemented by a civil and sexual ethics' (Gibbens 1998: 44).

As noted already, the ethic that currently supplements the law is largely conditioned by the overriding liberal metanarrative: a socially constructed understanding of that which promotes autonomy and maximizes happiness or pleasure. In addition, the intellectual roots of moral judgements become increasingly difficult to justify, as principles and laws are informed by the current norms in society, rather than an objective understanding of the intrinsic moral quality of sexual acts. As Burnside observes: 'The Sexual Offences Act 2003 points beyond itself to a loss within our social consciousness of how we understand the significance of sexual behaviour. This is something we are all caught up in because it affects all of us, both individually and collectively as a society' (2011: 385). It is this collective loss of meaning which is the final outcome of nihilism: 'The strands of epistemological, metaphysical and ethical nihilism weave together to make a rope long enough and strong enough to hang a whole culture. The name of the rope is Loss of Meaning' (Sire 2009: 111).

In conclusion, I have endeavoured in Part II to present a glimpse of the 'moral zeitgeist' currently shaping our understanding of sex. The purpose of doing so is to note that where public moral discourse increasingly defends the right to pursue self-constructed notions of the 'good' without any intrinsic understanding of the morality of sex, an inevitable consequence for the policy content and practice of SRE is that it follows suit. This includes, as Tatchell suggests, teaching young people that, within a socially defined understanding of ethical sex, in addition to orientation, the context is inconsequential: 'regardless of whether they are married, cohabiting or living apart; regardless of whether they are into one-night-stands or committed relationships; and regardless of whether they have sex for love or sex for pleasure' (2002: 66). The moral prerequisite is mutual consent. However, this principle in itself, no longer has a fixed application or boundary. In addition, the call for an inclusive SRE, which raises knowledge and awareness of the pluralities of sexualities in society (Biddulph 2012), does little to sharpen our social and moral consciousness.

Beyond the consequentialist interpretation of public and legal norms, Rivers warns of a new 'political absolutism' in which the state, through the power of the legal system, protects the individual's self-constructed notion of dignity. He points to the debate over same sex marriage as an example of this 'postmodern dignity' at work, representing 'a paradigm shift towards a denial of the "natural" in any normatively charged sense and to the universal mandate of the state to protect each individual in his or her vulnerable self-construction' (2012b: 150). Similarly, Sire – in his assessment of the implication of a postmodern worldview on ethics – notes: 'Ethics, like knowledge, is a linguistic construct. Social good is whatever society takes it to be' (2009: 228). If this is the case, it would appear that there is an even more urgent task to re-awaken public moral discourse around a vision of relational and sexual civic virtue. For within a climate of increased moral agnosticism about moral norms and values with regards to sexual behaviour, there remains a pressing need to understand and respond to young people's ethical questions within a renewed moral vision of human flourishing.

In light of this task, I shall move on in Part III to present a moral framework which, I will argue, provides a more coherent and enriched vision of a sexually and relationally educated young person, a vision shaped by a theological virtue ethic. It not only enriches liberal educational discourse, but re-invigorates a public sexual ethic which moves beyond a set of legal precepts. In what Tom Wright notes to be the evidenced lurch between 'deregulation' and 'reregulation' in major areas of life, such as sexual relationships, he highlights what he views to be the essential problem with this approach: '*introducing new regulations doesn't get to the heart of the problem*' (2010: 21, italics in original). The heart of the problem, he suggests, is a character deficit, in which we are more concerned with what to do, or not to do, than how to do it: 'Rules matter, it seems, but character matters more, and provides a framework within which rules, where appropriate, can have their proper effect' (2010: 44).

PART III

The Value of Virtue in Relationships and Sex Education (RSE)

CHAPTER 8

Cultivating Virtue in Moral Education: An Enriched Vision for RSE

> The story that liberalism teaches us is that we have no story, and as a result we fail to notice how deeply that story determines our lives.
>
> — STANLEY HAUERWAS (1981: 84)

> The danger with an approach to learning that focuses on values is that it can become a purely cognitive exercise where students simply engage in gaining cognitive knowledge and understanding of values. Teachers can be tempted to treat values as a check-list that they tick off when covered in the curriculum. However this is less likely to happen in an approach which focuses on developing virtues as a means of character formation.
>
> — TREVOR COOLING ET AL. (2016: 167)

So far in our discussion we have focussed our critique on the implicit and explicit moral values and principles within the current moral vision of SRE discourse – as reflected in Archard's philosophical approach to sex education. As explored in Chapter 4, the predominant place given to the process of moral enquiry, based on the assumptions presented within developmental psychology, have dominated the landscape of moral education. Kohlberg and his cognitive development theory of moral education became the 'holy grail' of liberal education (Carr and Steutel 1999b: 243). In response to the dominance and perceived inadequacy of this educational approach, James Davison Hunter, in *The Death of Character: Moral Education in an Age Without Good or Evil*, identifies the alternatives that have emerged in the US from the neoclassical[1] and communitarian critics, in particular, the practical 'character education' pedagogies[2] that have arisen out of both of these theories (Hunter 2000: 112).

Hunter concludes, however, that the alternative pedagogies have amounted more to political rhetoric than to a significant shift in educational approach – an approach to moral education that is 'repackaged' more than effectively challenged (Hunter 2000: 128). In short, moral education, as a reflection of the dramatic shifts in moral culture, has deeply shifted in its institutional character and its normative presuppositions and distinctions, framed no longer by a shared civic virtue but by a perceived liberal neutrality. What has resulted, Hunter argues, is an incoherent moral philosophy which boils down to the promotion of personal preferences. Without the binding influence of moral communities and creeds, what we are left with is 'virtue on the cheap' (2000: 201). The 'impoverished' nature of moral education in our schools, notes Richard Pring, has emerged on account of the emphasis on the cultivation of autonomy over virtue (2014: 48–49).

In addition to the shift in moral education, the dissolution of the normative link between sex and relationships, as discussed in Chapter 5, has stripped sexual activity of any inherent moral value and, as a consequence, has impoverished our understanding of sexual personhood. In light of this, the danger exists within our public sexual ethic that we lose a relational language in which to speak about the context of sex; at least, a relational language that moves beyond the limited, socially constructed understanding of respect and consent. This is reflective of an increased moral disorientation within policy discourse around an understanding of relationships: 'Many people are willing to agree that long-term stable

1 For example, William J. Bennett's *The Book of Virtues* as a neoclassical approach to moral education using stories from literature and history to teach the virtues. However, as Hunter notes, 'the question is, on whose terms will children be anchored? Which stories and whose history will provide the common frame of reference for society?' (Hunter 2000: 112).

2 For example, the work of Thomas Lickona in *Educating for Character: How our Schools Can Teach Respect and Responsibility*, London: Bantham Books, 1991.

relationships are, in principle, a good thing. But when it comes to defining a "good" relationship, or what kinds of relationship (if any) should be favoured by public policy, and whether things are getting worse or simply changing, agreement and even rationality can begin to disappear' (Ashcroft and Schluter 2005: 22).

In responding to this perceived liberal neutrality, and an impoverished understanding of sexual personhood and relationships, our discussion in this chapter will attempt to reinstate a politics of moral engagement within public debate – in particular, public discourse concerned with the development of future Relationships Education and Relationships and Sex Education policies and programmes. For if, as Sandel suggests, we are to deliberate within liberal democracy on the nature of the good life, and foster a vision of the common good, the inevitable result for future RSE policy is that we make judgements which move us beyond a position of liberal neutrality. In doing so, we must ask fundamental questions about the nature and purpose of health and moral education, and the nature and meaning of sex and relationships, and how they correspond with human flourishing. We must reimagine and recast a moral vision.

In doing so, and in presenting a vision of the common good in education with regards to children and young people's relationships and sexual behaviour, I echo what James Arthur refers to as a 'communitarian liberal position', which 'values both individual choice and action, but places it within the context of a rich and worthwhile common culture' (2000: 19). A communitarian approach to education as a means of forging and nurturing this common culture is particularly outworked in character and citizenship education, seeking to foster common civic values and build moral character. While caution is expressed in associating these educational fields too closely (see, for example, Davies et al. 2005), the common good in education is perceived to consist of two 'essential' and 'inseparable' aspects: 'the development of the capacities and powers of unique and irreplaceable human beings and the development of cooperative, fraternal, and mutually helpful ways of associating' (2000: 84). In light of this, I will present a case for why the cultivation of virtue offers important insights for moral education, more specifically Relationships and Sex Education.

Educating for Virtue in a Pluralistic Society

Since the foundations of Western civilization, moral philosophy has had a long-standing interest in the place of virtues in the moral life, and this tradition of rational engagement has significantly influenced and shaped the Christian tradition of virtue ethics and Christian character formation (Farley 1995: 3). Discovering the place of virtue in the moral life has also contributed to a rich tradition of moral discourse within the activities and purposes of moral education. Accompanying this long-standing tradition – the so-called 'project of acquiring virtue' (Herdt 2008: 1) – is a long-standing critique of it within both philosophy and theology; it is viewed on the one hand as a threat to moral autonomy by the perceived external imposition of virtues and, on the other, as presenting a false vision of the moral self (2008: 1).

As a normative ethical theory, a virtue ethic gives particular attention to the teleological character and function of the individual and the moral life, as well as to the moral life of the community. Particularly evidenced in an Aristotelian ethic, and arguably most fervently defended by Alasdair MacIntyre in modern philosophical discourse, the moral life is a trajectory towards the individual acting in accordance with the essential nature and function of a human being. MacIntyre notes that: 'Within that teleological scheme there is fundamental contrast between man-as-he-happens-to-be and man-as-he-could-be-if-he-realized-his-essential-nature' (2007: 52).

Aristotle believed that human action was ultimately directed towards 'eudaimonia', understood as 'happiness' or 'living well' (2004: 6–7, *NE* 1095a 17–20). Indeed, all the major schools of philosophy in Ancient Greece were eudaimonists, understanding that all practical reason requires a final end, where a vision of the good life incorporates '*human* fulfilment and *individual* fulfilment' (Russell 2013: 11, italics in original). However, the difference in the understanding of 'eudaimonia' – among ancient philosophers, between ancient and modern ethics and between contemporary virtue theories – has signified a 'fundamental divide' in approaches (Slote 2000: 327).

Nevertheless, there is broad agreement that the achievement of happiness amounts to acting virtuously, deliberating rationally on what will achieve the ultimate good, with an individual's reason informed by the virtues. As MacIntyre points out, 'the virtues are precisely those qualities the possession of which will enable an individual to achieve *eudaimonia* and the lack of which will frustrate his movement towards that *telos*' (2007: 148). Thus, understanding Aristotle's vision of happiness for the sexual life, Scruton points out, does not amount to the 'satisfaction of impulses, but to the fulfilment of the person' (2006: 326). Translated into our own public sexual ethic, a vision of human flourishing which focusses solely on the absence of pregnancy or disease may invariably fall short, as, indeed, would a vision which gives undue attention to satisfying sexual impulses. For, as Scruton suggests, 'health is the state in which I flourish as an animal; happiness is the state in which I flourish as a person' (2006: 327).

In noting the link between human flourishing and virtuous living, Foot states: 'Human beings do not get on well without them. Nobody can get on well if he lacks courage, and does not have some measure of temperance and wisdom, while communities where justice and charity are lacking are apt to be wretched places to live' (1978: 3). Wright echoes this observation by pointing out that 'the "virtues" are the different strengths of character which together contribute to someone becoming a fully flourishing human being' (2010: 31). Thus, in moving forward in our discussion, we affirm Jean Porter's definition of a virtue as 'a trait of character or intellect that is in some way praiseworthy, admirable or desirable' (2012: 87). The nurturing of such qualities of character is not only beneficial for the individual but for the community: '*Virtues are defined as qualities of a person that make that person a good person in community, and that contribute to the good of the community, or to the good that humans are designed for*' (Stassen and Gushee 2003: 32, italics in original).

In engaging with a theological virtue ethic as a means of enriching moral discourse – particularly as policy emphasis shifts from SRE to RSE – it is important to highlight two prerequisites that frame the conversation. First, as indicated in Chapter 1, I shall adopt what Cooling presents as a 'transformationalist strategy' in education, where Christian values, rather than being viewed as separatist, are welcomed as a means of enriching moral discourse and contributing to the common good in education. In light of this approach, and in view of modern accounts of the virtues within moral education, we will explore common ground with, in particular, the communitarian and neoclassical accounts of character formation, which Hunter suggests have emerged in direct challenge to the inadequacy of the 'sovereign self' account of moral education in psychological approaches to moral education (2000: 193).

In doing so, we heed MacIntyre's warning about the 'indeterminacy of meaning' (1991: 6) when it comes to the virtues, which can lead to discrepancy both in their understanding and application in a morally pluralistic context. As he rightly highlights, 'there is no theory-neutral, prephilosophical, yet adequately determinate account of the virtues to be given' (1991: 12). As such, 'there can be no theory-neutral education into the practice of the virtues' (1991: 13). This raises a particular challenge for character education in a pluralistic context: 'How is it possible in a heterogeneous society, composed of people who sharply disagree about basic values, to achieve a consensus about what constitutes character education for citizens in democracy? Can we agree on what constitutes character education, on what its content should be, and how it should be taught?' (Arthur 2008: 91). Within educational discourse, these questions and concerns have been noted (see, for example, Kristjánsson 2013; Katayama 2003).

In attempting to achieve an agreed understanding of character, therefore, the metaethical challenges raised in Chapter 4 around an 'informed choice' approach to moral education are not automatically resolved within a virtue account. Thus, 'it would be a mistake to suppose that thinking in terms of virtues resolves all the philosophical questions about moral education, let alone the practical issues about how to pursue moral education' (Haydon 2003: 326). As Halstead and McLaughlin warn: 'in the absence of an overall and adequately sophisticated characterisation of the nature and structure of the virtues, and a specification of the ingredients of the sort of practical reasoning with which they must be inseparably connected, proponents of "character education" are in danger of being left with a mere "bag of virtues" for transmission' (1999: 145). Thus, the difficulty of addressing and seeking to resolve 'questions of meaning, priority and coherence with respect to the virtues' is very evident (1999: 145). Concerning issues of particularity with regard to moral content and meaning, Hunter rightly suggests: 'These moral matters simply cannot be addressed without getting into the practicalities of moral commitment and the traditions and communities that ground those commitments' (2000: 210).

In light of this challenge, Carr and Steutel suggest that one solution has been to incorporate a broad Aristotelian conception of moral formation within the existing liberal-principled framework: 'The overall aim would be, in short, to have the liberal cake, but eat it communitarianly' (1999b: 249). In addition, key contributors to the debate have outworked the argument for educating in 'civic virtue' (Halstead and McLaughlin 1999: 149). After all, educating according to the principles and virtues required for participation within a democratic society is, for proponents like Gutmann, the primary purpose of public education (1987: 287). This involves teaching the 'morality of association' which incorporates such virtues as 'empathy, trust, fairness, and benevolence' (1987: 62). Recognizing that no morally neutral account of sex education can be found, she affirms the democratic process in deciding on the legitimacy of teaching the subject and the appropriate approach (1987: 111).

However, notwithstanding the value of the democratic process and virtues of association identified, there remains the same unanswered question concerning the ontological foundations of the possible virtues up for discussion. The nature, meaning and content of the virtues would appear to be self-evident or, perhaps, the hope exists that they might become self-evident after democratic deliberation. Yet for Robert Nash, in his call for a 'moral conversation' in response to the authoritative 'minsters of morality' within character education in the US, such foundational questions are irrelevant: 'I believe a nonfoundational, multifunctional, and non-exclusionary public moral language is a key in promoting reconciliation and eschewing division not just in a classroom, but in a democracy as well' (1997: 148). Adding to Gutmann's dispositions for democratic deliberation and decision-making, Nash presents his 'postmodern virtues' – including hope, confidence, courage, self-respect, friendship, trust, honesty, decency, humility, faith, self-denial and charity (1997: 163–166) – judged necessary for moral conversation. In view of his non-foundational position, he does so in the hope of avoiding accusations of being nihilistic or antireligious (1997: 163).

While Nash's emphasis on the need for a moral conversation within a pluralist, secular democracy is admirable, there should remain not only a concern that ultimate questions concerning moral truth remain unanswered, but that they deliberately remain so. Even those virtues such as humility, faith, self-denial and charity, which he acknowledges have religious or distinctly Christian foundations, can only have 'functional utility' if they are '"decoupled" from their religious roots and secularized' (1997: 166). It is necessary, therefore, for virtues to stand on their own perceived merit. Nash refuses, suggests Arthur, to acknowledge that 'all education rests on assumptions and beliefs and that a plurality of positions, including character education, can co-exist' (2008: 89). At the same time it is important to recognize, as Gutmann and Nash do, that it will be possible to find many common values and virtues in democratic society, values which are informed by, and continue to shape, the cultural narrative. In light of this, Halstead and McLaughlin note the overlap that exists between 'non-expansive' and 'expansive' conceptions of character education, with the latter enriching and expanding the former (1999: 154).[3]

Yet, at a philosophical level, the idea of any concept of citizenship being derived from a functional, rather than a foundational basis is to undermine the necessity of having a defence for the moral validity of that position and the necessity of showing one's 'moral workings'. This has been, from the start, a central critique of the current moral assumptions within existing SRE policy. As Hunter concludes: 'Of good intentions there is no end. The commitment to do well by our children is serious and unflagging. In the

3 A 'non-expansive' approach to character education, according to Halstead and McLaughlin, is one that offers an insufficient rationale for its conception of character, proposes fundamental traits that should be directly taught, and downplays the role of reason in moral decision-making (1999: 137). With 'expansive' conceptions of character education, in contrast, 'a fuller and more substantial account is offered of matters such as the nature and extent of its rationale, the qualities of character and virtue aimed at, and the role given to appropriate forms of reasoning on the part of students' (1999: 146).

end, however, while we desperately want the flower of morality to bloom and multiply, we have, at the same time, pulled the plant up out from the soil that sustains it' (2000: 226). Yet these sociological conclusions, Arthur notes, while important and valid, provide 'few practical solutions for character educators' (2003: 98).

Therefore, in engaging with theology as a 'partner for educators' (Sullivan 2014), I will make the case for how a theological virtue ethic can enrich moral discourse around RSE. While it may be regarded as a 'sectarian' position (Nash 1997: 58), it introduces a moral language, I will suggest, that presents a more human approach to moral education and human flourishing – not overtly focussed on a young person's capacity for moral reasoning, but offering a more embodied understanding of how directed loves and desires shape habits and contribute to personal formation.

In following on from the first, a second prerequisite to any public conversation on the place of virtue in the moral life – and, in particular, moral education in a pluralistic context – is to recognize and accept that there will be fundamental differences in the underlying presuppositions brought to bear in the discussion. In highlighting these differences, Robert C. Roberts, for example, points out that within a classical virtue ethic, a virtue is a 'realization or actualization of some aspect of human nature' (1995: 66) whereas virtues – ascribed and understood within the Christian narrative – are determined and formed in two ways: 'a. as a response to grace; and b. as imitation of God' (1995: 69). These foundational distinctions, particularly between a philosophical and a theological account of virtue, cannot and should not be overlooked. As Wright states: 'Virtue, in the great philosophical tradition, has always said, "Become what you will be." Christian virtue says, "What you will be is what you already are in Christ"' (2010: 102).

Therefore, in light of the narrative context that gives shape and meaning to virtues, I do not seek to present a theological virtue ethic as equivalent in meaning and practice to other virtue traditions. At the same time, I do not see a constructive conversation between these traditions as redundant. Stanley Hauerwas – who has arguably presented the most prolific and detailed contemporary examination of a theological virtue ethic within the Protestant tradition (Hauerwas 1975; 1981; 1983; Hauerwas and Pinches 1997) – acknowledges that the language of virtue or character 'might well be useful to *most* accounts of moral development' (1981: 132). He clarifies and qualifies this by saying that his own reflections are specifically concerned with moral growth in the Christian community, reiterating the importance of the narrative context for understanding moral growth. Indeed, he critiques a 'moral development that is independent of content', pointing out that the idea of moral development is 'seductive', on account of the fact that it presupposes an understanding of what accounts as moral (1981: 129). Yet Hauerwas and Pinches acknowledge that the differences in virtue traditions do not make 'a conversation between Christian and ancient pagan or modern liberal accounts of the virtues impossible or irrelevant' (1997: x). Instead, the differences make the conversation 'all the more necessary as well as interesting' (1997: x).

In light of this, and embracing the constructive spirit that is inherent in a 'transformationalist' approach to SRE, I will seek to be faithful to a theological account of human personhood and human sexuality, recognizing that no virtue account is 'ideologically neutral' (Roberts 1995: 67). In the development of our discussion, we will point out where modern accounts of virtue are incompatible with this account, and in the spirit of tolerant and open public engagement, it will be for public moral discourse to make a judgement on whether the 'moral orientation' of a theological virtue ethic should contribute towards a public vision of human flourishing within RSE policy and practice as, indeed, it should do so with every other 'moral orientation' represented. The end purpose of this discussion is to make the case for how such a vision can enrich the moral discourse of SRE policy: a vision outworked in practical terms through the re-introduction of a moral language that engages with the relational good of sexual behaviour and human flourishing. This a vision in which, as Volf suggests, the love of pleasure gives way to the pleasure of love (2011: 145).

Christian Virtue and the Virtue Tradition

It is evident within historic and contemporary theological discourse that the case has been made for why the virtues offer a particularly suitable framework within which to present a Christian understanding of the moral life (see, for example, Porter 2012: 87–102; Kallenberg and Tousley 2011: 814–819). This tradition can be traced back, in particular, to the significant contribution made by Thomas Aquinas in the thirteenth century in the *Summa Theologica*, and was informed by, and developed in response to, other moral traditions, in particular the Hellenistic tradition. Indeed, the 'theoretical structure' that the ancient tradition of virtue ethics provides is arguably unsurpassed, and offers the structure within which to examine other theories 'that call themselves virtue ethics' (Annas 2006: 515–516). In his extended critique of the ethic of Aristotle and Aquinas, Hauerwas affirms this: 'Their thought, in spite of obvious difficulties and ambiguities, continues to be the most adequate systematic account of the nature of character in the history of ethics' (1975: 35). In light of this philosophical virtue tradition, Porter points to two formative sources for a Christian understanding of the virtues – the Hellenistic tradition and those presented in Scripture (2012: 88). Indeed, as a precursor to his exploration of the New Testament scriptural understanding of Christian virtue, Wright points out that it was the experience of early Christians that 'in and through Jesus they had discovered *both* a totally different way of being human *and* a way which scooped up the best that ancient wisdom had to offer and placed it in a framework where it could, at last, make sense' (2010: 13, italics in original). Consequently, earliest accounts of ethical teaching and learning within the church evidence the place the virtues occupied in the curriculum, interpreting, in particular, the Greek philosophical tradition in light of the Christian faith, for example, in the curriculum of Origen (Young 2006: 485–500).

More recently, Hauerwas has expounded a defence for a virtue ethic within the Protestant tradition, suggesting that every theological ethic adopts a metaphor in which an understanding of the nature of God and man's moral experience is understood. Pointing to the dominance of the 'command-obedience' metaphor within Protestant theological ethics, he adopts instead virtue and character as his central metaphors (1975: 2). Hauerwas indicates that the language of character and virtue does not 'exclude the language of command but only places it in a larger framework of moral experience' (Hauerwas and Pinches 1997: 3). In accounting for the relationship between our beliefs and subsequent behaviour, he states: 'Our moral life is not comprised of beliefs plus decisions; our moral life is the process in which our convictions form our character to be truthful' (1983: 16). Wells points out that, for Hauerwas, the efficient rather than the final cause of moral decisions is his primary concern and, as such, 'the stuff of ethics lies further upstream in the formation of the agents who are to become the efficient causes' (1998: 25). This understandably leaves Hauerwas open to criticism that he fails to adequately outwork his theological beliefs (Healy 2014: 102).

Consequently, while narrative can give content and meaning to our existence, questions arise as to whether it can provide a sufficient foundation for ethics. Instead, Hollinger suggests that we need both the 'broad strokes' of narrative and the 'specific pointers' of commands and principles (2002: 59). He points, in particular, to a 'transcendent reality' beyond the context of community which can be known through the revelation of God in the 'written and incarnate Word' (2002: 60). As applied to a Christian sexual ethic, while Hollinger affirms the 'foundation, motivation, and substance' that narrative provides, he yet points to the fact that 'principles are a significant part of divine revelation and show us the directions and boundaries our sexual lives ought to reflect' (2009: 42). Therefore, attention given to the virtues must be done alongside an understanding of the commands and principles that shape a theological ethic: 'An ethic that focuses on both character and decisions, the internal (who we are) and the external (what we do), is far more holistic and representative of biblical guidance' (2009: 42). Similarly, Porter notes that the language of virtue and the language of moral rules may indeed provide different roles within moral discourse, neither replacing nor reducing the necessity for the other (1995: 137).

In reflecting on the role of Scripture in shaping the moral life, William Spohn observes that the ethics of principles and consequences are subordinate to the ethics of character as a source of moral knowledge (Spohn 2005: 94). In addition, those who advocate a theological virtue-centred approach to ethics do not dismiss the authority of Scripture or the implications of the Incarnation for Christian ethics, but recognize that both provide the content and context which give form and meaning to community (Hauerwas 1981: 36–71). Thus, in view of the narrative context within which a virtue ethic is understood, it is the community that is given an elevated place and influence in shaping the meaning of the moral life and determining an understanding of moral character (1981: 129–152; 1983: 17–34).

More specifically, in reflecting on the place of an ethic of character within the biblical narrative, Benjamin F. Farley points out that central to any biblical understanding is the affirmation of humanity created in the image of God. This, he suggest, has two implications: '(1) the high human potential for intellectual development and moral sensitivity, (2) the uniquely human capacity for fellowship and cooperation with God and neighbor' (1995: 5). The fall, he contends, did not completely destroy God's image in us, and 'men and women alike are capable of impressive moral and intellectual achievement' (1995: 6). Of course, this touches on one of the fundamental internal critiques of a Christian virtue ethic within theological discourse: that of recognizing and reconciling the ethical theory with the nature of our corrupted moral agency and the effect of sin on our understanding of personhood (see, for example, Lane 2006).

This leads us to make the distinction between a philosophically informed and theologically informed understanding of human *telos*. MacIntyre suggests that Aristotle's scheme is 'complicated and added to, but not essentially altered, when placed within a framework of theistic beliefs' (2007: 53). One addition was the concept of sin. Indeed, as MacIntyre notes, 'there is no word in the Greek of Aristotle's age correctly translated "sin", "repentance", or "charity"' (2007: 174). However, the doctrine of sin fundamentally alters our theological understanding of human nature and the outworking of moral theory. In defence of a distinctly theological ethic of virtue, John Millbank, for example, argues that the 'counter-history', 'counter-ethics' and 'counter-ontology' of Christianity makes MacIntyre's assertion refutable in its presumptions and presuppositions

(1990: 326–438). However, while the content of virtue and virtuous living is fundamentally altered, there is inevitable continuity in the conceptual framework of human *telos*, even if MacIntyre concedes that 'only grace enables us to respond to and obey its precepts' (2007: 54).

In his assessment of an ethic of character within an evangelical ethic, O'Donovan acknowledges the soteriological discrepancy between a Catholic and Protestant understanding of character formation within the respective moral traditions; this does not deem either one redundant, nor indeed the outcome of the moral deliberation: 'We shall not learn how to save our souls by talking about the formation of virtuous characters. Nevertheless, such talk may teach us better than anything else what it is for a soul to be lost or saved, and so teach us to care about it for ourselves and others' (1994: 224). As Farley points out, the gospel truth behind a biblical virtue ethic is clear: '*no one is saved by exercising virtue; nor is anyone damned for the lack of it. God and God's grace come first*' (1995: 3, italics in original).

Nevertheless, as a result of this discrepancy, Arthur claims that there are few ethicists and moral philosophers from the Protestant tradition engaged in thinking around character education and virtue ethics (2003: 47). In light of this, Arthur notes: 'It is both interesting and strange that some Protestant writers in the field are suspicious of Aristotle and not Piaget, and that they trust Kohlberg and not Aquinas' (2003: 54). Virtue theory is largely associated with a Catholic moral tradition and arguably remains a 'neglected concept in protestant ethics' (Herms 1982: 481). When it comes to educating for virtue and character, Arthur suggests that the Catholic Church thus 'appears to have a clear, definite and intelligible theory of character formation which is strengthened by religious motive' (2003: 57).

In contrast, a Protestant approach is not so clearly understood and still lacks an adequate theological framework within which to construct a vision of educating in virtue. Those whom he does identify fit into one of two communities: 'the neo-orthodox who lean towards separatism and isolationism in their view of character within their own Christian communities, and another liberal group who have been too open to non-Christian accounts of character' (2003: 47). Thus, Gilbert C. Meilaender identifies the challenge faced by Protestant educators in giving credence to both their belief that virtues can be shaped by habit and yet the assertion that the virtuous life is only possible on account of divine initiative (1984: 123).

In light of this tension, Herdt, in addressing in particular the fundamental objection posed by a Lutheran position, i.e. that of seeking to foster virtuous habits and communities before firstly exhibiting a total reliance on God's gift of grace (2008: 174), points out: 'Luther is forced to concede that children must be transformed from outside in, at least in the sense that the beauty of external practices can render them receptive hearers of the Word' (2008: 189). This is echoed in Gerald Strauss's account of the pedagogical principles that defined Luther's approach to education and learning: 'Still, one may find in his assertions enough encouragement to support the conclusion that educational efforts are by no means wasted or without object and direction' (1978: 35). In particular, and interesting for our own discussion, were the efforts made to prolong the perceived innocence of childhood when it came to a young person's acknowledgement and understanding of their sexual nature, in order to allow time for the forming and shaping of thoughts and habits (1978: 101).

Virtue and Moral Education

The language of virtue has shaped a rich philosophical and theological landscape within which an ethic of character has been understood, and in which an approach to moral education has been formed (Carr 2000b; Carr 2000c). In understanding virtues as qualities of character that are acquired, character is not equivalent to temperament or natural trait, but it is something that an individual chooses (Hauerwas 1975: 16). Thus, in exploring the interest of character in moral education, R. S. Peters noted: 'A craving for a beef-steak, a lust for a pretty girl reveal a man's nature, not his character. His character is revealed in what he does about them, in the manner in which he regulates, or fails to regulate them' (1974: 246). In light of this, actions are not devoid of motivation or reason, but instead virtues are character traits that must manifest a commitment to 'some ethical *value*' such as justice, where the moral agent does not simply perform actions that are deemed to be just, but is disposed, engaging practical reasoning, to act accordingly (Annas 2006: 519). In doing so, 'the various virtues receive their particular form through the agent's character' (Hauerwas 1975: 16).

It is important for our own discussion to identify key features of this ethical theory, both through a theological and a philosophical lens, and its implication for a virtue approach to moral education: in particular, the emphasis it places on the moral agent, and the role and effectiveness of virtue as a moral guide. In doing so, we will strengthen our case for why a theological virtue ethic offers a justifiable guide to the moral life, and how and why the cultivation of virtue offers important insights for moral education and, in turn, Relationships and Sex Education.

The Moral Agent: Being versus Doing

Dennis Hollinger offers a succinct definition of a virtue approach to ethics: 'The key issue is not What ought we to do? but rather What ought we to be? The kind of people we are as evidenced by our virtues, firmly implanted within, is the heart and essence of ethics' (2002: 45). It follows that a virtue ethic, in comparison to other ethical traditions, places particular importance on human agency. In doing so, Hauerwas notes that 'to attribute agency to a person is to assume that he is capable of changing the circumstances around himself' (1997: 83). Carr echoes this point by affirming necessary qualities of moral agency: 'one cannot understand what it is to engage in appropriate moral reasoning and deliberation apart from some grasp of what it is to be a moral agent – conceived in terms of the possession of broader qualities of moral character, perception and sensibility' (Carr 2008: 101).

In light of this emphasis on human agency, the morality of an action is measured more by the character and motivation of the moral agent than by a consequentialist judgement, or compliance with law and duty. While other ethical theories, i.e. those within a Kantian or utilitarian tradition, offer an account of the moral agent and recognize the importance of cultivating the virtues, their point of departure is not the moral agent, but the nature of the moral reasoning needed in order to be accorded status as a moral agent (Carr 2008: 101). In expounding a virtue approach to moral education, Carr and Steutel highlight the distinctions in differentiating a virtue ethic from other ethical approaches. They note, for example, a broad and narrow interpretation of a virtue approach: 'On the broad interpretation, a virtue ethics certainly requires us to provide an ethical justification of virtues – some account of their moral significance – but on a narrow interpretation, the ethics of virtue points to a justification of a particular kind: one which grounds moral life and the aims of education in other than utilitarian and Kantian considerations' (1999a: 6–7).

Therefore, while other moral traditions may have a theory of virtue, a moral theory that treats virtue as just one aspect of that theory, does not count as a virtue ethic (Slote 2000: 326). Hauerwas acknowledges that a theological ethic of character is problematic for those who view command as central to ethics, reflecting a more general concern about the danger of ethics seeking to understand the Christian life apart from God's grace (1975: 130–131). In addition, one 'vice' of the longer-term, virtue-centred approach, suggests Louden, is that it may lead to a 'peculiar sort of moral backsliding', due to the focus on good or bad agents, rather than right or wrong actions (1997: 209).

Nonetheless, in comparison to other theories of moral education, a virtue approach advocates that moral education and engagement has an intrinsic, rather than just an extrinsic, benefit in that life is enriched by the possession of virtues and young people are brought to appreciate the moral life for its own sake (see, for example, Putman 1995). In contrast to trait or character-utilitarianism, for example, character traits are good, not in so far as they maximize utility, but for their own intrinsic merit and that they constitute a vision of human flourishing (Carr and Steutel 1999a: 14). Thus where the motivation of an act-centred ethic is the concept of duty or the maximization of utility, the motivation of a virtue theorist is the virtues themselves (Louden 1997: 205). Carr highlights characteristics such as honesty, self-control and justice, as exemplified in the moral virtues, as dispositions which carry their own intrinsic value (2004: 15). Yet, despite the presumed value of these traits, Carr and Steutel also note 'a surprising dearth' in contemporary philosophical thinking on virtue theory (1999b: 241).

In envisioning the moral life and the moral agent through a theological lens, a biblical understanding of virtue is often equated with teachings concerning the disposition of 'the heart'. As Hollinger states: 'The word *heart* occurs hundreds of times in English translations of the Bible, and it is clearly the closest concept to character, the innate moral dispositions of the moral actor' (2002: 56, italics in original). O'Donovan cautions, however, against an understanding of the biblical teaching on the heart overlooking the place of moral action, substituting 'agent-evaluation for act-evaluation' (1994: 205). Instead, he suggests, it is important to recognize the correlation between the two: '(a) the subject's character must not be reduced to a function of his acts; (b) the subject's acts must be allowed to disclose his character, which will make itself known only through them' (1994: 206). On the first point, Hauerwas points to a similar conclusion drawn by Aristotle's ethic, in that 'the mere fact that a man performs certain acts does not mean that he is a man of good character' (1975: 39). Additionally, Louden notes the fact that nobody is morally infallible, for 'even the best person can make the wrong choices' (1997: 206). Also, moral characters, he suggests, are vulnerable to change (1997: 208).

O'Donovan's second point is of particular importance for an understanding of virtue within the moral life, for in noting the 'epistemological priority of act', O'Donovan suggests that knowledge of a person's character is important, not for deliberative moral reasoning, but for the moral evaluation of an act (1994: 215). At the same time, Louden points out that 'we cannot always know the moral value of a person's character by assessing his or her actions' (1997: 211). Virtue-based theories are open, he suggests, to the charge of 'style over substance' in terms of the ends to which they are directed (1997: 215), and thus argues that a virtue ethic is 'particularly weak in the areas of casuistry and applied ethics' (1997: 205). Nevertheless, when it comes to moral reasoning, while an act-centred ethic is concerned with devising a particular formula of rules to resolve moral dilemmas, an agent-centred ethic is more concerned with the long-term impact of choices on the agent's character (1997: 209; see also Carr 2003). Thus, preceding epistemological questions concerned with the content of moral reasoning, a virtue ethic identifies a reciprocal relationship between character and action.

In view of this long-term lens, character is understood as something that is not fixed or permanently determined, but accounts for the 'continuing qualification of our agency' (Hauerwas 1975: 120). Georg Henrik von Wright notes: 'Because of the lack of an essential tie between a virtue and an act-category, *the path of virtue is never laid out in advance*. It is for the man of virtue to determine where it goes in the particular case' (1963: 145, italics in original). At the same time, a philosophical and theological account recognize the impact of habitual virtuous behaviour on one's long-term character, where virtuous acts are done, among other things, notes Aristotle, from a 'fixed and permanent disposition' (2004: 37, *NE* 1105a 32). Thus, as Hollinger notes, while character may inform our decisions, the decisions, in turn, inform our character (2002: 58–59).

We can see that a particular understanding of human agency and the formation of moral character is presented within a virtue ethic – a theory, Joseph Kotva suggests, is positioned between behaviourism and voluntarism: 'We are not, as the behaviourist account suggests, simply at the mercy of forces outside our control; we help form our own and each other's character. We also are not, contrary to the voluntarist account, free from the constraints of character. Past choices and actions influence the kind of person we become, and the kind of persons we become informs our choices and actions' (1996: 28). Therefore, based on a progressive understanding of the moral self, Hauerwas notes that 'the ethics of character is concerned with the self's duration, growth, and unity' (1975: 179) and, within a theological account, accords with the doctrine of sanctification. As Wright states: '*virtue* is what happens when wise and courageous choices have become "second nature"' (2010: 9, italics in original).

Virtue as Moral Guide

The interaction between judgement and action lies at the heart of morality and moral education (Straughan 1988). Carr and Steutel note that a virtue ethic moves moral education beyond the acquisition of knowledge and the ability to process cognitively to understanding the role motivation plays in appreciating and outworking moral principles (1999b: 245). In doing so, it seeks to present a more coherent picture of the interplay between 'reason, affect and behaviour in virtuous conduct' (1999b: 252). Therefore, it remains a central task of virtue ethicists, Slote suggests, to give an account of how people should act, 'giving a *distinctively virtue-ethical account* of the rightness or wrongness, goodness or badness, of human actions' (2000: 326, italics in original).

Drawing on the place of virtue in Aristotle's moral philosophy, Carr highlights three key contributions that a virtue ethic can make to philosophical reflections on moral education. First, it brings focus to the practical and habitual nature of the moral life and emphasizes the need for practical training in the moral virtues, grounded in the exercise of temperance and self-control (2008: 114). Aristotle advanced that the 'intellectual virtues are acquired through teaching, the virtues of character from habitual exercise' (MacIntyre 2007: 154; see Curren et al. 2007). Secondly, a virtue ethic stresses the responsibility of parents, teachers and responsible adults in presenting examples of model conduct (Carr 2008: 115; Carr and Steutel 1999b: 253). Thirdly, full virtue is achieved when moral habituation is accompanied by the exercise of moral deliberation, practical wisdom (2008: 115). As such, a particular emphasis is placed on the acquisition and habitual exercise of practical wisdom and the relation of virtue to character (Carr and Steutel 1999b: 252). This can be traced to Aristotle's understanding of *phronesis* where 'it is not possible to be fully good without having practical wisdom, nor practically wise without having excellence of character' (Halstead and McLaughlin 1999: 135, *NE* 1144b 31–32).

Rosalind Hursthouse's neo-Aristotelian virtue ethic responds to the perceived weakness of a virtue ethic in providing specific moral guidance. She argues that moral rules and virtues both require an account of morality in order to guide moral decision and are, therefore, both open to the danger of relativism or moral scepticism (1999: 32–34). In effect, whether a moral evaluation is centred on the agent or the act, without a narrative account of reality, this leaves principally unanswered the criteria against which an evaluative account of their behaviour is given or, indeed, a guide as to what the moral agent should do or be. For example, in exploring a virtue ethics approach to sexuality, Halwani questions whether there are sexual acts that a virtuous person would not engage in and, equally, whether there are acts that stem from vice, that are deemed wrong (2006: 280). As such, Louden points to the necessity of morally condemning some acts in view of their intolerable nature, (1997: 207–208) emphasizing that acts, rather than agents, should sometimes be the locus of moral evaluation (210). As Linville points out: 'We should be able to say simply that rape and genocide are wrong because people ought neither to be raped nor exterminated' (2009a: 431).

It is important to note that a virtue ethic does not demote the value of moral reasoning. Instead, a virtue is concerned with the disposition to act for a reason: 'The exercise of the agent's practical reasoning is thus essential to the way a virtue is both built up and exercised' (Annas 2006: 516). According to the classical understanding, a virtuous agent, engaging their affective and intellectual nature, chooses to do the right thing for the right reason (2006: 517). For example, Aristotle recognized 'an essential connection between the idea of man capable of action and his existence as a rational being' (Hauerwas 1975: 46). Thus, Aristotle's moral agent discerns the end towards which reasoning is directed: 'Now the origin of action (the efficient, not the final cause) is choice, and the origin of choice is appetition and purposive reasoning' (2004: 146, 1139a 30). Accordingly, the reason which precedes moral judgement is informed by the virtues, and the virtues informed by the corresponding vision of the good life and human flourishing. As Geach states: 'But if (and this is what I believe) all men can attain their last end, but only by right choices, then it is reasonable to suppose that the right choice must be guided be a right view of things' (1977: 18).

In addition, on both a philosophical and theological account of moral action, reasoning and choice are not devoid of desire. Hauerwas points out that both Aristotle and Aquinas were 'aware of the interdependence of reason and desire' (1975: 47), integrating an understanding of the moral and intellectual virtues (1975: 59). Virtue is distinguished from the 'mere capacity' required for a skill or an art, for it must engage the will (Foot 1978: 8). Choice, therefore, is an intentional outcome of man's rational and desiring self, and engages the agent's will: 'In choice man's will receives its particular determination, for it is in choice that man is committed to act in the concrete, that in electing the act he elects to be a particular kind of man' (Hauerwas 1975: 65, citing Aquinas, *ST*, I-II.13.2).

As such, even though intentions are not always realized, agency and action cannot be separated within an idea of character, in view of the agent's self-determining nature and the embodied nature of his choices and actions: 'Man's very ability to engage the world, shaping it in accordance with his intentions and projects, determines who he is' (Hauerwas 1975: 114). This echoes Thielicke's vision of sexual personhood, in which sexual behaviour is not viewed in isolation, but is understood alongside our thinking, feeling and willing attributes. Therefore, while Gushee and Stassen warn against the 'fundamental error' of distinguishing between the importance of being and doing (2003: 73), acquiring character through determined action lies at the heart of what Hauerwas understands it to mean to have character (1975: 79).

In light of the multi-dimensional nature of character formation and the moral life, Gushee and Stassen, in their theological account, suggest a move from talking of virtue ethics to 'holistic character ethics' (2003:55) presenting four dimensions of a character ethic which they advance as faithful to Jesus's teaching and a broader biblical ethic: 'our passions/loyalties, our perceptions, our way or reasoning and our basic convictions' (2003: 59). The first dimension appears to echo Smith's anthropological presuppositions – that we are more than autonomous minds, but our passions and related loyalties to people, practice, and communities and ultimately to God, deeply shape our character. This reflects what van der Ven notes to be the inter-relational dynamic of character development: 'Character does not unfold from within the person in isolation, but is called out through interaction with others in that situation, and through the grappling with tasks and challenges that are part of that situation' (1998: 354). A holistic model, Gushee and Stassen suggest, avoids ethics deteriorating into 'inward emigration', overtly focussed on private morality and failing to take account of the social context in which character is shaped (2003: 74).

Conclusion

Cultivating virtue within moral education requires a vision of the moral agent within a vision for the moral life, in particular, a concept of human *telos* informed by an understanding of what it is to flourish as a human being. Thus, the question emerges over whether it is in fact possible in a pluralistic society to find a 'unifying concept of a virtue'; as Halstead and McLaughlin note, 'whether some virtues are universal and fundamental with respect to their significance for human life or whether virtues in general are inherently relativistic and particularistic' (1999: 134). In order to enrich moral discourse around future RSE policies and programmes with a constructive language of virtue, these questions must invariably be addressed, questions which are of a philosophical nature. Therefore, while recognizing that the discipline of psychology has an interest in moral growth and the development of moral character as outworked within moral education, our particular focus on character and virtue is of a philosophical and theological kind. At the same time, we acknowledge that the interplay between the disciplines cannot go unnoted, particularly in view of what Carr notes to be the analytical 'revolution' in the philosophy of education, and the integration of the empirical theories of social science with philosophical discourse, including the focus on rationality in deriving moral norms (2010: 44).

In presenting *The Christian Case for Virtue Ethics*, Kotva notes three points on which he suggests consensus has been reached on human *telos*: first, that the human good is embodied in the practice of virtue; secondly, that the embodied virtues are an inclusive part of the human good; and thirdly, that the human good is an individual and corporate activity (1996: 20–21). On the third point, he highlights that the functional nature of moral growth inevitably involves others and, in addition, he argues for the interconnectedness of the human good: 'The human *telos* is found in common projects, shared activities, and intimate relationships' (1996: 21). As such, he points out that many virtues lose their function and purpose outside of social relationships.

Essential for our own discussion is his observation concerning our social and relational nature, as understood within a virtue theory: 'virtue theory views us as creatures who fully flourish as individuals in relationships. The human *telos*, the best kind of life for humans, is one in which we become fully individuated in the midst of various kinds of intrinsically worthwhile relationships' (Kotva 1996: 22). The definition of an 'intrinsically worthwhile relationship' will inevitably be shaped and determined by the moral community, for as we have already established, there can be no neutral account of virtue. All virtues are determined by the moral narrative from which they arise. Gushee and Stassen point out that, for Kotva, this is an ethic grounded in biblical and theological understanding and convictions which view the moral end of the Christian life as that of being conformed into the image of Christ (2003: 70).

Thus, where different virtue theories will identify different values, what is central in a classical virtue ethic is that one's actions are understood within a broader conception of the whole of life (Annas 2006: 520). This is why '*vision* is likely to be a central theme in any ethic of virtue. Our virtues do not simply fit us for life; they help shape life' (Meilaender 1984: 11, italics in original). Echoing this, and of particular relevance for our own discussion, Herms points out that making the connection between action and a vision of the moral subject lies at the very heart of moral education (1982: 491). Therefore, we will continue to explore how our social nature and the corresponding virtues can be faithful to a Christian understanding of personhood and the outworking of grace. On this basis, and in light of basic Christian ethical convictions, such as Christlikeness and justice, Gushee and Stassen note that a discussion within a secular context may not prove redundant: 'The trick is to figure out how and where the way of Jesus can be normative for public ethics by persuasion' (2003: 61).

Indeed, re-imaging a language of virtue within the context of future RSE policy may simply re-awaken a moral language, the remnant of which remains within contemporary moral discourse. For, as Wright suggests, Western culture has already been shaped for centuries by elements of Christian teaching on what constitutes good character. As a consequence, what we explore in terms of Christian character, he claims, 'will overlap considerably with wider questions about the "character" that our whole society urgently needs to rediscover and develop' (2010: 27). Surely, in responding to the insufficiencies of a liberal approach to sex education, it is for the critic to argue why this would not or could not offer a worthwhile, enriching and, arguably, much needed contribution to the current and future moral discourse around Relationships Education and Relationships and Sex Education.

CHAPTER 9

Common Virtue in Moral Education: A Theological Defence

> From the outset, Christians have identified certain traits of character as virtues that are distinctively characteristic of their way of life, while condemning others as vices that undermine the life of the soul and the well-being of the community.
>
> — JEAN PORTER (2012: 87)

> Actively promoting the welfare, the shalom, of the larger human community will require us also to speak in the public square about policies and practices that can restrain sin and even contribute to positive patterns of civic righteousness.
>
> — RICHARD MOUW (2001: 84)

Throughout this book I have articulated the theological premises that underscore my arguments, particularly as they understand and offer a critique to the current liberal metanarrative around the nature of moral knowledge and sexual personhood. In addition to this, I have engaged with other disciplines to highlight the inconsistencies and weaknesses of the current moral approach to SRE. In engaging with a theological virtue ethic as a means of presenting a constructive contribution to the moral vision of future RSE policy, I must again more carefully show my 'moral workings'. In particular, in drawing on the elements of a virtue theory, as discussed already, and, in particular, exploring the philosophical logic and moral foundations of a virtue approach to RSE, our attention must turn to the theological implications of such an approach and its internal coherence as outworked in public policy.

On this point it is essential to note that the purpose of our discussion is not to directly engage with the Christian community's own commitment to its specific Christ-reflecting and Holy Spirit-empowered qualities of character and practices, nor indeed to offering a theological critique of the current understanding and outworking of its own sexual virtue – though this is an important and necessary task. The theological distinctiveness of Christian character is clear. In his exploration of the New Testament vision of Christian character, and answering the question of how Christians should behave, Wright asserts: 'Once Christian faith is in place, you need to develop Christian character by practicing the specifically Christian "virtues"' (2010: 12). Indeed, at a societal level Hauerwas suggests that the most important social task is for the church to be truthful to itself, to operate its own 'school of virtue' (1981: 84). This opens him up to the accusation of being 'ecclesiocentric' in his approach (Healy 2014: 38); nevertheless, Hauerwas affirms that: 'The challenge is always for the church to be a "contrast model" for all polities that know not God' (1981: 84).

In light of this social task, Hauerwas points out that the church must critique its own commitment to virtuous living as much as it critiques that of secular society for, as he suggests, the moral education of the young in church is often limited to 'conventional pieties coupled with a few unintelligible "don'ts"' (1981: 86). Indeed, research points to Christian young people developing a moral vision that is influenced more by a Western consumerist mindset, in pursuit of self-authenticated choice, than by the Christian moral narrative. For example, the creed of 'Moral Therapeutic Deism' that emerged from Christian Smith's large-scale study of the religious and spiritual lives of American teenagers revealed, amongst other things, the moral assumptions that God wants people to be good, nice and fair to each other and that the main goal of life is to be happy and feel good about oneself (2009: 162–163).

Thus, giving renewed attention to the distinctiveness of Christian virtuous living is not mutually exclusive from the contribution the church can make to the public good. Indeed, in affirming the distinct nature and practices of the Christian community, Walter Brueggemann suggests that when it comes to the church's engagement with society, 'the church has gifts to give when it acts out of its own peculiarity, out of its "new self", when it comes to "the other" out of its own being loved and forgiven' (2006: 195). As such, the exhibition of a distinctive virtuous character that arises out of a renewed life in Christ, and the practices that flow from it, have implications for the common good of wider society: 'The biblical virtues are keys to community well-being: peacemaking, hungering for justice, doing mercy, integrity, humility and caring for the poor and the mourning. And they are the way of participation in community with God' (Gushee and Stassen 2003: 53). Living within and according to this distinctive Christian narrative, Hauerwas suggests, offers 'a beacon to others illuminating how life should be lived well' (2003: 34).

However, in seeking to cultivate theological virtues, not within the context of Christian community, but within the context of public moral education, we open ourselves up to the accusations of moving outside of a coherent understanding of a theological ethic. Clearly, 'what it is to be a person in the fullest and deepest sense is a matter of controversy between different moral traditions' (Roberts 1995: 65). As a result, understandings of human nature and human flourishing are fundamentally different, as are the individual virtues that constitute the moral life (1995: 66). Thus, a theological virtue, understood apart from the process of sanctification which begins after union with Christ, 'seems meaningless or, at least, seriously lacking in integration with Christian doctrine and the human condition' (Varma 2010: 179). Indeed, the proponents of 'Radical Orthodoxy' claim that there is a 'deep antithesis that brokers no overlapping consensus' between what a Christian narrative defines as 'good' and what modern liberals describe as 'good' (Smith, 2004: 241). Herdt notes, however, that such a view, as exemplified by John Milbank, tends to 'collapse modern into pagan'; she suggests that Milbank 'is far too critical of both pagan and modern to be an advocate of virtue ethic as such' (Herdt 2008: 348).

In response to these criticisms, I will present a vision of human flourishing within RSE policy discourse that attempts to avoid what Herdt identifies as the very real temptation of contemporary Christian virtue ethics: 'on the one hand, that of falsely idealizing the church and its practices, and, on the other, that of denouncing secular modernity rather than discerning God at work within it' (2008: 347). In addressing this temptation, I affirm the dynamic reality of the church's dual citizenship: 'Pending the final disclosure of the Kingdom of God, the church and society are in dialectical relation, distant from each other as well as identified' (O'Donovan, 1996: 251).

This re-orientates the locus of our discussion, which is specifically concerned with a theological ethic of character in the context of public moral education. Presenting a Christian vision of personhood, and the virtues that correspond to it, can be viewed as a central part of moral education, while at the same time readily recognizing the theological tensions therein. Meilaender suggests that this tension evidences the practical outworking of the now but not yet of the Christian story: 'These virtues do at least foster human life together and fashion human behaviour – if not character in the fullest sense – in a way which more closely approximates God's will for human life' (1984: 125). The *What If Learning* concept of teaching and learning provides an example of a recent initiative within Christian education to explore the role of character in education, presenting a 'distinctive vision of what it means to be a person made in God's image'.[1]

In a wider sense, a focus on the examined life provided by virtue discourse can be seen as an apologetic opportunity. Presenting God in His full attractiveness, Alister McGrath suggests, includes presenting the morality which the Christian faith offers: 'Christianity offers a world-view, which leads to the generation of moral values and ideals which are able to give moral meaning and dignity to our existence' (1992: 226). As such, he views our perception of moral obligation as a 'point of contact for the gospel' (1992: 68). In adopting a constructive approach to public theological engagement, therefore, I will advance a position of 'holiness as relational engagement' rather than 'holiness as separation' (Brueggemann 2006: 188) when it comes to a public vision of moral education.

1 'Developing Christian Character', <http://www.whatiflearning.co.uk/files/_cache/pdf/Page-12-uk.pdf> accessed 20 March 2013. See also Cooling 2012; Cooling 2016.

A Natural Account of Common Virtue

We noted in Chapter 8 that a challenge arises for moral education in presenting a vision of character that, in view of the pluralistic context, avoids a subjective and relativistic evaluation of the virtues to be cultivated. What is needed instead is the articulation of virtues within a narrative that brings substance and meaning to their content. One approach is to adopt a neo-naturalist understanding of virtue – an understanding of virtue ethics in moral education where 'virtues are natural human dispositions conducive to objectively determinable goals of human flourishing' (Carr 2008b: 467). This suggests that there are common virtues across cultures and creeds which are objective, universal and therefore applicable to all, discernible through human reason and necessary to human flourishing. As Geach states, 'men need virtues as bees need stings' (1977: 17). This may at least be viewed as one response to the relativist danger presented by MacIntyre's social constructivist position (Carr 2003: 111), or as an alternative evaluation of virtue to the 'non-foundational' position evidenced in accounts of civic virtue. Within theological discourse, such a position accords with a natural law approach to ethical theory.

A natural law understanding of human nature and the moral life has a rich theoretical tradition which extends beyond the realm of theological discourse. In its origin and evolution, it was evident in Graeco/Roman philosophical thinking, and incorporated into an account of Christian ethics from the early church and Patristic period onwards (Pope 2012). While strongly associated with theological ethics, particularly within a Catholic tradition, the language of natural law has also been associated with a long-established philosophical and political tradition. Indeed, Charles Curran points to the fact that natural law 'involves three distinct but overlapping considerations – the strictly theological, the philosophical and the legal' (1996: 595). Despite the diversity of uses, Pope suggest that 'natural-law ethicists share a belief that there is such a thing as the human good, commensurate with human nature, however complex its manifestations and various its possible modes of fulfilment' (2012: 83). While acknowledging the rich tradition in which it has developed, observing natural theology and, in particular, natural law theory through a theological lens will narrow the frame in which our discussion is located.

Porter points to the resurgence of thinking on natural law theory among Catholic and Protestant ethicists alike, in response to modern moral discourse (1999: 27–28). In noting a previous reluctance among Christian ethicists and theologians to engage with this theory, she argues that if we 'avoid talking about the moral significance of human nature, both theological ethics and the wider social discourse will be impoverished' (1999: 27). Moreover, Pope identifies two central reasons why natural law is attractive to theological ethics: first, it affirms an objective, realist understanding of moral standards and, secondly, it affirms a morality that is universal in its scope (2005: 149).

For our own discussion, it is of interest to note that the rediscovery of the natural law tradition in Reformed theological ethics, particularly since the 1990s, is viewed as a resource for talking about moral issues in the public square (Grabill 2006: 6).[2] This is echoed in David VanDrunen's exploration of the place of natural law in Reformed social thought, noting that 'the fledgling renaissance of natural law and two kingdoms thinking among some Reformed writers today may provide a fresh and coherent contribution to wider discussions about Christianity and culture' (2010: 12). Indeed, J. Daryl Charles strongly asserts that, without an affirmation of natural law in the public square, our apologetic bridge is lost: 'We have consequently cut ourselves off at the knees in terms of developing a "public philosophy," at the heart of which lie natural law and "common grace"' (2008: 22).

In view of the potential resource for public engagement on moral issues, it is important to affirm that a theologically informed understanding of nature stands in contrast to the contemporary scientific and evolutionary understanding of human nature and behaviour, where nature is judged to be 'purposeless and amoral' (2005: 153; see also McGrath 2011). This is not to say that the same moral norms and values – regarded as an intrinsic part

2 Grabill points to a list of scholars whom he evidences as engaging with the natural law tradition – Nigel Biggar, Rufus Black, Carl Braaten, J. Budziszewski (now Roman Catholic), Michael Cromartie, Jean Bethke Elshtain, Arthur F. Holmes, Paul Helm, Alister McGrath, Susan Schreiner, David VanDrunen, and Daniel Westberg.

of human nature and valuable to present-day culture – are not valued by representatives of both a theistic and naturalistic worldview, merely that the ontological defence for their existence is fundamentally different: 'A materialistic, deterministic view of nature and natural events, for example, is incompatible with nearly all theistic affirmations' (Bangert 2006: 2).

As explored in Chapter 6, a theistic worldview can, where a naturalistic worldview cannot, provide a defence for the moral principles and virtues it ascribes to. More specifically, naturalism, in contrast to natural law theory, does not infer a morality that points to a transcendent reality. Instead, through the exercise of moral reasoning, humanly-constructed norms and values are established, applicable to a particular place and time (Pope 2005: 154). Thus, it is important to heed Pope's challenge for contemporary moral discourse: in deriving normative conclusions from the natural order, the notion of 'natural' changes (2005: 149). Indeed, where 'nature' is a culturally construed notion, our Western Enlightenment tradition has mistakenly believed that rationality is 'independent of culture and history' (McGrath 2008: 165).

Therefore, in deriving moral conclusions on human nature through a theological lens, it is important to adopt an understanding of the relationship between God and His creation. This, for Gustafson, is the most important 'base point' in developing a theological ethic (1984: 144). Within John Stott's 'fourfold scheme of biblical history', the account of creation is 'foundational to the Christian faith': 'The godlikeness of humankind emerges as the story unfolds: Men and women are rational and moral beings (able to understand and respond to God's commands), responsible beings (exercising dominion over nature), social beings (with a capacity to love and be loved), and spiritual beings (finding their highest fulfilment in knowing and worshipping their Creator' (2006: 62).

Our understanding of human virtue is thus related to our doctrine of creation. However, within Stott's 'fourfold scheme', the fall follows creation. This raises at least two points which require greater exploration and clarity in our discussion: How can human nature and the natural world be regarded as a source of moral knowledge? How do we give a theological defence for human reason having the capacity, not only to discern moral knowledge, but to do so in view of the corruption of moral agency as a consequence of sin? These are important considerations if we are to give a theological defence for the pursuit and cultivation of common virtue in moral education. According to Porter at least, 'if we take the doctrine of creation seriously – if we regard everything that exists, including ourselves, as creations of a good God – then it is problematic, at best, to claim that human virtue is altogether and without qualification false and evil' (2005: 212). Thus, she raises an important question for a theological virtue ethic, relevant to our own discussion: 'what kind of value should we ascribe to humanly attainable virtues, and by extension, to the moral life generally considered?' (2005: 213).

Human Reason and Moral Knowledge

Alister McGrath highlights the importance of understanding how nature is 'seen': 'the Christian "sees" nature through a lens which is shaped by the fundamental themes of the Christian faith' (2008: 306). He identifies three major approaches to discerning God in nature within the Christian tradition: 'human reason, the ordering of the world, and the beauty of the world' (2007: 164). Such discernment is fundamental, he argues, to a renewed understanding of goodness in nature (2008: 307). Thus, this epistemological claim that the moral order can be discerned by human reason is based on what McGrath identifies as a main theme in a Christian approach to understanding the natural world: 'The principle that humanity is created in the image of God, and thus endowed with some capacity to discern traces of God within or through nature' (2008: 178; 2008: 291–313). Indeed, this understanding of the *imago Dei* has shaped both Catholic and Protestant approaches to natural theology.

In light of this, James Bretzke draws the distinction between the ontological and the epistemological premise of natural law theory. While the ontological premise points to an objective moral order, the epistemological premise claims that this can be discerned with the application of 'right reason' (2011: 542). Indeed, the capacity for human reason itself, 'the height of human nature', is said to evidence God in nature (McGrath 2007: 164), and within the order of creation, knowledge of God's eternal law has been written on to human hearts by means of human conscience (Bretzke 2011: 542). The implications of these premises can be evidenced in a Catholic approach to character education in which the 'development of conscience' becomes one of its central aims (Arthur 2003: 53).

However, understood as an intuitionist approach, it has received much criticism. D. J. O'Connor, for example, in critiquing Aquinas's theory of natural law claims that 'we must have *some* set of axioms as our starting-point' (1967: 66, italics in original). In addition, if these 'natural inclinations', discerned by reason, were able to provide moral precepts by which to live, it is unclear why we ought to pursue them (1967: 72). Particular concern is also raised over how this understanding of nature impacts on an understanding of grace. In tracing back the distinction between autonomous nature and grace to the 'philosophic-theology' of Aquinas, Frances Schaeffer argued that, as a result of this distinction, 'nature began to "eat up" grace' (1968: 12–13). In Aquinas's defence, Porter argues that the distinction Aquinas made between nature and grace in understanding human virtue was due to his belief that both were directed towards different ends, 'naturally attainable happiness, and the supreme happiness of personal union with God' (2005: 217). Rather than eating up grace, she asserts, Aquinas repeatedly asserted that 'grace does not destroy nature, but rather perfects it' (2005: 217). Thus, a wider understanding of God's grace at work in all aspects of the natural order is needed. For, as David Nicholls suggests, while it may be important to distinguish grace from the natural realm of ideas, the cross-contamination is inevitable: 'God's Spirit is present in all authentic instances of the natural' (1996: 414).

In understanding natural law theory through the lens of the Christian faith, and thus within the 'economy of salvation', McGrath points out that nature and the human observer must also be understood within the narrative of the fall and the redemptive process initiated by the Incarnation (2008: 198). Subsequently, if our understanding of virtue is related to the doctrine of creation, then in viewing virtue through the lens of the Christian faith, it must also be reconciled with the doctrine of sin and the doctrine of salvation. Gustafson is also clear that the doctrine of sin cannot be overlooked. In his discussion on the appropriate understanding of God's relation to humanity and the world, in particular the aspects of what he calls the 'human fault', Gustafson points out that the distortion and corruption that resulted extends beyond the moral: 'The human fault keeps us from proper understanding of our proper relations by construing our trusts and loyalties, our loves and desires, our rational construing of the world, and our moral interests' (1981: 306). Nevertheless, while holding to an understanding of the depravity of human nature as a consequence of sin, it is acknowledged within natural law theory that human reason was not totally destroyed in the fall (Bretzke 2011: 542).

It is due to a 'radically different understanding of grace', Grabill notes, that Karl Barth, in his infamous rejection of natural theology and the natural law tradition – described as a 'subtext' to mainstream Protestant criticism of the tradition – took the position that Protestant and Catholic ethics stood in conflict with one another (2006: 22). As noted already, critics of natural theology have, in particular, questioned the reliability of human reason, having been corrupted by sin, in discerning moral truth. Barth pointed, not only to human reason as an unreliable source of moral knowledge, reflective of his wider critique of moral philosophy (Porter 1999: 169), but to the ontological supposition that our knowledge of God's creation and of the Creator can only be known through a Christological lens, as evidenced in Scripture (1928: 19–45; 1957: 533, 536). McGrath observes: 'Barth's hostility towards natural theology thus rests on his fundamental belief that it undermines the necessity and uniqueness of God's self-revelation' (2007: 166). For this reason, Barth did not offer an explanatory Christian account of God and His creation, for he 'sought nothing other than to be a witness to God's reconciling and redeeming work in Jesus Christ' (Hauerwas 2002: 146).

In his well-known response to Barth's rejection of natural theology, Emil Brunner emphasized the distinction between Catholic and Reformed thinking, suggesting that while the former makes no distinction between the objective and subjective concept of nature, maintaining the preservation of the *imago Dei* in an '*unrefracted theologia naturalis*' (1946: 48) the latter cannot view nature 'unless Christ be taken into account' (1946: 46). Barth critiques Brunner's assertion that, within Catholic doctrine, nature can stand as a moral order independent of grace (1946: 96). Nevertheless, Brunner believed a 'point of contact' (*Anknüpfungspunkt*) between divine revelation and human nature offered a renewed vision of natural theology, a vision which was outrightly rejected by Barth. In addition, where Brunner points to evidence of God's 'preserving grace' within fallen creation, present, for example, in the function of the state (1946: 28), Barth rejects any notion of 'grace of creation or preservation' (1946: 74). Nevertheless, Thielicke points out that Barth did acknowledge the necessary functioning of some form of natural law in civil society, and concurs that as such, it deserves some level of respect: 'For in the secular sphere what can we put in place of natural law?' (1979: 431).

When it comes to discerning moral truth, objections to the natural law tradition continue to be raised, not least in its apparent stand over against the role and authority of Scripture. For example, Burnside argues that drawing a distinction between 'divine law' and 'natural law' creates an 'epistemological problem' by creating two distinct sources of moral knowledge, namely Scripture and nature (2011: 94–95). However, while natural law theory may be seen to dissuade from the place of scriptural authority within a theological ethic, Porter argues for a more interconnected understanding, highlighting the practice within the medieval scholastic tradition of natural law which treated nature, reason and Scripture as 'three mutually interpreting sources of moral norms' (1999: 121). In addition, it is suggested that moral conclusions are not so neatly derived from the scriptural text. For example, in a comparative discussion of his 'theocentric ethic' positioned alongside Barth's ethical claims, Gustafson suggests that Barth's doctrine of Scripture assumes a coherency of the divine command that is not always self-evident: 'I find Barth's singular Christological interpretation too simple and neat. The theology of the Bible backs and warrants more diversity in ethics than Barth permits' (1984: 35).

In response to these objections and counterclaims, we can affirm that when natural law theory is understood through the lens of Scripture and the Christian faith, the authority of Scripture remains unchallenged. As Hauerwas states: 'We do not seek a philosophical truth separate from the book's text' (1983: 70). Thus, our understanding of natural law is defended on the basis of Scripture. Susan E. Schreiner, for example, notes that Calvin, like his predecessors, 'assumed the existence of natural law from Romans 2:14–15' (1997: 55), in addition to it being evidenced in the Decalogue

(1997: 57). In light of this, Scripture does not stand alone in mediating a knowledge of God, but is complemented by nature and reason. Grabill, for example, points out that for Calvin, 'his doctrine of the natural knowledge of God is founded on two principal sources: creation and the natural means by which God is known in Scripture' (2006: 70). Also, in adopting an incarnational approach to natural theology, McGrath notes how God uses nature to reveal himself to humanity: 'Revelation takes place in and through nature and history, not beyond them' (2008: 174; 2007: 153–172). Highlighting the natural theology expounded by Calvin, McGrath points to the Reformed belief in the full revelation of God mediated through Christ, which can only be known through Scripture, with nature 'clarifying, confirming, and extending what may be known through the former' (2007: 163).

'Common Grace' and Common Virtue

Despite a strong critique, the Protestant tradition has not been united in their rejection of the notion that God and His divine precepts can be discerned through the natural order, or that sin has corrupted all aspects of nature and reason. Indeed, Schreiner deems it ironic that natural law theory has derived so much critical attention, in view of the fact that it was uncontroversial in Calvin's day (1997: 55). As part of the theological endeavour to understand God's relationship with His creation – in particular within cultural and political life – the doctrine of common grace has been articulated within Reformed theological discourse as a means of interpreting the ability of human reason to discern moral norms in the natural order. Abraham Kuyper (1998) is acclaimed for developing and expanding this Reformed doctrine into thinking on engagement in public life. Kuyper appealed to Calvinist thinking in the development of his so-called 'theology of culture' (see van der Kooi 1999; Heslam 1998; Molendijk 2008), and he used the term 'neo-Calvinist' to indicate that he was bringing Calvinist thinking up-to-date (Heslam 1998: 87–88). Thus, in initiating the 'neo-Calvinist' movement, he drew on and developed the diverging strands of Calvinist thinking into a public theology (Mouw 2009: 439).

Herman Kuiper affirmed that the notion of common grace is evident in Reformed thinking and was evident within Calvin's writings: 'He attributes to all men a certain love of truth, a certain knowledge of the principles which underlie civil order, and a disposition to cherish and preserve society' (1928: 16). Therefore, in developing his public theology, Kuyper used the doctrine of common grace to make 'explicit an element that was implicit in Calvin's thought' (Heslam 1998: 140). Despite this apparent coherence, others, like VanDrunnen, suggest that Kuyper stands 'ambiguously' in the Reformed tradition of social thought (2010: 278), while at the same time conceding that the influence of Kuyper on Reformed social thinking is undisputed: 'Abraham Kuyper's theological vision of cultural and political life is arguably the most thorough and complex ever constructed in the history of Reformed Christianity' (2010: 314).

Thus, in locating our own presuppositions within this theological vision, the following questions arise for our discussion: can a 'common grace' understanding of public morality accord, in particular, with the development of a constructive virtue ethic approach to moral education and RSE? More specifically, in taking account of the natural law Reformed tradition – in both ethics and cultural and political life – can human and civic virtue be understood as God's grace at work within the created order? Further to this, can a theological understanding of virtue be developed within the life of the moral agent, apart from union with Christ?

In response to these questions, and in exploring Kuyper's doctrine more explicitly, Vincent Bacote points to three definitive aspects of his thinking: '(1) God is merciful and beneficent toward all humanity in the provision of life and various blessings; (2) all humans have a capacity for morality that manifests itself in actions of justice and virtue; and (3) because humans have the ability to reason and understand, the study of nature and history, persons and societies is possible and useful to believers and non-believers alike' (2005: 92).

Building from these doctrinal beliefs, it is possible to see that for Kuyper, nature and grace were inseparable: 'You cannot see grace in all its riches if you do not perceive how its tiny roots and fibres everywhere penetrate into the joints and cracks of the life of nature' (1998: 197). In building this into a public theology, he adopted a constructivist theological approach, where 'common grace was thus a theology of public responsibility, of Christians' shared humanity with the rest of the world' (Bratt 1998: 165). In view of this shared humanity, Kuyper believed that the divine image is reflected not only in the individual but in humanity as a whole, and our social nature creates the capacity for human development: 'in creating human beings in his likeness God deposited an infinite number of nuclei for high human development in our nature and that these nuclei cannot develop except *through the social bond between people*' (Kuyper 1998: 178, italics in original). In light of this propensity for social relationship, common grace is at work in all spheres of society: 'every view that would confine God's work to the small sector we might label "church life" must be set aside. There is beside the great work of God in *special* grace also that totally other work of God in the realm of *common* grace' (1998: 176, italics in original). Michael De Moor notes that an understanding of common grace enables agreement and affirmation of common goods within the political community (2014: 76).

Importantly, we can observe that Kuyper distinguished this 'life of nature' as separate from the task of salvation (Bacote 2005: 104), making a distinction between common and special grace. This understandably raised theological questions and concerns, the majority of which questioned the Christological foundations of Kuyper's doctrine (Bacote 2005: 112; see, for example, Kaltwasser 2011). Yet Kuyper made clear that his doctrine does not demote the status of Christ but instead makes the link between nature and grace by maintaining the status of Christ as Creator and Re-Creator (Kuyper 1998: 173). VanDrunen points to the development of neo-Calvinist thinking in this direction, where creation is not so much being '*preserved* as it is' but 'God's redeeming the creation order and moving it toward its eschatological goal of a new heavens and a new earth' (2010: 4, italics in original). In addition, a narrow Christological view is judged to overlook the role and function of the Holy Spirit: 'we need the Spirit's guidance in our hearts and minds as we seek to identify traces of the Spirit's work in the larger creation' (Mouw 2001: 28; Bacote 2005: 112). This larger work of the Holy Spirit, evidenced in Kuyper's doctrine, 'supplements' the salvific plans of God (Mouw 2001: 43–44).

In addition to his public theology, the understanding and application of Kuyper's common grace is commended within Christian ethics. In particular, Gene Haas remarks that his neo-Calvinist position provides a valuable resource for interacting with a virtue ethic; it can 'recognize and incorporate the important emphases found in virtue ethics at the same time that it exposes the problems and relativistic tendencies in this approach to ethics' (1998: 349). For example, concerning the life of virtue, Kuyper makes a distinction in the 'operations' of common grace – one aimed at the interior and one at the exterior part of our existence (Kuyper 1998: 181). With regard to the interior, Kuyper suggests that this is operative 'wherever civic virtue, a sense of domesticity, natural love, the practice of human virtue, the improvement of the public conscience, integrity, mutual loyalty among people, and a feeling for piety leaven life' (Kuyper 1998: 181).

In understanding the place of virtue and 'common grace' within the Reformed tradition, it is helpful to note the distinction with a traditional Catholic ethic. Notably, in reconciling an account of the virtues and God's grace within a natural law tradition, Aquinas made the distinction between those virtues that are acquired and discerned by reason in pursuit of the human good and those that are infused, given by God for union with Him and therefore necessary for salvation (Porter 2012: 93–94). 'Pagan virtues', as such, amounted to pride and self-love because they were not informed by and directed towards God (Porter 2012: 91; Herdt 2008: 45–48). Calvin, in contrast, held to the Augustinian view that the 'natural gifts', including reason, had been corrupted by sin; in light of this, his theology was highly critical of the unregenerate mind (Mouw 2009: 435; 2001: 17). Nevertheless, he believed that the unredeemed were not entirely devoid of the ability to discern moral knowledge (Calvin 1960a: 270). In view of this position, Grabill suggests that Calvin's '*epistemological* modifications to the realist theory of natural law', in contrast to Aquinas, attributed greater priority to the 'the post-lapsarian conscience than to the pre-lapsarian reason' (2006: 90, italics in original). In a similar vein, Paul Sigmund suggests that Kuyperianism can still be distinguished from Catholic social thinking on natural law by the greater emphasis it places on the distorting impact of sin on human reason (Sigmund 2000: 219; see also van den Brink 1999).

Thus, while Barth claimed that Calvin believed only in the 'hypothetical possibility' of a natural knowledge of God – 'one might call it an objective possibility, created by God, but not a subjective possibility, open to man' (1946: 106) – Schreiner instead points to the important distinction that Calvin made between the spiritual and the natural realm, where the law of nature accords with Calvin's second table of the law (1997: 60). This second table concerns commands on how we are to treat others (Reuschling 2011: 243). When it came to the spiritual realm, however, Schreiner notes that 'Calvin was perfectly clear and consistent; his condemnation of our natural gifts as directed to God was unrelenting' (1997: 60). Calvin indeed affirmed that 'true virtue' was obtained through union with Christ and the process of sanctification (1960: 770–771). Nevertheless, while knowledge of the natural law, through the functioning of the conscience, was to 'render man inexcusable', Schreiner notes that this distinction between the spiritual and natural realm moves beyond an individual's standing before God to their function in the world, moving from the 'sphere of theological anthropology and epistemology to the sphere of providence' (1997: 61).

In noting the significance of Calvinist thinking for public theology, Bacote (2005: 95) points in particular to Calvin's understanding of the work of God's grace to restrain sin, which includes the capacity of the individual to act morally:

> In every age there have been persons who, guided by nature, have striven toward virtue throughout life. I have nothing to say against them even if many lapses can be noted in their moral conduct. For they have by the very zeal of their honesty given proof that there was some purity in their nature ... These examples, accordingly, seem to warn us against adjudging man's nature wholly corrupted, because some men have by its prompting not only excelled in remarkable deeds, but conducted themselves most honorably throughout life. But here it ought to occur to us to us that amid this corruption of nature there is some place for God's grace; not such grace as to cleanse it, but to restrain it inwardly. (Calvin 1960: 292, *Institutes, Volume XX*, 2:3:3)

Thus, Calvin's account of human nature evidences an understanding of the operation of common grace, an understanding of virtuous behaviour for the bridling of sin and the preservation of society. As Kuiper observes, such are the 'divine gifts which are granted with a view to the preservation of society and that God rewards the unregenerate who cultivate virtue with many temporal blessings' (1928: 39). In addition, Grabill notes that, according to Calvin's explication of the natural knowledge of God, 'the human conscience continues to provide moral knowledge of moral precepts; the created order continues to reflect God's wisdom, goodness, and power; and God continues to nourish civic virtues among the unregenerate' (2006: 96).

Conclusion

Our discussion in this chapter has given particular attention to presenting a theological defence for the application of a virtue ethic within RSE discourse. The purpose of doing so is to ensure that, in presenting a case for a theological contribution to public discourse, we are endeavouring to offer a defence for the theological premise on which such a position is founded. This is particularly in response to the criticism that there are few ethicists and moral philosophers from the Protestant tradition engaged in thinking around character education and virtue ethics. In engaging with a natural law understanding of common virtue, I have made the case for how the discernment and application of common virtue can be understood within the doctrine of creation, and, in particular, the doctrine of 'common grace'.

Thus, in recognizing Kuyper's common grace understanding of faith outworked in the public square, an important distinction is made between common grace and salvific grace: 'This grace does not bring salvation, but it invites the recognition of validity and excellence from many sources, and the relative capacity of all, including the "little people" and unbelievers, to contribute to the general welfare' (Stackhouse 2006: 2). As such, Christ's redemption was not just about the salvation of individuals but the redemption of the whole of creation, and Kuyper's common grace doctrine, points out Mouw, developed the notion that the 'natural man' can serve 'God's cultural goals' (2009: 441).

Therefore, in acknowledging that a theological understanding of common grace comes with a certain theological 'messiness' (Mouw 2001: 87), Mouw proposes that it yet provides a means by which the

Christian community can contribute to the wellbeing and flourishing of the community: 'If God's deep love for humanity persists even despite the effects of sin, then the theology of common grace is an important resource for our efforts as Christians to respect and reflect that love' (2001: 101). This involves, he suggests, finding those places of commonality and consensus (2001: 99).

In seeking to develop a constructive approach to moral education, in particular RSE, we echo Herdt's position in arguing against the false dichotomy between nature and grace, and presenting a more holistic model of the moral life:

> We can affirm the radical dependence of all human agency on divine sustenance while also insisting that the quality of that dependence is transformed when acknowledged and embraced. We can affirm the redemptive activity of the Word at work throughout created-but-fallen nature while also insisting that the quality of that redemptive activity is transformed when the Word is known as Jesus Christ and His Spirit is known in the church. (2008: 97)

In doing so, we affirm the intrinsic good of social relationships in understanding human *telos* and flourishing – the created capacity to love and be loved. This is articulated in Kotva's understanding of the human good in terms of 'intrinsically worthwhile relationships', and the virtues that correspond with this (1996: 22). In light of these, I will, in our final chapter, expound on those virtues that correspond with a Christian moral vision of human good – human good that is particularly relevant to a moral understanding of relationships and sex.

CHAPTER 10

Educating for Sexual Virtue: Christian Love and Chastity

> Emerging adults can jump into intimate relationships, assuming that sex is just another consumer item, recreational thrill, or lifestyle commodity. But many of them soon discover the hard way that sex is much more profound and precious than that.
>
> — CHRISTIAN SMITH ET AL. (2011: 193)

> To be loved but not known is comforting but superficial. To be known and not loved is our greatest fear. But to be fully known and truly loved is, well, a lot like being loved by God. It is what we need more than anything.
>
> — TIMOTHY AND KATHY KELLER (2011: 95)

In light of the theological tradition of identifying specific virtues understood within the Christian narrative that contribute to the good of the community and contribute to the flourishing of the individual, we have come in our final chapter to name those virtues that accord with a Christian vision of personhood, and dispositions that, I will argue, enrich the vision of a sexually and relationally educated young person. The virtues that we will explore in this chapter – Christian love and chastity – are specific to an understanding of sexual virtue, but our understanding is not limited to these two. Other virtues, for example, justice and wisdom could also contribute to an enriched vision of a sexually and relationally educated young person.

Therefore, the virtues discussed here should be understood within the larger moral framework of character education, and educating in sexual virtue should not be detached from educating for the whole of life. For if we are to present a coherent and integrated vision of a sexually and relationally educated young person, sexual choices and behaviours cannot be separated from the rest of the moral life or moral commitments. We also heed the warning against narrowing our understanding of virtue to one that is exclusively concerned with sexuality: 'Having displaced virtue from the central position it once occupied, as the defining attribute of the good life and the good society, we have relegated it to the bedroom and boudoir' (Himmelfarb 1995: 15). Instead, the moral content of the virtues in any future Relationships Education and Relationships and Sex Education programme should equip children and young people for moral unity and moral growth in the whole of life.

That said, any exploration of the virtues within the Christian narrative must be framed by the virtue of Christian love, for as the 'greatest virtue' (Wright 2010: 156) it has long been understood that all other virtues are understood and perfected through its exercise. Aquinas believed that it is the theological virtues (faith, hope and charity), above all charity, which would secure the inner unity of the virtues, and to which the cardinal virtues of justice, prudence, temperance and fortitude are directed (Porter 1990: 169).

As we noted in Part II, shaping the current moral narrative is a normative disjuncture between sex and love in modern philosophical accounts of both: 'The claim that sex without love has *some* value, even potentially significant value, is no longer thought wrong by very many (though some within certain religious traditions still reject it)' (Jollimore 2006: 614, italics in original). This is an understanding of sex and love that is also emerging in SRE discourse; for while 'love' and 'loving' appear only once each in the *Sex and Relationships Education (SRE) for the 21st Century* (2014) advice to schools, 'consent' appears twenty-two times, highlighting where the moral emphasis on young people's sexual behaviour currently lies.

In addition, promoting a subjective understanding of morality that gives precedence to an outcome which is predisposed to securing individual autonomy, compromises a Christian vision of personhood. Indeed, as Kotva points out, many of the Christian virtues are intrinsically other-regarding (1996: 152). The goal of Christian behaviour is neither autonomy nor independence, and the Christian life 'is substantively at odds with any account of morality that makes autonomy the necessary condition and/or goal of moral behavior' (Hauerwas 1981: 130). Therefore, while love may not be completely absent from policy discourse, any hint of a narcissistic vision of sexual love is inherently problematic within a Christian worldview. As MacIntyre observes: 'Charity is not of course, from the biblical point of view, just one more virtue to be added to the list. Its inclusion alters the conception of the good for man in a radical way' (2007: 174). He continues: 'the story of the thief on the cross is unintelligible in Aristotelian terms. It is unintelligible precisely because charity is not a virtue for Aristotle' (2007: 175). Consequently, it is understandable why a Christian understanding of 'loving your neighbour as yourself' along with 'loving your enemies' bewildered the atheistic Freud (Nicholi 2002: 175) whereas within the narrative content of Lewis's Christian worldview, it was 'Divine Gift-love' that made such love possible (2002a: 155). In re-echoing Smith's philosophical anthropology, the narrative that shapes our understanding of love ultimately shapes our identity: 'I cannot answer the question, what do I love? without (at least implicitly) answering the question, what story do I believe?' (2013: 129–130).

In view of the fact that the virtue of love is narrative dependent, it is increasingly nonsensical to suggest that when it comes to determining a public sexual ethic, we resort to the mantra that love is simply love; the meaning of love thus becomes a culturally constructed romantic ideal aimed at morally justifying sexual freedom. This is reflected in a recent newspaper article advocating: 'A new way to love: In praise of Polyamory'.[1] While this understanding of love may be logically consistent with the worldview commitment of our cultural moral narrative – and we have argued in Part II why this naturalistic narrative is inherently problematic in shaping a public sexual ethic – we will show that it is not consistent with the meaning of love within the Christian narrative.

1 < https://amp.theguardian.com/lifeandstyle/2017/jul/23/polyamory-new-way-to-love-men-women-sex-relationships-elf-lyons > accessed 24 July 2017.

Christian Love

It is a mammoth task to draw together what has been understood by the virtue of love within Scripture and Christian tradition – a task which is certainly beyond the remit of this chapter. As a central norm of Christian ethics, it has had differing interpretations and applications, including being accorded supreme value in ethical decision-making – as exemplified in Fletcher's Situation Ethics (1966). Yet its importance in the Christian narrative is beyond dispute: 'Christian theologians from Augustine and Aquinas to Edwards and Wesley have consistently praised love as the singularly most important feature of the Christian life' (Boyd 2008: 4). Within a New Testament account, Wright points to the *agape* love – spoken of by Paul and the early Christians – as an interpretation which 'sets the bar as high as it can go' (Wright 2010: 158).

The word 'love' in the English language has multiple meanings, with C. S. Lewis's famous *The Four Loves* highlighting the multi-layered complexity of its nature (Wright 2010: 158). This complexity was explored in detail in Anders Nygren's two-volume seminal work, *Agape and Eros* (1953), noted as a key text in shaping the field, offering 'conceptual clarity' in its 'fourfold analysis of God's love for humanity, and humanity's for God, self-love, and the love of neighbour' (Werpehowski 2005: 434). In his argument, Nygren re-asserts that *agape* is the 'fundamental motif' with which to understand Christian love (1953: 46). It is affirmed in theological discourse as rooted in, and springing from, divine *agape* as exemplified in the sacrificial love of Christ (1953: 726).

Alongside this assertion, he contends that *agape* has been corrupted by an association with *eros*, for in his view the two understandings of love, in effect, stand in diametric opposition to one another. According to Nygren, 'Eros and Agape are the characteristic expressions of two different attitudes to life, two fundamentally opposed types of religion and ethics' (1953: 205). Nygren's discussion is credited with initiating significant scholarship on the notion of love (Hall 2005: 308), and while it is beyond the scope of our analysis to explore this in any length, what the following discussion will begin to introduce is a defence for how *eros* can be understood alongside *agape*, and how both can be enriched within an understanding of *philia*.

Agape *and* Eros

Edward Collins Vacek in *Love, Human and Divine: The Heart of Christian Ethics* suggests that 'eros springs from and is directed to fulfilling the interests or development of the self' (1994: 247). Akin to this definition of *eros*, we have, throughout this book, critiqued the current moral vision of the 'good' in SRE discourse – a vision predisposed to the realization of a self-authenticated choice, towards a self-determined end. In particular, in noting the dominance of the pleasure discourse, we heed Lewis's warning that the danger with the 'god-like' nature of *eros* is 'not that the lovers will idolise each other but that they will idolise Eros himself' (2002a: 135).

Yet, in view of Vacek's definition, disagreement arises within Christian tradition over how this 'development of the self' should be interpreted. Nygren, for example, rejects this self-centred pursuit, while Vacek points to Aquinas who affirmed love for one's own good (1994: 244). Therefore, while self-love is regarded with suspicion in Reformed thinking, as reflected in Nygren's position, classical theologians, including Augustine and Aquinas, 'posit that a proper love for self as God's creation would lead to the glorification of and right relation with God' (Maddalena 2011: 714).

However, the nature of, and the relationship between *agape* and *eros* comes into sharp focus when examined in the framework of a sexual ethic. Of course, it is important to note that *eros* and sexual activity are not mutually inclusive. Lewis, for example, notes that 'sexual experience can occur without Eros, without being 'in love', and that Eros includes others things besides sexual activity' (2002a: 111). Nevertheless, Thielicke, in his account of personhood, is critical of the excessive discourse within society on the 'details of *eros*', which, he notes, are outworked within sex education (1964: 37). Problems arise, he suggests, when sexual behaviour is reduced to mere self-driven impulse and instinct: 'For the farther we remove ourselves from the realm of the personal and the more we move into the realm of purely physical and psychic reactions the more we remove ourselves from the dimension of the "once-for-all" and move into the dimension of the general and interchangeable' (1964: 39).

Thielicke's critique echoes the transitory nature of Lewis's 'Need-love': like 'Need-pleasure', neither will 'last longer than the need' (2002a: 18). The resolution Thielicke offers is not to replace *eros* with *agape*, but to see their interconnection within a theologically informed anthropology. Unlike Nygren, Thielicke does not view the two concepts of love as dialectically opposed, but notes instead their intersection within the so-called 'sexual community' (1964: 28). Within Thielike's 'sex community', *agape* must always play a role because it involves a connection between two persons, respecting the 'alien dignity' in the other (1964: 33). In addition, the two are interrelated in that there are particular conditions set on who that 'object of my *eros*' can be: 'Sex community is a special case of human communication with conditions attached to it' (1964: 34).

In addition, Hollinger suggests that what Nygren's account overlooks is the 'creation-ordered' dimension of love, and in expounding the biblical teaching on *agape* and *eros*, he notes: 'Love in the Bible is never so spiritualized that it cannot include sexual love, and a sexual love that involves the passions' (2009: 107–108). Jollimore echoes this point by highlighting secular philosophers who have understood the value of sexual love in agapic terms (2006: 608). In referring to Lewis's discussion on the matter, he notes that *eros* is concerned not just with the satisfaction of desire, but with the particular person towards whom the desire is directed: 'Unlike hunger (or horniness), which might be satisfied by any dish or roast beef (or any accommodating person), Eros attaches to one particular person, for whom there can be no substitute' (2006: 611).

In light of this evaluation, it is mistaken to deny the interpersonal aim of sexual desire, as recognized by Scruton (2006), where love is the *telos* towards which sexual desire is directed. Yet in drawing a distinction between the two, Thielicke points to a different motivation between *agape* and *eros*: 'in *eros* the *worth* of the other person is the object; in *agape* the *authentic being [Eigentlichkeit]* of the other person is the object' (1964: 28, italics in original); this is an identity that transcends mere function (1964: 32).

Existence for the Other

It is important to recognize that *eros* does not remain unchecked within the philosophical discourse surrounding sex education. Ben Spiecker and Jan Steutel, for example, advocate a virtue of 'balanced caring', which incorporates 'emotions of benevolence' towards another's welfare (2007: 183). This follows through in educational outcomes to the extent that a failure of young people to demonstrate 'affective-motivational' qualities, such as respect and care, indicates 'possible stagnation in the child's moral-sexual development' (2007: 185). Thus, empathy is evidently viewed as playing an important role in a young person's emotional and moral development (see, for example, Cooper 2011; Skoe 2010; Van der Ven 1998: 313).

In translating theory into policy and practice, this emphasis on respect, care and empathy is reflected in current SRE policy advice for schools: 'SRE lays the foundations for developing empathy and understanding between girls and boys, young men and young women' (Brook et al. 2014: 10). Nevertheless, as discussed in Chapter 7, an understanding and articulation of empathy, situated within the overarching concept of consent, remains largely unchecked and under review. In contrast, Christian *agape* is not just benevolence towards another's welfare but is understood as 'existence-for-the-other-person' (Thielicke 1964: 90). This theological anthropology suggests that a person is 'determined by his neighbour' (1964: 90) and is only found in relation to others: 'genuine personhood is primarily derived from one's fidelity and commitment to others' (McFadyen 1990: 73). The implication for a sexual ethic is a 'trend towards monogamy' (Thielicke 1964: 90). Such a view of sexual faithfulness enriches a socially constructed notion of empathy and challenges the 'experiential satisfaction' currently shaping our vision of flourishing. It also challenges the idea of short-term recreational sexual relationships being consistent with a Christian vision of sexual virtue (McCarty 2015, 221).

Within a biblical sexual ethic, this existence-for-the-other is realized in the exclusive lifelong, one-flesh union between a husband and wife. In exploring this commitment, Hollinger suggests that love needs 'definition and a conviction that sexual love goes hand in hand with one-flesh consummation and a context of procreation' (2009: 110). The context and commitment of marriage, he suggests, avoids passion turning into 'self-serving objectification of the other person, using the other as a means for one's own selfish ends' (2009: 110). The vision of human flourishing within a Christian worldview, therefore, points to the fact that the sexual act signifies 'a permanent and exclusive type of relationship' (Geach 1994: 185).

In light of this narrative context, a Christian vision of the moral good of sexual behaviour would argue for the reinstatement of the normative link between sex and love within current and future RSE discourse, in particular between *eros* and *agape*, directed towards the moral end of marriage. Marriage, within the Christian narrative, is viewed as part of the moral order of creation. In light of this, and reflective of our discussion in Chapter 9, 'the moral structure of the world and the core anthropology of the human person, although flawed and spoiled , yet bear this order of creation, to which we must attend if we are wise' (Ash 2003: 640). While the meaning of marriage is now ideologically contested, this should not, however, amount to the exclusion of the orthodox Christian understanding from present and future discourse around RSE policies and programmes. After all, according to this understanding, marriage – as constituted in the order of creation – is a 'good' for all.

Sexual faithfulness thus becomes a content- and context-specific aspect of the theological virtue of love. While in Chapter 5 we noted Primoratz's conclusion that 'there is casual sex, but love is never casual' (1999: 31), within a Christian understanding of sexual love, 'casual sex is a contradiction in terms' (Smedes 1994: 67). Our understanding of love moves beyond a mere fleeting, romantic or self-fulfilling notion. Instead, as Rowan Williams points out, it takes time for this 'mutual recognition that my partner and I are not simply passive instruments to each other' (2002: 315). The more time spent, he suggests, the greater the element of risk in exposing oneself to being formed by the other: 'properly understood, sexual faithfulness is not an avoidance of risk, but the creation of a context in which grace can abound because there is a commitment not to run away from the perception of another' (2002: 315). This context opens up the opportunity for vulnerability as a counterbalance to the human tendency to pursue control and self-sufficiency. As Lewis asserted, 'to love at all is to be vulnerable' (2002a: 147).

In summary, the virtue of Christian love centres on the 'existence for the other' by engaging an understanding of the relationship between *agape* and *eros*. In so doing, it moves future RSE discourse and the public sexual ethic beyond a socially constructed notion of consent, towards a transcendent narrative of commitment and fidelity. It follows that such a script does not accommodate a casual, self-seeking approach to relationships or sexual encounters, nor does it diminish the value of sexual love: 'Agape gives will and backbone to the soft tissues of eros. Christian love, far from snuffing out passion, fuels the flames' (Smedes 1994: 82).

Philia

In developing further our exploration of the virtue of love, it is possible to enrich our understanding by taking into account the nature and importance of *philia*. Again, Vacek presents a case for why *agape* and *eros*, while both having a place in the Christian life and distinct in their own right, are incomplete without *philia*, described as 'mutual love' – a love that does not work '*for* the other', nor one that lives '*from* others', but 'a love that means being *with* others' (1994: 280, italics in original).

Friendship appears to be an aspect of love that in modern times has been neglected. Meilaender (1985), for one, points to a dearth of Christian reflection on the subject. He notes this to be the case particularly in comparison to the attention it received in the ancient world. Lewis directed a similar critique at modernity: 'To the Ancients, Friendship seemed the happiest and most fully human of all loves; the crown of life and the school of virtue. The modern world, in comparison ignores it' (2002a: 69). It is proposed that this difference is on account of the understanding that people had of the political nature of their relationships. Herdt, for example, notes that with an Aristotelian vision of friendship, the virtues – as excellences of the individual – are viewed in terms of their contribution to the common good, instituting the political nature of friendship (2008: 37).[2] In contrast, MacIntyre

2 Aristotle devoted two books in *The Nicomachean Ethics* to friendship – Book 8 is dedicated to 'The Kinds of Friendship', Book 9 to 'The Grounds of Friendship'.

suggests that in our modern world of liberal individualism, '"Friendship" has become for the most part the name of the type of emotional state rather than of a type of social and political relationship' (2007: 156).

Viewed through the lens of a theological ethic, Meilaender is critical of the idea of civic friendship, as it points to a different form of human community in which the boundaries of love are limited: 'We do not receive our life and being, finally, from the political community' (1985: 77). In his own reflection, he offers an exploration of what he suggests to be the 'central tension' between *agape* and *philia*: the understanding of friendship as 'preferential love', with the related problems of reciprocity and fidelity in friendship (1985: 3). In particular, in viewing friendship as reciprocal love he notes the tension between 'wishing the other well for the other's sake and desiring union with the other' (1985: 48). This desire for the other, he points out, is a 'desire to enjoy the *friend*, not the pleasure which accompanies the presence of the friend' (1985: 48, italics in original). However, by their very nature, preferential and reciprocal love 'must be subject to change', which would appear to make them incompatible with the faithful love of Christian friendship (1985: 54). Nevertheless, he acknowledges that 'a love which lacks these marks of philia – its deep intimacy, mutuality, and preference – seems too impersonal and cold to satisfy the needs of our nature' (1985: 65).

This echoes the criticism directed against the 'equal regard' of Gene Outka's *agape* love, which calls for an 'independent and unalterable' regard for one's neighbour (1972: 12). Such an account, according to Gushee and Stassen, seems too 'abstract' and 'incomplete', failing to give enough importance to the moral obligations towards family and those closest to us (2003: 333). Instead, Meilaender suggests that 'friendship, with its warmth and mutuality, should be the internal fruition of agape' (1985: 65). Indeed, Liz Carmichael places friendship at the heart of *agape* love: 'The love of friendship [...] is love that sets people free to be and to become in their own individual uniqueness, and which is essentially directed towards, hopes for and invites, reciprocal love and the joy of fulfilment in mutual relationship: but without possessively demanding it' (2004: 200). Also, within the Christian narrative, *philia* is credited to be the context in which Christian love is learnt (Wadell 1989: 119).

Alongside *agape*, *philia* also enriches our understanding of *eros* and the relationship between them. In critiquing the dominance of *eros* at the expense of *philia* within the church, Kenneth Leech notes: 'The obsession with anatomy and genitalia has made many Christians timid about deep, passionate and committed friendships, and this has had a detrimental effect on the whole area of solidarity and communion' (1997: 31). Outside of the church, an 'ambiguity' in the relationship between sex and friendship is also noted (Vernon 2005: 31). This could be on account of the direct influence or interpretation of ideas put forward by theorists like Freud, who seemingly diminished friendship and other forms of 'higher love' as merely 'aim-inhibited' forms of *eros*, the product of a repressed sexual instinct (Badhwar 2006: 390).

In arguing for an appropriate and enriching understanding of the relationship between *philia* and *eros*, James McEvoy suggests that friendship within marriage, 'loving the other for the goodness of character that is his or hers, teaches *eros* a restraint, an exclusiveness and a fidelity, that belong to the full human accomplishment of living' (1994: 201). Thus, all three aspects of the virtue of love come together in a shared life, one mark of which, notes Vacek, is the dialogue and interaction between free people: 'A true encounter is always with someone whom we cannot control' (1994: 290). In each *philia* encounter, we realize a different aspect of one's personal self in a process of 'mutual self-disclosure' (1994: 290). Thus, friendship 'is a relation between men at their highest level of individuality' (Lewis 2002a: 72). Once again, a vision of the good of community and the good that human beings were designed for accords with Kotva's assertion that we become fully individuated and fully flourish in the midst of 'intrinsically worthwhile relationships' (1996: 22).

In summary, our discussion has offered only a brief exploration of *eros*, *agape* and *philia* – their distinctiveness and relatedness – and therefore presents only an initial reflection on the multi-faceted nature of the virtue of love and the mutuality that is inherent within a Christian understanding of living in community. Suffice to say, in the face of a culture overtly focussed on *eros*, a Christian contribution to current and future RSE discourse would introduce an understanding of these multi-layered facets, in order to enrich a vision of moral education and human flourishing. In doing so we would move beyond a policy discourse of perceived 'neutrality', towards a relational narrative on which to build a vision of a sexually and relationally educated young person. Ultimately, within a Christian narrative, friendship with God lies at the heart of that vision.

Chastity

In addition to the place of Christian love in a vision of human flourishing, the virtue of chastity is an enriching virtue within a vision of Christian personhood. This is the virtue that Lewis pointed to as denoting a Christian morality of sex.[3] Its exploration addresses, in particular, the negative press that 'abstinence' currently receives in current SRE discourse, and responds to the judgement that there exists a void in policy articulating why delaying sex might be a good and worthwhile choice. It also confronts the cultural narrative that promotes an unbounded pursuit of sexual pleasure or, as Lewis noted, the 'propaganda in favour of unchastity' (2002b: 86).

Chastity is a virtue that is distinct to sexual activity (Carr 2007). On account of this, Carr draws an insightful distinction between the concepts of abstinence, celibacy, chastity and virginity, presenting the possibility, for example, 'that one might be chaste in the absence of celibacy or virginity' (2006: 7). He suggests that a distinction can be made, in particular, between 'religious and secular forms of abstention' in view of the different understandings of the concept of chastity: 'What mainly seems to distinguish consecrated celibacy from secular celibacy (aesthetically or pragmatically motivated avoidance of sexual relations) is a commitment of abstention as a moral or spiritual ideal of human growth' (2006: 9). For Carr, 'consecrated celibates' are committed to more than just sexual abstinence, but to 'the cultivation of certain attitudes toward sexual life – a certain purity of

3 In Book Three and Chapter 5 of *Mere Christianity*, Lewis devotes a chapter to sexual morality.

heart or mind – that is not reducible to even complete celibate abstinence' (2006: 9). In light of this, he asserts, 'it is possible to be celibate without being chaste, insofar as one might abstain totally from sex yet cultivate lewd thoughts and desires' (2006: 9).

Similarly, in viewing chastity as a 'form of the virtue of faithfulness' which, as we noted earlier, is inherent to an understanding of Christian love, Hauerwas suggests that it is as equitable to married life as to the single life (1981: 195). Thus, where the evidence shows that people are having less sex today – 'that the revolution's promise of more sex is not being delivered' (Harrison 2016: 93) – this does not necessarily equate with more people being chaste. However self-controlled and temperate a moral agent might be, it is their attitude, values, or feelings towards sex which marks their moral vision out as distinctive: 'The key difference between the chaste and the sexually continent is that the former do not entertain such inclinations as viable or honourable prospects; they regard lustful, adulterous or promiscuous promptings as unworthy and demeaning and are therefore free from the moral struggle of the continent' (Carr 2007: 97). However, one person's promiscuity is another person sexual freedom and, as such, 'chastity is the most unpopular of the Christian virtues' (Lewis 2002b: 84). In light of this, such 'unworthy' and 'demeaning' attitudes and feelings may merely be viewed as hang-ups from our 'anti-sex' tradition and therefore no longer understood or embraced as part of our contemporary social narrative.

Indeed, the virtue of chastity may no longer be regarded as an '*honourable* quality' (Adams 2006: 57, italics in original). Instead, in noting chastity to be 'deeply political' (2008: 4), Jenny Taylor suggests that it is 'not just invalid as an ideal, but has effectively dropped out of the lexicon because few understand its wider social meaning' (2008: 12). This is due, she suggests, to a loss of connection between sexuality and spirituality, a loss which she observes is also evident in the church (2008: 83). This, for Wright, is a consequence within the Christian community of a wider neglect in the understanding of virtue: 'Do you think, as a "normal" young person growing up in today's sex-soaked Western world, that you could attain chastity of heart, mind, and body just through praying one prayer about it?' (2010: 61).

Chastity has also been denounced as an 'instrument of social control' and amounting to the denial of human sexual instinct, which according to the interpretation of psychoanalytic theory, is 'liable to lead to serious psychological harm or damage' (Carr: 2007: 98). Freud, in his assessment of sexual instinct, observed: 'Experience shows that the majority of the people who make up our society are constitutionally unfit to face the task of abstinence' (1985a [1908]: 45). He noted, in particular, the challenge faced 'during the period of ardent and vigorous youth' (1985a: 45). As explored in Chapter 5, interpretations of these psychoanalytical conclusions have significantly shaped the master narrative in which SRE policy has been shaped. However, Carr suggests that Freud was not advocating for sexual liberation or the 'free pursuit of essentially selfish auto-erotic goals', but instead he acknowledged 'certain definite constraints of a psychological and social kind on sexual life' (Carr 1987: 366). Carr claims that the exercise of other-regarding virtues were, for Freud, to be the measure of sexual growth. Accordingly, 'the sexually adult or mature individual is able to locate his sexuality in a context of altruistic consideration and concern for others whereas the sexually immature or "abnormal" individual exhibits a relatively egocentric unconcern' (Carr 1987: 372). Such an interpretation requires some constraint on sexual impulse and instinct.

Indeed, despite the negative or silent press, abstention from sexual activity – even within our sex-saturated culture – is not such a strange phenomenon. As Lewis points out, 'every sane and civilised man must have some set of principles by which he chooses to reject some of his desires and to permit others' (2002a: 87). He draws attention to the difference between 'repressed' sex, as understood within psychology, and 'suppressed' sex, a conscious restraint, where the second leads to an intimate understanding of one's sexuality. He concludes: 'Virtue – even attempted virtue – brings light; indulgence brings fog' (2002a: 88). Moreover, Anscombe (1972) highlighted how unrestrained sexual instinct provides a poor barometer of moral character: 'The idea lacks any foundation, that the people who are bent upon and who get a lot of sexual enjoyment are more gentle, merciful and kind than those who live in voluntary continence'.

As noted throughout, it is the end to which sexual activity is directed which will inevitably determine the virtues that are cultivated, the moral reasoning engaged in, and the choices made. In view of this moral end, temperance, in particular, has long been associated with the need to regulate, control and direct the sexual appetite. Indeed, Foot suggests that all the virtues can be seen as '*corrective*, each one standing at a point at which there is some temptation to be resisted or deficiency of motivation to be made good' (1978: 8). Virtues, as such, direct our emotions: 'temperance is directly about desires, courage about fears. How we act outwardly comes from how we feel inwardly, and so temperate behaviour depends on well-tempered emotions' (Aquians 1968: 15, citing *ST* II-II.141.3).

In adopting an Aristotelian 'doctrine of the mean', Scruton suggests that 'education is directed towards the special kind of temperance which shows itself, sometimes as chastity, sometimes as fidelity, sometimes as passionate desire, according to the "right judgement" of the subject' (2006: 340). This understanding of the 'mean' is echoed in Geach's understanding of temperance, where its exercise is 'a common-sense matter of neither being distracted from great ends by short-term enjoyments, nor damaging oneself by excessive abstinence' (1977: xxvi). In adopting this approach to education, we once again shift our understanding and *telos* of human sexuality beyond the mere biological towards a thinking, feeling and willing understanding of our personhood.

In translating these ideas into educating for character, Van der Ven notes that the passions must be given their 'proper place' (1998: 381). This involves the rejection of the idea of 'suppressing, controlling, and neutralizing' them, pointing instead to their 'ordering and processing' (1998: 381). As such, education should be directed towards the complementary process of living according to reason and passions, where rational engagement is directed towards the processing of emotions towards the vision of the moral good (1998: 382). This has included, within modern philosophical discourse, a defence for the compatibility of temperance with casual sex and promiscuity, with the qualification that such desires exclude 'wrong-making features' such as paedophilia, adultery and deception (Halwani 2007: 217). Only a more explicit articulation of the vision of the inherent moral goodness of sexual activity in future RSE discourse will determine whether casual sex and promiscuity are behaviours that accord with a right ordering and processing of sexual desire. Within a Christian moral vision, they are clearly incompatible with the virtue of Christian love.

In recognizing its unpopularity, and before it is completely rejected from contemporary discourse, we should note Carr's proposition that chastity – 'broadly conceived as decent and honourable self- and other-regarding sexual association' within secular, liberal discourse – can be viewed by educationalists as 'part of the rich tapestry of any flourishing moral life' (2007: 100). In re-engaging with the interpersonal nature of sex, Scruton suggests 'it becomes not foolish but admirable to ignore the promptings of a desire that brings no intimacy or fulfilment' (2006: 341). Thus, the challenge remains for future RSE discourse to identify a moral language and present a moral vision which gives young people, not only a moral reason to say no to sex, but also a moral vision of the ideal context in which to say yes, a vision which cannot be derived from experience or instinct. Only then will we truly be educating for sexual virtue.

Conclusion

In ensuring the provision of Relationships Education and Relationships and Sex Education, the government has expressed its commitment to provide young people with the 'full set of knowledge and life skills' necessary to support them to be 'safe, healthy, happy and successful' (Department for Education 2017: 2). However, in order to do this, it must first articulate a moral vision of a sexually and relationally educated young person – a vision which will give definition and meaning to the knowledge and skills to be appropriated. In this chapter I have argued that in the face of the incoherent and inadequate vision of moral education and human flourishing that is currently evident in SRE discourse, a virtue ethic approach to moral education and future RSE will articulate the qualities or character that are praiseworthy, admirable and desirable, that contribute both to the good of community and to what human beings are designed for.

In particular, we have identified Christian love and chastity as two virtues which are distinct but yet intertwined within the Christian moral narrative of sex. In so doing, we have begun to reconstruct a moral framework that gives meaning and dignity to the moral agent and their sexual personhood. We also introduce a framework within which it is possible to place other virtues. For example, the virtue of courage can be seen to engage the moral agent in making moral decisions that move them towards a vision of human flourishing in which their dignity as decision-maker is enhanced. As Wells suggests: 'Freedom means being able to go from saying "it happened" to "I did it". If people are able to face their lives without illusion or deception, they need courage' (1998: 27). In expounding on the 'unity of the virtues' in Aquinas's theory, Porter notes that prudence is also needed, alongside temperance, courage and justice, to ground and direct actions and reactions towards a vision of the human good (1990: 121).

Therefore, if the moral end of government policy is 'wise and informed choices', a critical awareness of the moral good of sex is necessary in order to direct actions, alongside the formation of moral character in order to achieve it. To have moral character, suggests Roberts, is to be a person of integrity, which means 'to be, and to be able to remain, a moral entity – that is, a person in the fullest and deepest sense' (1995: 65). Thus, a vision of Relationships and Sex Education that integrates the biological with a vision of the moral and spiritual is one in which the moral character of the young person, and corresponding virtues, is understood within a wider understanding of sexual personhood. I propose that a theological virtue ethic not only provides a vision of the moral agent as an embodied learner, but provides a moral narrative from which to derive virtues that are directed towards a more coherent vision of what it is to be truly human. Within this moral vision, choices around sex and relationships are inspired rather than merely informed.

Bibliography

Adams, R. M. (2006). *A Theory of Virtue: Excellence in Being for the Good*. Oxford: Clarendon Press.

Addo, F. R., Lichter, D. T., and Sassler, S. (2012). 'The Tempo of Sexual Activity and Later Relationship Quality', *Journal of Marriage and Family*, 74 (4), 708–725.

Adeney, D. (2006). 'Liberalism', In A. Soble (ed.), *Sex from Plato to Paglia: A Philosophical Encyclopedia, Vol. 1: A-L*, pp. 598–606. London: Greenwood Press.

Alldred, P., and David, M. E. (2007). *Get Real About Sex: The Politics and Practice of Sex Education*. Maidenhead: Open University Press.

Allen, A., and Carmody, M. (2012). '"Pleasure Has No Passport": Re-visiting the Potential of Pleasure in Sexuality Education', *Sex Education*, 12 (3), 455–468.

Allen, L. (2005). *Sexual Subjects: Young People, Sexuality and Education*. Basingstoke: Palgrave Macmillan.

—— (2011). *Young People and Sexuality Education: Rethinking Key Debates*. Basingstoke: Palgrave Macmillan.

—— (2014). 'Pleasure's Perils? Critically Reflecting on Pleasure's Inclusion in Sexuality Education'. In L. Allen, K. Quinlivan and M. L. Rasmussen (eds), *The Politics of Pleasure in Sexuality Education: Pleasure Bound*, pp. 169–185. London: Routledge.

Allen, L., Quinlivan, K., and Rasmussen, M. L. (2014). 'Introduction: Putting Pleasure under Pressure'. In L. Allen, K. Quinlivan and M. L. Rasmussen (eds), *The Politics of Pleasure in Sexuality Education: Pleasure Bound*, pp. 1–11. Abingdon: Routledge.

Almond, B. (2006). *The Fragmenting Family*, Oxford: Oxford University Press.

—— (2010). 'The Value of Knowledge'. In R. Bailey, R. Barrow, D. Carr, C. McCarthy (eds), *The SAGE Handbook of Philosophy of Education*, pp. 297–306. London: SAGE.

Anderson, E. (2009). 'John Stuart Mill: Afterword'. In S. M. Cahn (ed.), *Philosophy of Education: The Essential Texts*, pp. 355–360. London: Routledge.

Annas, J. (2006). 'Virtue Ethics'. In D. Copp (ed.), *The Oxford Handbook of Ethical Theory*, pp. 515–536. Oxford: Oxford University Press.

Anscombe, E. (1972). 'Contraception and Chastity', <http://www.orthodoxytoday.org/articles/AnscombeChastity.php> accessed 16 July 2014.

—— (1981). 'You can have Sex without Children: Christianity and the new Offer', *The Collected Philosophical Papers of G. E. M. Anscombe, Vol. 3: Ethics, Religion and Politics*, pp. 82–96. Oxford: Basil Blackwell.

—— (1983). *Ethics, Religion and Politics*. Oxford: Blackwell.

Aquinas, T. (1968). *Summa Theologiae, Vol. 42, Courage (II-II.123–40)*. Translated by A. Ross and P. G. Walsh. London: Blackfriars.

—— (1968). *Summa Theologiae, Vol. 43, Temperance (II-II.141–54)*. Translated by T. Gilby. London: Blackfriars.

Arai, L. (2009). *Teenage Pregnancy: The Making and Unmaking of a Problem*. Bristol: The Policy Press.

Archard, D. (1998a). 'How Should We Teach Sex?', *Journal of Philosophy of Education*, 32 (3), 437–449.

—— (1998b). *Sexual Consent*. Oxford: Westview Press.

—— (2000). *Impact (No.7): Sex Education*. In J. White (ed.). Philosophy of Education of Great Britain.

—— (2003). 'Sex Education'. In R. Curren (ed.), *A Companion to the Philosophy of Education*, pp. 540–547. Oxford: Blackwell.

—— (2006). 'The Moral and Political Status of Children', *Public Policy Research*, March–May 2006, 6–12.

—— (2010). *The Family: A Liberal Defence*. Basingstoke: Palgrave Macmillan.

Aristotle (2004). *The Nicomachean Ethics*. Translated by J. A. K. Thomson. London: Penguin Books.

Arthur, J. (2000). *Schools and Community: The Communitarian Agenda in Education*. London: Falmer Press.

—— (2003). *Education with Character: The Moral Economy of Schooling*. London: RoutledgeFalmer.

—— (2008). 'Traditional Approaches to Character Education in Britain and America'. In L. P. Nucci and D. Narvaez (eds), *Handbook of Moral and Character Education*, pp. 80–98. Abingdon: Routledge.

Ash, C. (2003). *Marriage: Sex in the Service of God*. Nottingham: IVP.

Ashcroft, J., and Schluter, M. (2005). 'A New Framework for the Social Order'. In J. Ashcroft and M. Schluter (eds), *Jubilee Manifesto: A Framework, Agenda and Strategy for Christian Social Reform*. pp. 17–33. Leicester: IVP.

Aspin, D., and Williams, G. (1981). 'The Philosophy of Health Education Related to Schools'. In J. Cowley, D. David and T. Williams (eds), *Health Education in Schools*, pp. 38–55. London: Harper and Row.

Atkinson, R. (1965). *Sexual Morality*. London: Hutchinson & Co.

Augustine, St (1955) [401]. 'Holy Virginity'. In R. J. Deferrari (ed.), *The Fathers of the Church. Saint Augustine: Treatises on Marriage and Other Subjects, A New*

Translation, Volume 27, pp. 133–212. Washington: Catholic University of America Press.

—— (1955) [401]. 'The Good of Marriage'. In R. J. Deferrari (ed.), *The Fathers of the Church. Saint Augustine: Treatises on Marriage and Other Subjects, A New Translation, Volume 27*, pp. 1–51. Washington: Catholic University of America Press.

Badhwar, N. K. (2006). 'Friendship'. In A. Soble (ed.), *Sex from Plato to Paglia: A Philosophical Encyclopedia, Vol. 1: A-L, pp. 390–397*. London: Greenwood Press.

Bacote, V. E. (2005). *The Spirit in Public Theology: Appropriating the Legacy of Abraham Kuyper*. Grand Rapids: Baker Academic.

Ball, C., Jambon, M., and Smetana, J. G. (2014). 'The Social Domain Approach to Children's Moral and Social Judgements'. In M. Killen and J. G. Smetana (eds), *Handbook of Moral Development* (2nd edn), pp. 23–45. London: Psychology Press.

Bangert, B. C. (2006). *Consenting to God and Nature: Toward a Theocentric, Naturalistic, Theological Ethic*. Eugene: Pickwick Publications.

Barth, K. (1928). *Ethics*. Edited by D. Braun (ed.), translated by G. W. Bromiley. Edinburgh: T. & T. Clarke.

—— (1946). *'No!', Natural Theology: Comprising "Nature and Grace" by Professor Dr. Emil Brunner and the Reply "No!" by Dr. Karl Barth*. Translated by Peter Fraenkel, pp. 67–128. London: Geoffrey Bles: The Centenary Press.

—— (1957). *Church Dogmatics, The Doctrine of God, Volume II, Part 2*. In G. W. Bromily and T. F. Torrance (eds). Translated by G. W. Bromily, J. C. Campbell, H. Knight, J. Strathearn McNaB, R. A. Stewart and I. Wilson. Peabody: Hendrickson Publishers.

Basinger, K. S., Berkowitz, M. W., Gibbs, J. C., Grime, R. L., and Moshman, D. (2009). 'Taking Development Seriously: Critique of the 2008 *JME* Special Issue on Moral Functioning', *Journal of Moral Education*, 38 (3), 271–282.

Bauman, Z. (2003). *Liquid Love: On the Frailty of Human Bonds*. Cambridge: Polity Press.

Beattie, A. (1996). 'The Health Promoting School: From Idea to Action'. In J. Orme and A. Scriven (eds), *Health Promotion: Professional Perspectives*, pp. 129–143. Basingstoke: Macmillan Press.

Beauchamp, D. (1987). 'Life-style, Public Health and Paternalism'. In S. Doxiadis (ed.), *Ethical Dilemmas in Health Promotion*, pp. 69–80. Chichester: John Wiley & Sons.

Beauchamp, T. L., and Childress, J. F. (2013). *Principles of Biomedical Ethics* (7th edn). Oxford: Oxford University Press.

Beckford, M. and Jamieson, A. (2008). 'Britain is among Casual Sex Capitals of the Western World, Research claims', *The Daily Telegraph*, 30 November, <http://www.telegraph.co.uk/health/healthnews/3536598/

Britain-is-among-casual-sex-capitals-of-the-Western-world-research-claims.html> accessed 10 February 2012.
Bentham, J. (2004) [1824]. 'An Introduction to the Principles of Morals and Legislation'. In A. Ryan (ed.), *John Stuart Mill and Jeremy Bentham: Utilitarianism and Other Essays*, pp. 65–111. London: Penguin Books.
Biddulph, M. (2012). 'Sexualities and Citizenship Education'. In J. Arthur and H. Cremin (eds), *Debates in Citizenship Education*, pp. 100–114. Abingdon: Routledge.
Biggar, N. (2009). 'Saving the "Secular": The Public Vocation of Moral Theology', *Journal of Religious Ethics*, 37 (1), 159–178.
Blair. A., and Monk, D. (2009). 'Sex Education and the Law in England and Wales: The Importance of the Legal Narrative'. In R. Davidson and L. D. H. Sauerteig (eds), *Shaping Sexual Knowledge: A Cultural History of Sex Education in Twentieth Century Europe*, pp. 37–51. London: Routledge.
Blake, S. (2014). *Talking of Sex: SRE is not and should not be controversial*, <http://simonatbrookcharity.blogspot.co.uk/2014/06/sre-must-not-be-controversial-or-overly.html> accessed 15 March 2017.
Blake, S., and Frances, G. (2001). *Just Say No! to Abstinence Education: Lessons learnt from a Sex Education Study Tour to the United States*. London: National Children's Bureau.
Board of Education. (1943). *Sex Education in Schools and Youth Organisations: Education Pamphlet No. 119*. London: HMSO.
Bottery, M. (1998). 'Can Schools in a Liberal Society satisfy Conservative Views on Sex Education? : A Preliminary but Necessary Discussion'. In S. A. Mabud and M. J. Reiss (eds), *Sex Education and Religion*, pp. 150–167. London: Islamic Academy.
Boyd, C. A. (2008). 'Introduction: Perspectives on Love and *Agapé*'. In C. A. Boyd (ed.), *Visions of Agapé: Problems and Possibilities in Human and Divine Love*, pp. 1–13. Aldershot: Ashgate Publishing.
Brandon, G. (2009). *Just Sex: Is it ever just Sex?* Nottingham: IVP.
—— (2011). 'Free Sex: Who Pays? Moral Hazard and Sexual Ethics', *Cambridge Papers: The Jubilee Centre*, 20 (4).
Bratt, J. D. (1998). 'Common Grace' In J. D. Bratt (ed.), *Abraham Kuyper: A Centennial Reader*, pp. 165–201. Cumbria: The Paternoster Press.
Bretzke, J. T. (SJ) (2011). 'Natural Law'. In J. B. Green (ed.), *Dictionary of Scripture and Ethics*, pp. 542–544. Grand Rapids: Baker Academic.
Bridgeman, J. (2006). 'Commentary: Young People and Sexual Health: Whose Rights? Whose Responsibilities?', *Medical Law Review*, 14, 418–424.
Brook (2011). *UK Sex and Relationships Education fails to Prepare Young People for Modern Day Life*, <http://www.brook.org.uk/professionals/application/

brookpr/index.php?option=com_brookpr&view=article&id=91&Itemid=640> accessed 5 September 2012.

Brook, PSHE Association and Sex Education Forum (2014). *Sex and Relationships Education (SRE) for the 21st Century: Supplementary Advice to the Sex and Relationship Education Guidance DfEE (0116/2000)*, <http://www.sexeducationforum.org.uk/media/17706/sreadvice.pdf> accessed 7 July 2014.

Brueggemann, W. (2006). *The Word That Redescribes the World: The Bible and Discipleship*. Minneapolis: Augsburg Fortress.

Brunner, E. (1946). 'Nature and Grace'. *Natural Theology: Comprising "Nature and Grace" by Professor Dr. Emil Brunner and the Reply "No!" by Dr. Karl Barth*. Translated by Peter Fraenkel. pp. 15–64, London: Geoffrey Bles: The Centenary Press.

Burge-Hendrix, B. (2007). 'The Educative Function of Law'. In M. Freeman and R. Harrison (eds), *Law and Philosophy: Current Legal Issues Volume 10*, pp. 243–354. Oxford: Oxford University Press.

Burgess-Jackson, K. (2006). 'Anscombe, G. E. M. (1919–2001)'. In A. Soble (ed.), *Sex from Plato to Paglia: A Philosophical Encyclopedia, Vol. 1: A-L*, pp. 50–56. London: Greenwood Press.

Burnside, J. P. (2011). *God, Justice and Society: Aspects of Law and Legality in the Bible*. Oxford: Oxford University Press.

Callan, E., and White, J. (2003). 'Liberalism and Communitarianism'. In N. Blake, P. Smeyers, R. Smith and P. Standish (eds), *The Blackwell Guide to the Philosophy of Education*, pp. 95–109. Oxford: Blackwell.

Calvin, J. (1960). *The Library of Christian Classics (Volume XX: Books I.i to III.xix), Calvin: Institutes of the Christian Religion*. Edited by J. T. McNeill, translated by Ford Lewis Battles. Philadelphia: The Westminster Press.

Campbell, A. V. (1990). 'Education or Indoctrination? The Issue of Autonomy in Health Education'. In S. Doxiadis (ed.), *Ethics in Health Education*, pp. 15–27. Chichester: John Wiley and Sons.

Carmichael, L. (2004). *Friendship: Interpreting Christian Love*. London: T. & T. Clarke International.

Carmody, M. (2009). *Sex and Ethics: Young People and Ethical Sex*. South Yarra: Palgrave Macmillan.

Carr, D. (1987). 'Freud and Sexual Ethics', *Philosophy*, 62 (241), 361–373.

—— (1998a). 'Between the Rock and the Hard Place: The Contemporary Dilemma of Sex Education'. In S. A. Mabud and M. J. Reiss (eds), *Sex Education and Religion*, pp. 168–185. London: The Islamic Academy.

—— (1998b). 'Moral Education and the Objectivity of Values'. In D. Carr (ed.), *Education, Knowledge and Truth: Beyond the Postmodern Impasse*, pp. 114–128. London: Routledge.

—— (1999). 'Cross Questions and Crooked Answers: Contemporary Problems of Moral Education'. In J. M. Halstead and T. H. McLaughlin (eds), *Education in Morality*, pp. 23–42. London: Routledge.
—— (2003a). 'Character and Moral Choice in the Cultivation of Virtue'. *Philosophy*, 78 (2), 219–232.
—— (2003b). *Making Sense of Education: An Introduction to the Philosophy and Theory of Education and Teaching*. London: RoutledgeFalmer.
—— (2003c). 'Three Conceptions of Spirituality for Spiritual Education'. In D. Carr and J. Haldane (eds), *Spirituality, Philosophy and Education*, pp. 213–225. London: RoutledgeFalmer.
—— (2004). 'Problems of Values Education'. In J. Haldane (ed.), *Values Education and the Human World: Essays on Education, Culture, Politics, Religion and Science*, pp. 14–30. Exeter: Imprint Academic.
—— (2006). 'Abstinence'. In A. Soble (ed.), *Sex from Plato to Paglia: A Philosophical Encyclopedia, Vol. 1: A-L*, pp. 7–14. London: Greenwood Press.
—— (2007). 'On the Prospects of Chastity as a Contemporary Virtue'. In R. Halwani (ed.), *Sex and Ethics: Essays on Sexuality, Virtue, and the Good Life*, pp. 89–100. Basingstoke: Palgrave Macmillan.
—— (2008a). 'Character Education as the Cultivation of Virtue'. In D. Narvaez and L. P. Nucci (eds), *Handbook of Moral and Character Education*, pp. 99–116. Abingdon: Routledge.
—— (2008b). 'Virtue Ethics'. In T. C. Hunt, D. K. Lapsley, D. Narvaez, R. J. Nuzzi and F. Clark Power (eds), *Moral Education: A Handbook, Vol. 2: M-Z*, pp. 467–468. London: Praeger.
—— (2008c). 'Virtue Theory'. In T. C. Hunt, D. K. Lapsley, D. Narvaez, R. J. Nuzzi and F. Clark Power (eds), *Moral Education: A Handbook, Vol. 2: M-Z*, pp. 468–469. London: Praeger.
—— (2010). 'The Philosophy of Education and Educational Theory'. In R. Bailey, R. Barrow, D. Carr and C. McCarthy (eds), *The SAGE Handbook of Philosophy of Education*, pp. 37–53. London: SAGE.
Carr, D., and Steutel, J. (1999a). 'Virtue Ethics and the Virtue Approach to Moral Education'. In D. Carr and J. Steutel (eds), *Virtue Ethics and Moral Education*, pp. 3–18. London: Routledge.
—— (1999b). 'The Virtue Approach to Moral Education: Pointers, Problems and Prospects'. In D. Carr and J. Steutel (eds), *Virtue Ethics and Moral Education*, pp. 241–255. London: Routledge.
Cates, W., Genuis, S. J., and Steiner, M. (2008). 'Are Condoms the Answer to Rising Rates of Non-HIV Sexually Transmitted Infection?', *British Medical Journal*, 336, 184–185.

Charles, J. D. (2008). *Retrieving the Natural Law: A Return to Moral First Things*. Grand Rapids: Eerdmans.
Chitty, C. (2004). *Education Policy in Britain*. Basingstoke: Palgrave MacMillan.
Coleman, E. (2010). 'From Sexology to Sexual Health'. In P. Aggleton and R. Parker (eds), *Routledge Handbook of Sexuality, Health and Rights*, pp. 135–144. Abingdon: Routledge.
Collyer, J. (1995). *Sex Education in Primary Schools: A Guide to Policy Development in Primary Schools*. London: Forbes Publications.
Cooling, T. (1994). *A Christian Vision for State Education*. London: SPCK.
—— (2010). *Doing God in Education*. London: Theos.
—— (2012). 'The Distinctiveness of Christian Learning in Church of England Schools'. In H. J. Worsley (ed.), *Anglican Church School Education: Moving Beyond the First Two Hundred Years*, pp. 167–185. London: Bloomsbury Academic.
Cooling, T., Green, B., Morris, A., and Revell, L. (2016). *Christian Faith in English Church Schools: Research Conversations with Classroom Teachers*. Bern: Peter Lang.
Cooper, B. (2011). *Empathy in Education: Engagement, Values and Achievement*. London: Continuum.
Cribb, A., and Duncan, P. (2002). *Health Promotion and Professional Ethics*. Oxford: Blackwell.
Crick, B. (2000). *In Defence of Politics* (5th edn). London: Continuum.
Crisp, R. (1997). *Mill on Utilitarianism*. London: Routledge.
Cummings, R., and Richmond, A. S. (2004). 'In Support of the Cognitive-developmental Approach to Moral Education: A Response to David Carr', *Journal of Moral Education*, 33 (2), 197–205.
Cunningham-Burley, S., and MacIntyre, S. (1993). 'Teenage Pregnancy as a Social Problem: A Perspective from the United Kingdom'. In A. Lawson and D.L Rhode (eds), *The Politics of Pregnancy: Adolescent Sexuality and Public Policy*, pp. 59–73. London: Yale University Press.
Curran, C. E. (1996). 'Natural Law'. In P. B. Clarke and A. Linzey (eds), *Dictionary of Ethics, Theology and Society*, pp. 594–597. London: Routledge.
Curren, R. (2007). 'Cultivating the Moral and Intellectual Virtues'. In R. Curren (ed.), *Philosophy of Education: An Anthology*, pp. 507–516. Oxford: Blackwell.
Curren, R., Hager, P., and Robertson, E. (2003). 'The Analytical Movement'. In R. Curran (ed.), *A Companion to the Philosophy of Education*, pp. 176–191. Oxford: Blackwell.
David, K., and Wise, C. (1987). 'Challenges for Sex Education in Schools'. In K. David and T. Williams (eds), *Health Education in Schools* (2nd edn), pp. 191–214. London: Harper and Row.

Davies, I., Gorard, S., and McGuinn, N. (2005). 'Citizenship Education and Character Education: Similarities and Contrasts', *British Journal of Educational Studies*, 53 (3), 341–358.

Dawkins, R. (2006). *The God Delusion*. London: Transworld.

DeMoor, M. (2014). 'Legitimacy, Public Justice, and Deliberative Democracy'. In J. Bowlin (ed.), *The Kuyper Center Review. Volume Four: Calvinism and Democracy*, pp. 104–133. Grand Rapids: Eerdmans.

Denman, S., Moon, A., Parsons, C., and Stears, D. (2002). *The Health Promoting School: Policy, Research and Practice*. London: RoutledgeFalmer.

Dennison, C., and Hadley, A. (2005). 'Teenage Pregnancy'. In L. Ewles (ed.), *Key Topics in Public Health. Essential Briefings on Prevention and Health Promotion*, pp. 135–156. London: Elsevier.

Department for Education (1986). *Education (No. 2) Act 1986*, <http://www.legislation.gov.uk/ukpga/1986/61/pdfs/ukpga_19860061_en.pdf> accessed 2 May 2012.

—— (2010). *The Importance of Teaching: The Schools White Paper*, <https://www.education.gov.uk/publications/eOrderingDownload/CM-7980.pdf> accessed 14 February 2013.

—— (2013a). *Consultation on PSHE: Summary Report*, <http://media.education.gov.uk/assets/files/pdf/p/pshe%20cons%20report.pdf> accessed 20 June 2014.

—— (2013b). *Guidance: Personal, Social, Health, and Economic Education*, <https://www.gov.uk/government/publications/personal-social-health-and-economic-education-pshe/personal-social-health-and-economic-pshe-education#personal-social-health-and-economic-education> accessed 7 July 2014.

—— (2017a). *Press Release: Schools to Teach 21st Century Relationships and Sex Education*, <https://www.gov.uk/government/news/schools-to-teach-21st-century-relationships-and-sex-education> accessed 3 July 2017.

—— (2017b). *Policy Statement: Relationships Education, Relationships and Sex Education, and Personal, Social, Health and Economic Education*, <https://www.gov.uk/government/uploads/system/uploads/attachment_data/file/595828/170301_Policy_statement_PSHEv2.pdf> accessed 3 July 2017.

Department for Education and Employment (2000). *Sex and Relationship Education Guidance DfEE (0116/2000)*. London: DfEE.

Department of Education and Science (1968). *A Handbook of Health Education*. London: HMSO.

—— (1977). *Health Education in Schools*. London: HMSO.

—— (1987). *Sex Education at School: Circular No 11/87*. London: HMSO.

Department of Health (2004). *Best Practice Guidance for Doctors and other Health Professionals on the Provision of Advice and Treatment to Young People under 16 on Contraception, Sexual and Reproductive Health*, <http://www.dh.gov.uk/en/Publicationsandstatistics/Publications/PublicationsPolicyAndGuidance/DH_4086960> accessed 10 October 2012.

—— (2013). *A Framework for Sexual Health Improvement in England*, <https://www.gov.uk/government/uploads/system/uploads/attachment_data/file/142592/9287-2900714-TSO-SexualHealthPolicyNW_ACCESSIBLE.pdf > accessed 3 July 2017.

Dewey, J. (1975) [1909]. *Moral Principles in Education*. Illinois: Southern Illinois University Press.

Diorio, J. A. (2006). 'Sex Education'. In A. Soble (ed.), *Sex from Plato to Paglia: A Philosophical Encyclopedia, Vol. 2: M-Z*, pp. 986–997. London: Greenwood Press.

Downey. M., and Kelly, A. V. (1978). *Moral Education. Theory and Practice*. London: Harper and Row.

Downie, R. S., Tannahill, C., and Tannahill, A. (1996). *Health Promotion: Models and Values* (2nd edn). Oxford: Oxford University Press.

Dworkin, R. (2011). *Justice for Hedgehogs*. London: Harvard University Press.

Egan, R. D., and Hawkes, G. L. (2010). 'Why a History of Childhood Sexuality?'. In P. Aggleton and R. Parker (eds), *Routledge Handbook of Sexuality, Health and Rights*, pp. 127–144. Abingdon: Routledge.

Eisenberg, L. (1987). 'Value Conflicts in Social Policies for Promoting Health'. In S. Doxiadis (ed.), *Ethical Dilemmas in Health Promotion*, pp. 99–116. Chichester: John Wiley and Sons.

Elias, J. L. E. (1989). *Moral Education. Secular and Religious*. Malabar: Robert E. Krieger.

Ellis, H. (1931). *Studies in the Psychology of Sex, Volume VI, Sex in Relation to Society*. Philadelphia: F. A. Davis Company.

Equality and Human Rights Commission (2014). *The Marriage (Same Sex Couples) Act 2013: The Equality and Human Rights Implications for the Provision of School Education*, 24 March 2014, <http://www.equalityhumanrights.com/sites/default/files/gd.13.103-4_schools_24-03-14.pdf> accessed 20 June 2017.

Ewles, L., and Simnett, I. (1992). *Promoting Health: A Practical Guide* (2nd edn). London: Scutari Press.

Family Planning Association (1994). *Sex, Education, Values and Morality*. London: Health Education Authority.

Farley, B. J. (1995). *In Praise of Virtue: An Exploration of the Biblical Virtue Context*. Grand Rapids: Eerdmans.

Feinberg, J. (1984). *Harm to Others: The Moral Limits of the Criminal Law*. Oxford: Oxford University Press.

Field, J., Johnson, A., Wadsworth, J., and Wellings, K. (1994). *Sexual Behaviour in Britain: The National Survey of Sexual Attitudes and Lifestyles*. London: Penguin Group.

Fine, M. (1988). 'Sexuality, Schooling and Adolescent Females: The Missing Discourse of Desire', *Harvard Educational Review*, *58 (1)*, 29–53.

Finnis, J. (1994). 'Rights and Equality of Concern and Respect'. In G. Dworkin (ed.), *Morality, Harm, and the Law*, pp. 43–45. Oxford: Westview Press.

—— (1998). *Aquinas*. Oxford: Oxford University Press.

Fischer, N. (2011). 'Purity and Pollution: Sex as a Moral Discourse'. In N. Fischer, C. Meeks and S. Seidman (eds), *Introducing the New Sexuality Studies* (2nd edn), pp. 38–44. Abingdon: Routledge.

Fisher, R. (2000). 'Philosophy for Children: How Philosophical Enquiry can foster Values Education in Schools'. In R. Gardner, J. Cairns, and D. Lawton (eds), *Education for Values: Morals, Ethics, and Citizenship in Contemporary Teaching*, pp. 50–66. London: Kogan Page.

Fitzjames Stephen, J. (1967) [1873]. *Liberty, Equality, Fraternity*. Edited by R. J. White. Cambridge: Cambridge University Press.

Fletcher, G., Simpson, J. A., Campbell, L., and Overall, N. C. (2013). *The Science of Intimate Relationships*. Chichester: Wiley-Blackwell.

Fletcher, J. (1966). *Situation Ethics*. London: SCM Press.

Foot, P. (1978). *Virtues and Vices and Other Essays in Moral Philosophy*. Oxford: Blackwell.

Foucault, M. (1978) [1976]. *The History of Sexuality: An Introduction, Volume One*. Translated by R. Hurley. New York: Random House.

—— (1986) [1984]. *The Uses of Pleasure: The History of Sexuality, Volume Two*. Translated by R. Hurley. Harmondsworth: Penguin Books.

Freud, S. (1949). *An Outline of Psycho-Analysis*. London: The Hogarth Press.

—— (1985a) [1908]. '"Civilized" Sexual Morality and Modern Nervous Illness'. *Civilization, Society and Religion: Group Psychology, Civilization and its Discontent and Other Works*, pp. 27–55. London: Penguin Books.

—— (1985b) [1930]. 'Civilization and its Discontents'. *Civilization, Society and Religion: Group Psychology, Civilization and its Discontent and Other Works*, pp. 243–340. London: Penguin Books.

—— (2010) [1927], *The Future of an Illusion*. Seattle: Pacific Publishing Studio.

Furedi, A. (1996). *Unplanned Pregnancy: Your Choices*. Oxford: Oxford University Press.

Geach, M. (1994). 'Marriage: Arguing to a Fist Principle in Sexual Ethics'. In L. Gormally (ed.), *Moral Truth and Moral Tradition: Essays in Honour or Peter Geach and Elizabeth Anscombe*, pp. 177–193. Dublin: Four Courts Press.

Geach, P. T. (1977). *The Virtues*. Cambridge: Cambridge University Press.
Gebhard, P. H., Kinsey, A. C., Martin, C. E., and Pomeroy, W. B. (1953). *Sexual Behaviour in the Human Female*. London: W. B. Saunders Company.
Gibbens, J. R. (1998). 'Sexuality and the Law: The Body as Politics'. In T. Carver and V. Mottier (eds), *Politics of Sexuality: Identity, Gender, Citizenship*, pp. 36–45. Abingdon: Routledge.
Giddens, A. (1990). *The Consequences of Modernity*. Cambridge: Polity Press.
Giesinger, J. (2012). 'Kant's Account of Moral Education', *Educational Philosophy and Theory*, 44 (7), 775–786.
Glanzer, P. L., and Ream, T. C. (2009). *Christianity and Moral Identity in Higher Education*. New York: Palgrave Macmillan.
Goldman, A. H. (1977). 'Plain Sex', *Philosophy and Public Affairs*, 6 (3), 267–287.
Gormally, L. (2011). 'Marriage and the Common Good'. In H. Watt (ed.), *Fertility and Gender: Issues in Reproductive and Sexual Ethics*, pp. 28–44. Oxford: The Anscombe Bioethics Centre.
Grabill, S. J. (2006). *Rediscovering the Natural Law in Reformed Theological Ethics*. Grand Rapids: Eerdmans.
Grayling, A. C. (1997). *The Future of Moral Values*. London: Phoenix.
—— (2010). *Thinking of Answers: Questions in the Philosophy of Everyday Life*. London: Bloomsbury.
—— (2011). *The Good Book: A Secular Bible*. London: Bloomsbury.
Green, J. (2002). 'Psychological Factors in Sexually Transmitted Diseases'. In J. Green and D. Miller (eds), *The Psychology of Sexual Health*, pp. 21–37. London: Blackwell Science.
Greslé-Favier, C. (2013). 'Adult Discrimination against Children: The Case of Abstinence-Only Education in Twenty-First-Century USA', *Sex Education*, 13 (6), 715–725.
Griffith, E. F. (1947a). 'The Road to Maturity'. In E. F. Griffith (ed.), *The Road to Maturity*, pp. 13–33. London: Methuen & Co.
—— (1947b). 'Towards Maturity'. In E. F. Griffith (ed.), *The Road to Maturity*, pp. 200–227. London: Methuen & Co.
Groothuis, D. (2000). *Truth Decay: Defending Christianity against the Challenges of Postmodernism*. Nottingham: IVP.
Gruen, L. (2006). 'Law, Sex and the'. In A. Soble (ed.), *Sex from Plato to Paglia: A Philosophical Encyclopedia, Vol. 2: M-Z*, pp. 583–589. London: Greenwood Press.
Gushee, D. P., and Stassen, G. H. (2003). *Kingdom Ethics: Following Jesus in Contemporary Context*. Downers Grove: IVP.
Gustafson, J. M. (1981). *Theology and Ethics*. Oxford: Basil Blackwell.

—— (1984). *Ethics from a Theocentric Perspective, Volume Two: Ethics and Theology.* London: The University of Chicago Press.

Gutmann, A. (1987). *Democratic Education.* Princeton: Princeton University Press.

Haas, G. (1998). 'Kuyper's Legacy for Christian Ethics', *Calvin Theological Journal,* 33, 320–349.

Haidt, J. (2012). *The Righteous Mind: Why Good People are Divided by Politics and Religion.* London: Penguin Books.

Hall, A. L. (2005). 'Love: A Kinship of Affliction and Redemption'. In G. Meilaender and W. Werpehowski (eds), *The Oxford Handbook of Theological Ethics,* pp. 307–321. Oxford: Oxford University Press.

Hall, G. S. (1914). *Adolescence: Its Psychology and its Relations to Physiology, Anthropology, Sociology, Sex, Crime, Religion and Education, VOL II.* London: D. Appleton and Company.

Halstead, J. M. (1998). 'Values and Sex Education in a Multicultural Society'. In S. A. Mabud and M. J. Reiss (eds), *Sex Education and Religion,* pp. 232–259. London: The Islamic Academy.

—— (2005a). 'Liberal Values and Liberal Education'. In W. Carr (ed.), *The Routledge-Falmer Reader in Philosophy of Education,* pp. 111–123. Abingdon: Routledge.

—— (2005b). 'Teaching about Love', *British Journal of Educational Studies,* 53 (3), 290–305.

—— (2010). 'Moral and Citizenship Education'. In R. Bailey, R. Barrow, D. Carr and C. McCarthy (eds), *The SAGE Handbook of Philosophy of Education,* pp. 253–268. London: SAGE.

—— (2011). 'Is Moral Education Working? Extracts from the Diary of a Twenty-First Century Moral Educator', *Journal of Moral Education,* 40 (3), 339–347.

Halstead, J. M., and McLaughlin, T. H. (1999). 'Education in Character and Virtue'. In J. M. Halstead and T. H. McLaughlin (eds), *Education in Morality,* pp. 132–163. London: Routledge.

Halstead, J. M., and Reiss, M. J. (2003). *Values in Sex Education: From Principles to Practice.* London: RoutledgeFalmer.

Halwani, R. (2003). *Virtuous Liaisons: Care, Love, Sex and Virtue Ethics.* Chicago: Open Court.

—— (2006). 'Ethics, Virtue'. In A. Soble (ed.), *Sex from Plato to Paglia: A Philosophical Encyclopedia, Vol. 1: A-L,* pp. 279–285. London: Greenwood Press.

—— (2007). 'Casual Sex, Promiscuity, and Temperance'. In R. Halwani (ed.), *Sex and Ethics: Essays on Sexuality, Virtue, and the Good Life,* pp. 215–225. Basingstoke: Palgrave Macmillan.

Harmin, M., Raths, L. E., and Simon, S. B. (1966). *Values and Teaching: Working with Values in the Classroom.* Columbus: Charles E. Merrill Books.

Harries, R. (2010). *Faith in Politics: Rediscovering the Christian Roots of our Political Values*. London: Darton, Longman and Todd.
Harris, A. (1971). 'What does "Sex Education" mean?', *Journal of Moral Education*, 1(1), 7–11.
—— (1976). *Teaching Morality and Religion*. London: George Allen and Unwin.
Harris, J. (1985). *The Value of Life: An Introduction to Medical Ethics*. London: Routledge and Kegan Paul.
Harris, S. (2010). *The Moral Landscape: How Science Can Determine Human Values*. New York: Free Press.
Harrison. J. K. (2000). *Sex Education in Secondary Schools*. Buckingham: Open University Press.
Hart, H. L. A. (1963). *Law Liberty and Morality*. Oxford: Oxford University Press.
Hartley, C. G. (1920). *Sex Education and National Health*. London: Leonard Parsons.
Haste, H. (1996). 'Communitarianism and the Social Construction of Morality', *Journal of Moral Education*, 25 (1), 47–55.
Hauerwas, S. (1975). *Character and the Christian Life*. San Antonio: Trinity University Press.
—— (1981). *A Community of Character: Toward a Constructive Christian Social Ethic*. Notre Dame: University of Notre Dame Press.
—— (2002). *With the Grain of the Universe: The Church's Witness and Natural Theology*. London: SCM.
—— (2003). *The Peaceable Kingdom: A Primer in Christian Ethics* (2nd edn). London: SCM Press.
Hauerwas, S. and Pinches, C. (1997). *Christians among the Virtues: Theological Conversations with Ancient and Modern Ethics*. Notre Dame: University of Notre Dame Press.
Haydon, G. (1993). *Education and the Crisis in Values: Should we be Philosophical about it? – The London File – Papers from the Institute of Education*. London: Tufnell Press.
—— (1997). *Teaching about Values: A New Approach*. London: Cassell.
—— (2003). 'Moral Education'. In R. Curran (ed.), *A Companion to the Philosophy of Education*, pp. 320–331. Oxford: Blackwell.
—— (2004). 'Values Education: Sustaining the Ethical Environment', *Journal of Moral Education*, 33 (2), 115–129.
—— (2010). 'Personal and Social Education'. In R. Bailey, R. Barrow, D. Carr and C. McCarthy (eds), *The SAGE Handbook of Philosophy of Education*, pp. 503–515. London: SAGE.
Health Development Agency (2001). *Teenage Pregnancy: An Update on Key Characteristics of Effective Interventions*. London: Health Development Agency,

<http://www.nice.org.uk/niceMedia/documents/teenpreg.pdf> accessed 20 September 2013.

Healy, N. M. (2014). *Hauerwas: A (Very) Critical Introduction*. Cambridge: Eerdmans.

Hendry, L. B., Philip, K., and Shucksmith, J. (1995). *Educating for Health: School and Community Approaches with Adolescents*. London: Cassell.

Herdt, J. A. (2008). *Putting on Virtue: The Legacy of the Splendid Vices*. London: University of Chicago Press.

Herms, E. (1982). 'Virtue: A Neglected Concept in Protestant Ethics', *Scottish Journal of Theology*, 35, 481–495.

Heslam, P. S. (1998). *Creating a Christian Worldview: Abraham Kuyper's Lectures on Calvinism*. Grand Rapids: Eerdmans.

Heywood, R. (2008). 'Mature Teenagers and Medical Intervention Revisited: A Right to Consent, a Wrong to Refuse', *Common Law World Review*, 37 (2), 191–203.

Hill, B. V. (1990). *That They May Learn: Towards a Christian View of Education*. Exeter: Paternoster.

Hill, D. B. (2006). 'Psychology, Twentieth- and Twenty-First Century'. In A. Soble (ed.), *Sex from Plato to Paglia: A Philosophical Encyclopedia, Vol. 2: M-Z*, pp. 784–793. London: Greenwood Press.

Himmelfarb, G. (1995). *The De-moralization of Society: From Victorian Virtues to Modern Values. Choice in Welfare Series No. 22*. London: IEA Health and Welfare Unit.

Hirst, J. (2013). '"It's got to be about enjoying yourself": Young People, Sexual Pleasure, and Sex and Relationships Education', *Sex Education*, 13 (4), 423–436.

Hirst, P. H. (1967). 'The Logical and Psychological Aspects of Teaching a Subject'. In R. S. Peters (ed.), *The Concept of Education*, pp. 44–60. London: Routledge & Kegan Paul.

—— (1973). 'Liberal Education and the Nature of Knowledge'. In R. S. Peters (ed.), *The Philosophy of Education*, pp. 87–111. Oxford: Oxford University Press.

—— (1974). *Moral Education in a Secular Society*. London: University of London Press.

Hirst, P. H., and Peters, R. S. (1970). *The Logic of Education*. London: Routledge and Kegan Paul.

Hollenbach, D. (SJ) (2002). *The Common Good and Christian Ethics*. Cambridge: Cambridge University Press.

Hollinger, D. P. (2002). *Choosing the Good: Christian Ethics in a Complex World*. Grand Rapids: Baker Academic.

—— (2009). *The Meaning of Sex: Christian Ethics and the Moral Life*. Grand Rapids: Baker Academic.

Home Office (2004). *Guidance on Part 1 of the Sexual Offences Act 2003, Circular 021/2004*. London: Criminal Law and Policy Directorate, <http://www.

homeoffice.gov.uk/about-us/corporate-publications-strategy/home-office-circulars/circulars-2004/021-2004/> accessed 10 October 2012.

Hook, S. (2009). 'John Dewey: Afterword'. In S. M. Cahn (ed.), *Philosophy of Education: The Essential Texts*, pp. 490–497. London: Routledge.

Hume, D. (1902) [1777]. *Enquiries Concerning the Human Understanding and Concerning the Principles of Morals* (2nd edn). Edited by L. A. Selby-Bigge. Oxford: Clarendon Press.

—— (1975) [1740]. *A Treatise of Human Nature*. London: Oxford University Press.

Hunter, J. D. (2000). *The Death of Character: Moral Education in an Age Without Good or Evil*. New York: Basic Books.

—— (2010). *To Change the World: The Irony, Tragedy, and Possibility of Christianity in the Late Modern World*. Oxford: Oxford University Press.

Hursthouse, R. (1999). *On Virtue Ethics*. Oxford: Oxford University Press.

Ingham, R. (2014). 'A Well-Kept Secret; Sex Education, Masturbation, and Public Health'. In L. Allen, K. Quinlivan and M. L. Rasmussen (eds), *The Politics of Pleasure in Sexuality Education: Pleasure Bound*, pp. 57–77. London: Routledge.

Ingham, R., and Stammers, T. (2000). 'For and Against: Doctors Should Advise Adolescents to Abstain from Sex', *British Medical Journal*, 321, 1520–1522.

Ingham, R., and Stone, N. (2006). 'Young People and Sex and Relationships Education'. In P. Aggleton and R. Ingham (eds), *Promoting Young People's Sexual Health: International Perspectives*, pp. 192–208. Abingdon: Routledge.

Irvine, J. M. (2006). 'Sexology'. In A. Soble (ed.), *Sex from Plato to Paglia: A Philosophical Encyclopedia, Vol. 2: M-Z*, pp. 1002–1009. London: Greenwood Press.

Jacobsen, R. (2006). 'Desire, Sexual'. In A. Soble (ed.), *Sex from Plato to Paglia: A Philosophical Encyclopedia, Vol. 1: A-L*, pp. 222–229. London: Greenwood Press.

James, S. (1997). *British Government: A Reader in Policy Making*. London: Routledge.

Jennings, B. (2007). 'Public Health and Civic Republicanism: Toward an Alternative Framework for Public Health Ethics'. In A. Dawson and M. Verweij (eds), *Ethics, Prevention and Public Health*, pp. 30–58. Oxford: Oxford University Press.

Jollimore, T. (2006). 'Love'. In A. Soble (ed.), *Sex from Plato to Paglia: A Philosophical Encyclopedia, Vol. 1: A-L*, pp. 606–620. London: Greenwood Press.

Jones, R. (1989). 'Sex Education in Personal and Social Education'. In P. White (ed.), *Personal and Social Education: Philosophical Perspectives*, pp. 54–70. London: Kogan Page.

Jones, T. M. (2011). 'Saving Rhetorical Children: Sexuality Education Discourses from Conservative to Post-Modern', *Sex Education*, 11 (4), 369–387.

Jones, L., and Cribb, A. (2000). 'Ethical Issues in Health Promotion'. In J. Douglas, J. Katz and A. Peberdy (eds), *Promoting Health: Knowledge and Practice* (2nd edn), pp. 95–107. Basingstoke: Macmillan Press.

Kallenberg, B. J., and Tousley, N. C. (2011). 'Virtue Ethics', In J. B. Green (ed.), *Dictionary of Scripture and Ethics*, pp. 814–819. Grand Rapids: Baker Academic.

Kaltwasser, C. J. (2011). 'Assessing the Christological Foundation of Kuyper's Doctrine of Common Grace'. In J. Bowlin (ed.), *The Kuyper Center Review. Volume Two: Revelation and Common Grace*, pp. 200–220. Grand Rapids: Eerdmans.

Kant, I. (1929) [1787]. *Immanuel Kant's Critique of Pure Reason*. Translated by N. K. Smith. London: Macmillan Education.

Katayama, K. (2003). 'Is the Virtue Approach to Moral Education Viable in a Plural Society?', *Journal of Philosophy of Education*, 37 (2), 325–338.

Keller, T., and Keller, K. (2011). *The Meaning of Marriage: Facing the Complexities of Commitment with the Wisdom of God*. London: Hodder & Stoughton.

Kinsey, A. C., Martin, C. E., and Pomeroy, W. B. (1948). *Sexual Behaviour in the Human Male*. London: W. B. Saunders Company.

Kirkendall, L. (1976). *A New Bill of Sexual Rights and Responsibilities*. Bufallo: Prometheus Books.

Kohlberg, L. (1981). *Essays in Moral Development. Volume 1: The Philosophy of Moral Development*. New York: Harper and Row.

Kotva, J. J. Jr (1996). *The Christian Case for Virtue Ethics*. Washington, DC: Georgetown University Press.

Kristjánsson, K. (2013). 'Ten Myths about Character, Virtue and Virtue Education – Plus Three Well-Founded Misgivings', *British Journal of Education Studies*, 61 (3), 269–287.

Kuehne, D. (2009). *Sex and the iWorld: Rethinking Relationship beyond an Age of Individualism*. Grand Rapids: Baker Academic.

Kuiper, H. (1928). *Calvin on Common Grace*. Goes: Oosterbaan & Le Cointre.

Kuyper, A. (1998). 'Common Grace'. In J. D. Bratt (ed.), *Abraham Kuyper: A Centennial Reader*, pp. 165–201. Cumbria: Paternoster.

Laing, J. (2012). 'The Connection between Law and Justice in the Natural Law Tradition'. In Nick Spencer (ed.), *Religion and Law*, pp. 125–134. London: Theos.

Lamb, S., Lustig, K., and Graling, K. (2013). 'The Use and Misuse of Pleasure in Sex Education Curricula', *Sex Education*, 13 (3), 305–318.

Lane, A. N. S. (2006). 'Lust: The Human Person as Affected by Disordered Desires', *Evangelical Quarterly*, 78 (1), 21–35.

Leach, R. (1995). 'Political Ideas'. In M. Mullard (ed.), *Policy-making in Britain: An Introduction*, pp. 13–32. London: Routledge.

Leech, K. (1997). *The Sky is Red: Discerning the Signs of the Times*. London: Darton, Longman and Todd.

Lennox, J. (2004). *Utilitarianism's Critique of the Sanctity of Life Doctrine: A World-View Perspective.* Unpublished MA Thesis: St Mary's University College, Twickenham.
—— (2011). *Gunning for God: Why the New Atheists are Missing the Target.* Oxford: Lion Hudson.
Levinson, M. (1999). *The Demands of Liberal Education.* Oxford: Oxford University Press.
Lewis, C. S. (2002a) [1960]. *The Four Loves.* London: HarperCollins.
—— (2002b) [1943]. 'Mere Christianity', *The Complete C. S. Lewis Signature Classics*, pp. 1–177. New York: HarperCollins.
—— (2002c) [1947]. 'The Abolition of Man'. *The Complete C. S. Lewis Signature Classics*, pp. 689–738. New York: HarperCollins.
Linville, M. D. (2009a). 'The Moral Argument'. In W. L. Craig and J. P. Moreland (eds), *The Blackwell Companion to Natural Theology*, pp. 391–448. Chichester: Willey-Blackwell.
—— (2009b). 'The Moral Poverty of Evolutionary Naturalism'. In P. Copan and W. L. Craig (eds), *Contending with Christianity's Critics: Answering New Atheists and Other Objectors*, pp. 58–73. Nashville: B&H Publishing Group.
Louden, R. B. (1997). 'On Some Vices of Virtue Ethics', R. Crisp and M. Slote (eds), *Virtue Ethics*, pp. 201–216. Oxford: Oxford University Press.
—— (2009). 'Immanuel Kant: Afterword'. In S. M. Cahn (ed.), *Philosophy of Education: The Essential Texts*, pp. 281–292. London: Routledge.
Loughrey, J. (2008). 'Can you keep a Secret? Children, Human Rights, and the Law of Medical Confidentiality', *Child and Family Law Quarterly*, 20 (3), 312–334.
MacIntyre, A. (1987). 'The Idea of an Educated Public'. In G. Haydon (ed.), *Education and Values: The Richard Peters Lectures, Delivered at the Institute of Education, University of London, Spring Terms, 1985*, pp. 15–36. London: Institute of Education, University of London.
—— (1991). *How to Seem Virtuous Without Actually Being So.* Lancaster: Centre for the Study of Cultural Values.
—— (2007). *After Virtue* (3rd edn). London: Bloomsbury Academic.
Maddalena, J. M. (2011). 'Self-Love'. In J. B. Green (ed.), *Dictionary of Scripture and Ethics*, pp. 714–715. Grand Rapids: Baker Academic.
Mason-Jones, A. J., Sinclair D., Mathews, C., Kagee, A., Hillman, A., Lombard, C. (2016). 'School-based interventions for preventing HIV, sexually transmitted infections, and pregnancy in adolescents', *Cochrane Database of Systematic Reviews 2016*, Issue 11. Art. No.: CD006417. DOI: 10.1002/14651858.CD006417.pub3.

McCarty, R. W. (2015). *Sexual Virtue: An Approach to Contemporary Christian Ethics*. Albany: SUNY.

McEvoy, J. (1994). 'Friendship within Marriage: A Philosophical Essay'. In L. Gormally (ed.), *Moral Truth and Moral Tradition*, pp. 194–202. Dublin: Four Courts Press.

McFadyen, A. (1990). *The Call to Personhood: A Christian Theory of the Individual in Social Relationships*. Cambridge: Cambridge University Press.

McGrath, A. E. (1992). *Bridge-Building: Effective Christian Apologetics*. Leicester: IVP.

—— (2007). *Christian Theology: An Introduction* (4th edn). Oxford: Blackwell.

—— (2008). *The Open Secret: A New Vision for Natural Theology*. Oxford: Blackwell.

—— (2011). *Darwinism and the Divine: Evolutionary Thought and Natural Theology*. Oxford: Wiley-Blackwell.

McIlroy, D. (2009). 'The Role of Government in Classical Christian Political Thought'. In N. Spencer and J. Chaplin (eds), *God and Government*, pp. 81–107. London: SPCK.

—— (2012). 'Does the Law Need a Moral Basis?'. In Nick Spencer (ed.), *Religion and Law*, pp. 153–161. London: Theos.

McLaughlin, T. H. (1998). 'Sex Education, Moral Controversy and the Common School'. In S. A. Mabud and M. J. Reiss (eds), *Sex Education and Religion*, pp. 186–224. London: Islamic Academy.

—— (2001). 'A Spiritual Dimension to Sex Education?', *International Journal of Children's Spirituality*, 6 (2), 223–232.

—— (2005). 'Philosophy and Educational Policy: Possibilities, Tensions and Tasks'. In W. Carr (ed.), *The RoutledgeFalmer Reader in Philosophy of Education*, pp. 17–33. Abingdon: Routledge.

—— (2008). 'Education of the Whole Child?'. In D. Carr, M. Halstead and R. Pring (eds), *Liberalism, Education and Schooling: Essays by T. H. McLaughlin*, pp. 48–59. Exeter: Imprint Academic.

McLaughlin, T. H., and Halstead, J. M. (1999). 'Education in Character and Virtue'. In J. M. Halstead and T. H. McLaughlin (eds), *Education in Morality*, pp. 132–163. London: Routledge.

McQueen, D. (2010). 'The Evaluation of Health Promotion Practice: Twenty-First Century Debates on Evidence and Effectiveness', *A Reader in Promoting Public Health: Challenge and Controversy* (2nd edn), pp. 89–96. Milton Keynes: The Open University.

Measor, L., Miller, K., and Tiffin, C. (2000). *Young People's Views on Sex Education: Education, Attitudes and Behaviour*. London: RoutledgeFalmer.

Meilaender, G. C. (1984). *The Theory and Practice of Virtue*. Notre Dame: University of Notre Dame Press.

—— (1985). *Friendship: A Study in Theological Ethics*. Notre Dame: University of Notre Dame Press.

Meredith, P. (1989). *Sex Education: Political Issues in Britain and Europe*. London: Routledge.

Michaud, P.-A., Chandra-Mouli, V., and Patton, G. C. (2009). 'Adolescent Health'. In R. Detels, R. Beaglehole, M. A. Lansang and M. Gulliford (eds), *Oxford Textbook of Public Health* (5th edn), pp. 1452–1464. Oxford: Oxford University Press.

Milbank, J. (1990). *Theology and Social Theory: Beyond Secular Reason*. Oxford: Blackwell.

Mill, J. S. (1867). *Inaugural Address: Delivered to the University of St. Andrews, Feb. 1st 1867*. London: Longmans, Green, Reader and Dyer.

—— (2004) [1871]. 'Utilitarianism'. In A. Ryan (ed.), *John Stuart Mill and Jeremy Bentham: Utilitarianism and Other Essays*, pp. 272–338. London: Penguin Books.

—— (2006) [1859]. 'On Liberty'. In A. Ryan (ed.), *On Liberty and the Subjection of Women*, pp. 1–129. London: Penguin Books.

Ministry of Education (1963). *Half our Future: A Report of the Central Advisory Council for Education (England)*. London: HMSO.

Molendijk, A. L. (2008). 'Neo-Calvinist Culture Protestantism: Abraham Kuyper's Stone Lectures', *Church History and Religious Culture*, 88 (2), 235–250.

Montgomery, H. (2007). 'Child Sexual Abuse – An Anthropological Perspective'. In G. Rousseau (ed.), *Children and Sexuality: From the Greeks to the Great War*, pp. 319–347. Basingstoke: Palgrave Macmillan.

Moore, G. E. (1966). *Principia Ethica*. London: Cambridge University Press.

Moran, K. (2009). 'Can Kant Have an Account of Moral Education?', *Journal of Philosophy of Education*, 43 (4), 471–484.

Mouw, R., (2001). *He Shines in All That's Fair: Culture and Common Grace*. Grand Rapids: Eerdmans.

Mouw, R. J. (2009). 'Calvin's Legacy for Public Theology', *Political Theology*, 10 (3), 431–446.

Mulhall, S., and Swift, A. (1996). *Liberals & Communitarians* (2nd edn). Oxford: Blackwell.

Müller, A. W. (1994). 'Has Moral Education a Rational Basis?'. In L. Gormally (ed.), *Moral Truth and Moral Tradition. Essays in Honour or Peter Geach and Elizabeth Anscombe*, pp. 203–225. Blackrock: Four Courts Press.

Nagel, T. (1969). 'Sexual Perversion', *The Journal of Philosophy*, 66 (1), 5–17.

Nash, R. J. (1997). *Answering the "Virtuecrats": A Moral Conversation on Character Education*. New York: Teachers College Press.

Nelson, W. (2002). 'Liberal Theories and their Critics'. In R. L. Simon (ed.), *The Blackwell Guide to Social and Political Philosophy*, pp. 197–217. Oxford: Blackwell.

Nicholi, A. M. Jr (2002). *The Question of God: C. S. Lewis and Sigmund Freud debate God, Love, Sex, and the Meaning of Life*. New York: Free Press.
Nicholls, D. (1996). 'Grace'. In P. B. Clarke and A. Linzey (eds), *Dictionary of Ethics, Theology and Society*, pp. 410–414. London: Routledge.
Nietzsche, F. (1968) [1889]. 'Twilight of the Idols'. *Twilight of the Idols and The Anti-Christ*, Translated by R. J. Hollingdale. pp. 29–122. London: Penguin Books.
—— (1968) [1895]. 'The Anti-Christ'. *Twilight of the Idols and The Anti-Christ*. Translated by R. J. Hollingdale. pp. 123–199. London: Penguin Books.
Noble, C., and Toft, M. (2012). 'How Effective are Schools as a Setting for Health Promotion?' In M. Hodgins and A. Scriven (eds), *Health Promotion Settings: Principles and Practice*, pp. 140–152. London: SAGE.
Noddings, N., and Slote, M. (2003). 'Changing Notions of the Moral and of Moral Education'. In N. Blake, P. Smeyers, R. Smith and P. Standish (eds), *The Blackwell Guide to the Philosophy of Education*, pp. 341–355. Oxford: Blackwell.
Nozick, R. (1974). *Anarchy, State, and Utopia*. Oxford: Basil Blackwell.
Nucci, L. (2006). 'Education for Moral Development'. In M. Killen and J. G. Smetana (eds), *The Handbook of Moral Development*, pp. 657–682. London: Lawrence Erlbaum Associates.
Nygren, A. (1953). *Agape and Eros*. Translated by P. S. Watson. London: SPCK.
O'Connor, D. J. (1967). *Aquinas and Natural Law*. London: Macmillan.
O'Daly, G. (1999). 'Augustine'. In D. Furley (ed.), *Routledge History of Philosophy Volume II: From Aristotle to Augustine*, pp. 388–428. London: Routledge.
O'Donovan, O. (1984). *Begotten or Made?* Oxford: Oxford University Press.
—— (1994). *Resurrection and Moral Order: An Outline for Evangelical Ethics* (2nd edn). Leicester: Apollos.
—— (1996). *The Desire of the Nations: Rediscovering the Roots of Political Theory*. Cambridge: Cambridge University Press.
—— (2010). 'Reflections on Pluralism'. In G. Graham (ed.), *The Kuyper Center Review. Volume One: Politics, Religion and Sphere Sovereignty*, pp. 1–13. Grand Rapids: Eerdmans.
Odell, S. J. (2006a). 'Consequentialism'. In A. Soble (ed.), *Sex from Plato to Paglia: A Philosophical Encyclopedia, Vol. 1: A-L*, pp. 194–202. London: Greenwood Press.
—— (2006b). 'Russell, Bertrand (1872–1970)'. In A. Soble (ed.), *Sex from Plato to Paglia: A Philosophical Encyclopedia, Vol. 2: M-Z*, pp. 944–948. London: Greenwood Press.
Ofsted (2010). *Personal, Social, Health and Economic Education in Schools*. Manchester: Ofsted.
—— (2013). *Not Yet Good Enough: Personal, Social, Health and Economic Education in Schools*. Manchester: Ofsted.

Outka, G. (1972). *Agape: An Ethical Analysis*. London: Yale University Press.

Pahl, R. (2000). *On Friendship*. Cambridge: Polity Press.

Papadopoulos, L. (2010). *Sexualisation of Young People Review*, <http://drlinda.co.uk/wp-content/uploads/2015/09/Sexualisation-Review.pdf> accessed 25 June 2017.

Pearce, D. M. (1993). '"Children having Children": Teenage Pregnancy and Public Policy from the Women's Perspective'. In A. Lawson and D.L Rhode (eds), *The Politics of Pregnancy: Adolescent Sexuality and Public Policy*, pp. 46–58. London: Yale University Press.

Peters, R. S. (1970a). 'Concrete Principles and the Rational Passions'. In N. F. Sizer and T. R. Sizer (eds), *Moral Education. Five Lectures*, pp. 28–55. Cambridge: Harvard University Press.

—— (1970b). *Ethics and Education*. London: George Allen & Unwin.

—— (1973). *Authority, Responsibility and Education* (3rd edn). London: George Allen and Unwin.

—— (1974). *Psychology and Ethical Development: A Collection of Articles on Psychological Theories, Ethical Development and Human Understanding*. London: George Allen and Unwin.

—— (1981). *Moral Development and Moral Education*. London: George Allen and Unwin.

Pope, S. (2005). 'Reason and Natural Law'. In G. Meilaender and W. Werpehowski (eds), *The Oxford Handbook of Theological Ethics*, pp. 148–167. Oxford: Oxford University Press.

—— (2012). 'Natural Law and Christian Ethics'. In R. Gill (ed.), *The Cambridge Companion to Christian Ethics*, pp. 67–86. Cambridge: Cambridge University Press.

Porter, J. (1990). *The Recovery of Virtue: The Relevance of Aquinas for Christian Ethics*. London: SPCK.

—— (1995). *Moral Action and Christian Ethics*. Cambridge: Cambridge University Press.

—— (1999). *Natural Law and Divine Law: Reclaiming the Tradition of Christian Ethics*. Cambridge: Eerdmans.

—— (2005). 'Virtue'. In G. Meilaender and W. Werpehowski (eds), *The Oxford Handbook of Theological Ethics*, pp. 205–219. Oxford: Oxford University Press.

—— (2012). 'Virtue Ethics'. In R. Gill (ed.), *The Cambridge Companion to Christian Ethics* (2nd edn), pp. 87–102. Cambridge: Cambridge University Press.

Primoratz, I. (1997). *Human Sexuality*. Aldershot: Dartmouth.

—— (1999). *Ethics and Sex*. London: Routledge.

—— (2001), 'Sexual Morality: Is Consent Enough?', *Ethical Theory and Moral Practice*, 4 (3), 201–218.

—— (2006). 'Pedophilia'. In A. Soble (ed.), *Sex from Plato to Paglia: A Philosophical Encyclopedia, Vol. 2: M-Z*, pp. 755–763. London: Greenwood Press.

Pring, R. (1987). 'Education as Health Promotion: An Educational Perspective'. In G. Campbell (ed.), *Health Education, Youth and Community: A Review of Research and Developments*, pp. 14–20. Lewes: The Falmer Press.

—— (2014). 'In Defence of Virtue Teaching'. In J. Gingell (ed.), *Education and the Common Good: Essays in Honor of Robin Barrow*, pp. 40–49. Abingdon: Routledge.

Pruss, A. R. (2011). 'From Love to Union as One Body'. In H. Watt (ed.), *Fertility and Gender: Issues in Reproductive and Sexual Ethics*, pp. 17–27. Oxford: The Anscombe Bioethics Centre.

Public Health England (2015). 'Sexually Transmitted Infections and Chlamydia Screening in England, 2016', *Health Protection Report*, 11 (20), <https://www.gov.uk/government/uploads/system/uploads/attachment_data/file/617025/Health_Protection_Report_STIs_NCSP_2017.pdf > accessed 6 July 2017.

Putman, D. (1995). 'The Primacy of Virtue in Children's Moral Development', *Journal of Moral Education*, 24 (2), 178–183.

Rabie, G. (2009). 'Public Health and the Schools Community'. In M. Mabhala and F. Wilson (eds), *Key Concepts in Public Health*, pp. 241–246. London: SAGE.

Rachels, J. (2003). *The Elements of Moral Philosophy*. London: McGraw Hill.

Rawls, J. (1972). *A Theory of Justice*. Oxford: Oxford University Press.

—— (2000). *Lectures in the History of Moral Philosophy*. Edited by B. Herman. London: Harvard University Press.

Raz, J. (1986). *The Morality of Freedom*. Oxford: Clarendon Press.

Reiss, M. J. (1993). 'What are the Aims of School Sex Education?', *Cambridge Journal of Education*, 23, (2), 125–136.

—— (1996). 'Food, Smoking and Sex: Values in Health Education'. In J. M. Halstead and M. J. Taylor (eds), *Values in Education and Education in Values*, pp. 92–103. London: The Falmer Press.

—— (1998). 'The History of School Sex Education'. In S. A. Mabud and M. J. Reiss (eds), *Sex Education and Religion*, pp. 5–18. London: Islamic Academy.

—— (2007). 'Conflicting Philosophies of School Sex Education'. In R. Curren (ed.), *Philosophy of Education: An Anthology*, pp. 553–560. Oxford: Blackwell.

Reuschling, W. C. (2011). 'Divine Command Theories of Ethics'. In J. B. Green (ed.), *Dictionary of Scripture and Ethics*, pp. 242–246. Grand Rapids: Baker Academic.

Riches, V. (1998). 'Shortcomings of Present-Day Practice in School Sex Education'. In S. A. Mabud and M. J. Reiss (eds), *Sex Education and Religion*, pp. 35–52. London: Islamic Academy.

Richey, L. B. (2006). 'Schopenhauer, Arthur (1788–1860)'. In A. Soble (ed.), *Sex from Plato to Paglia: A Philosophical Encyclopedia, Vol. 2: M-Z*, pp. 967–973. London: Greenwood Press.

Ritchie, A. (2012). *From Goodness to God: Why Religion Makes Sense of our Moral Commitments*. London: Theos.

Rivers, J. (2006). 'The Abuse of Equality', *Ethics in Brief*, 11 (1), <http://klice.co.uk/uploads/Ethics%20in%20Brief/Rivers%20v11.1%20pub.pdf> accessed 15 August 2014.

—— (2012a). 'Redefining Marriage: The Case for Caution', *Cambridge Papers*, 21 (3).

—— (2012b). 'Is English Law Christian?'. In N. Spencer (ed.), *Religion and Law*, pp. 143–152. London: Theos.

Roberts, R. C. (1995). 'Character'. In D. J. Atkinson and D. H. Field (eds), *New Dictionary of Christian Ethics and Pastoral Theology*, pp. 65–71. Leicester: IVP.

Rorty, A. O. (1999). 'Morality as an Educational Institution'. In J. M. Halstead and T. H. McLaughlin (eds), *Education in Morality*, pp. 7–22. London: Routledge.

Rorty, R. (2007). 'Kant vs. Dewey: The Current Situation of Moral Philosophy', *Philosophy as Cultural Politics: Philosophical Papers*, pp. 184–202. Cambridge: Cambridge University Press.

Rowntree, F. (1971). 'The New Role of Sex Education'. In A. Le Meitour-Kaplun (ed.), *International Union for Health Education: Communication and Behaviour Change*, pp. 267–272. Geneva: International Journal of Health Education.

RSA (2014). *Schools with Soul: A New Approach to Spiritual, Moral, Social and Cultural Education*, <http://www.thersa.org/action-research-centre/learning,-cognition-and-creativity/education/reports-and-events/reports/schools-with-soul> accessed 20 June 2014.

Rubin, I. (1968a), 'A Balanced View of the "Sexual Revolution"'. In I. Rubin and L. A. Kirkendall (eds), *Sex in the Adolescent Years: New Directions in Guiding and Teaching Youth*, pp. 19–32. New York: Association Press.

—— (1968b). 'What Real Sex Education Means'. In I. Rubin and L. A. Kirkendall (eds), *Sex in the Adolescent Years: New Directions in Guiding and Teaching Youth*, pp. 13–19. New York: Association Press.

Rubin, G. S. (2007) [1984]. 'Thinking Sex: Notes for a Radical Theory of the Politics of Sexuality'. In R. Parker and P. Aggleton (eds), *Culture, Society and Sexuality: A Reader* (2nd edn), pp. 150–187. London: Routledge.

Russell, B. (2009) [1929]. *Marriage and Morals*. London: Routledge.

Russell, D. C. (2013). 'Virtue Ethics, Happiness, and the Good Life'. In D. C. Russell (ed.), *The Cambridge Companion to Virtue Ethics*, pp. 7–28. Cambridge: Cambridge University Press.

Ryan, A. (2006). 'Introduction'. In A. Ryan (ed.), *John Stuart Mill: On Liberty and The Subjection of Women*, pp. ix-xlvii. London: Penguin Books.

Samples, K. R. (2007). *A World of Difference: Putting Christian Truth-Claims to the Worldview Test*. Michigan: Baker Books.

Samuelson, P., and Snarey, J. (2008). 'Moral Education in the Cognitive Developmental Tradition: Lawrence Kohlberg's Revolutionary Ideas'. In D. Narvaez and L. P. Nucci (eds), *Handbook of Moral and Character Education*, pp. 53–79. Abingdon: Routledge.

Sandel, M. J. (1982). *Liberalism and the Limits of Justice*. Cambridge: Cambridge University Press.

—— (2010). *Justice: What's the Right Thing to Do?*. London: Penguin Books.

Sauerteig, L. D. H., and Davidson, R. (2009). 'Shaping Sexual Knowledge of the Young: Introduction'. In R. Davidson and L. D. H. Sauerteig (eds), *Shaping Sexual Knowledge: A Cultural History of Sex Education in Twentieth Century Europe*, pp. 1–15. London: Routledge.

Sauntson, H., and Sundaram, V. (2016). 'Discursive Silences: Critically Analysing the Presence/Absence of Sexual Diversity in the Sex and Relationships Education Guidance for England and Wales'. In V. Sundaram and H. Sauntson (eds), *Global Perspectives and Key Debates in Sex and Relationships Education: Addressing Issues of Gender, Sexuality, Plurality and Power*, pp. 100–114. London: Palgrave MacMillan.

Schaeffer, F. A. (1968). *Escape from Reason*. London: IVP.

Schreiner, S. E. (1997). 'Calvin's Use of Natural Law'. In Michael Cromartie (ed.), *A Preserving Grace: Protestants, Catholics, and Natural Law*, pp. 51–76. Grand Rapids: Eerdmans.

Scriven, A. (2010). *Promoting Health: A Practical Guide* (6th edn). Oxford: Baillière Tindall.

Scruton, R. (2006). *Sexual Desire: A Philosophical Investigation*. London: Continuum.

Seedhouse, D. (2004). *Health Promotion: Philosophy, Prejudice and Practice* (2nd edn). Chichester: John Wiley and Sons.

Sex Education Forum (2005). 'Sex and Relationships Education Framework', <http://www3.hants.gov.uk/ck001_sre_u1_pack_-_sre_forum_factsheet-2.pdf> accessed 5 September 2012.

—— (2008). *Key Findings: Young People's Survey on Sex and Relationships Education*, <http://www.ncb.org.uk/media/333301/young_peoples_survey_on_sex___relationships_education.pdf> accessed 5 September 2012.

Sexual Offences Act 2003 (c.42), <http://www.legislation.gov.uk/ukpga/2003/42/pdfs/ukpga_20030042_en.pdf > accessed 10 October 2012.

Sexual Offences Review Group (2000). *Setting the Boundaries: Reforming the Law on Sexual Offences*. London: Home Office Communications Directorate.

Shipley, H. (2017). 'Teaching Sexuality, Teaching Religion: Sexuality Education and Religion in Canada'. In L. Allen and M. L. Rasmussen (eds), *The Palgrave Handbook of Sexuality Education*, pp. 157–176. London: Palgrave Macmillan.

Shucksmith, J. (2004). 'A Risk Worth the Taking: Sex and Selfhood in Adolescence'. In E. Burtney and M. Duffy (eds), *Young People and Sexual Health: Individual, Social, and Policy Contexts*, pp. 5–14. Basingstoke: Palgrave Macmillan.

Sidgwick, H. (1898). *Practical Ethics: A Collection of Addresses and Essays*. London: Swan Sonnenschein & Co.

Sigmund, P. E. (2000). 'Subsidiarity, Solidarity, and Liberation: Alternative Approaches in Catholic Social Thought'. In Luis E. Lugo (ed.), *Religion, Pluralism and Public Life: Abraham Kuyper's Legacy for the Twenty-First Century*, pp. 205–220. Grand Rapids: Eerdmans.

Singer, P. (1979). *Practical Ethics*, Cambridge: Cambridge University Press.

—— (1997). *How are we to live?: Ethics in an Age of Self-interest*. Oxford: Oxford University Press.

—— (2001). 'Heavy Petting', <http://www.utilitarian.net/singer/by/2001----.htm> accessed 27 February 2013.

Sire, J. (2009). *The Universe Next Door* (5th edn). Nottingham: IVP.

Skoe, E. E. A. (2010). 'The Relationship between Empathy-related Constructs and Care-based Moral Development in young Adulthood', *Journal of Moral Education*, 39 (2), 191–211.

Slote, M. (2000). 'Virtue Ethics'. In H. LaFollette (ed.), *The Blackwell Guide to Ethical Theory*, pp. 325–347. Oxford: Blackwell.

Smart, J. C. C., and Williams, B. (1973). *Utilitarianism: For and Against*. Cambridge: Cambridge University Press.

Smedes, L. B. (1994). *Sex for Christians: The Limits and Liberties of Sexual Living*. Grand Rapids: Eerdmans.

Smith, J. K. A. (2004). *Introducing Radical Orthodoxy: Mapping a Post-secular Theology*. Milton Keynes: Paternoster.

—— (2009). *Desiring the Kingdom: Worship, Worldview, and Cultural Formation*. Grand Rapids: Baker Academic.

—— (2013). *Imagining the Kingdom: How Worship Works*. Grand Rapids: Baker Academic.

Smith, C., and Snell, P. (2009). *Souls in Transition: The Religious and Spiritual Lives of Emerging Adults*. Oxford: Oxford University Press.

Smith, C., Christofferson, K., Davidson, H., and Snell Herzog, P. (2011). *Lost in Transition: The Dark Side of Emerging Adulthood*. Oxford: Oxford University Press.

Soble, A. (2006a). 'Activity, Sexual'. In A. Soble (ed.), *Sex from Plato to Paglia: A Philosophical Encyclopedia, Vol. 1: A-L*, pp. 15–25. London: Greenwood Press.

—— (2006b). 'Philosophy of Sex, Overview of'. In A. Soble (ed.), *Sex from Plato to Paglia: A Philosophical Encyclopedia, Vol. 2: M-Z*, pp. 784–793. London: Greenwood Press.

—— (2008). *The Philosophy of Sex and Love* (2nd edn). St Paul: Paragon House.

Social Exclusion Unit (1999). *Teenage Pregnancy: Report by the Social Exclusion Unit.* London: HMSO.

Sorokin, P. A. (1992). *The Crisis of our Age* (2nd edn). Oxford: Oneworld.

Spencer, N. (2011). *Freedom and Order: History, Politics and the English Bible.* London: Hodder and Stoughton.

Spiecker, B., and Steutel, J. (2007). 'Components of Virtues and Stagnations in Moral-Sexual Development'. In R. Halwani (ed.), *Sex and Ethics: Essays on Sexuality, Virtue, and the Good Life*, pp. 177–189. Basingstoke: Palgrave Macmillan.

Spohn, W. C. (2005). 'Scripture'. In G. Meilaender and W. Werpehowski (eds), *The Oxford Handbook of Theological Ethics*, pp. 93–111. Oxford: Oxford University Press.

Stackhouse, M. L. (2006). *Theology in the Public Square: Kuyper's Contributions Highlighted in New PTS Center*, <http://www.ptsem.edu/uploadedFiles/Seminary_Relations/Communications_and_Publications/Publications/inSpire/2006_Winter_Spring/feature5.pdf> accessed 30 March 2014.

Stammers, T. G. (2007a). *Before Virtue: Does Sexual Goodness Exist?* Unpublished MA Thesis: St Mary's University College, Twickenham.

—— (2007b). 'The Imperative of Sexual Ethics', <http://www.bioethics.ac.uk/news/the-imperative-of-sexual-ethics.php> accessed 10 November 2011.

Stapleton, H. (2010). *Surviving Teenage Motherhood: Myths and Realities.* Basingstoke: Palgrave MacMillan.

Stott, J. (2006). *Issues Facing Christians Today* (4th edn). Grand Rapids: Zondervan.

Stout, J. (1990). *Ethics after Babel: The Language of Morals and Their Discontents.* Cambridge: James Clarke & Co.

Straughan, R. (1988). 'Judgement and Action in Moral Education'. In B. Spiecker and R. Straughan (eds), *Philosophical Issues in Moral Education and Development*, pp. 6–16. Milton Keynes: Open University Press.

Strauss, G. (1978). *Luther's House of Learning: Indoctrination of the Young in the German Reformation.* London: The John Hopkins University Press.

Stuart-Smith, S. (1996). 'Teenage Sex: Cognitive Immaturity Increases the Risk', *British Medical Journal*, 312, 390–391.

Sugarman, B., Williams, N., and Wilson, J. (1967). *Introduction to Moral Education.* Harmondsworth: Penguin Books.

Sundaram, V., and Sauntson, H. (2016). 'Introduction: Global Perspectives and Key Debates in Sex and Relationships Education: Setting the Scene'. In V. Sundaram and H. Sauntson (eds), *Global Perspectives and Key Debates in Sex and Relationships Education: Addressing Issues of Gender, Sexuality, Plurality and Power*, pp. 1–12. London: Palgrave MacMillan.

Tannahill, A. (2008). 'Beyond Evidence – To Ethics: A Decision-Making Framework for Health Promotion, Public Health and Health Improvement', *Health Promotion International*, 23 (4), 380–390.

Tatchell, P. (2002). *Teenage Sex: What Should Schools Teach Children?* London: Hodder and Stoughton.

Taylor, C. (1994). 'Justice after Virtue'. In J. Horton and S. Mendus (eds). *After MacIntyre: Critical Perspectives on the Work of Alasdair MacIntyre*, pp. 16–43. Cambridge: Polity Press.

—— (2007). *A Secular Age*. London: The Belknap Press of Harvard University Press.

Taylor, J. (2008). *A Wild Constraint: The Case for Chastity*. London: Continuum.

Teenage Pregnancy Independent Advisory Group (2010). *Teenage Pregnancy Independent Advisory Group Final Report. Teenage Pregnancy: Past Successes – Future Challenges*. London: Department for Education.

Thatcher, A. (2001). 'Sex Education "after Modernity"', *International Journal of Children's Spirituality*, 6 (2), 233–241.

Thielicke, H. (1964). *The Ethics of Sex*. Translated by J. W. Doberstein. Cambridge: James Clarke & Co.

—— (1979). *Theological Ethics. Volume 1: Foundations*. Edited by W. H. Lazareth. Grand Rapids: Eerdmans.

Thomson, R. (1993). *Religion, Ethnicity and Sex Education: Exploring the Issues*. London: National Children's Bureau.

—— (1997). 'Diversity, Values and Social Change: Regenerating a Consensus on Sex Education', *Journal of Moral Education*, 26 (3), 257–271.

Tones, K. (1987). 'Health Promotion, Affective Education and the Personal-Social Development of Young People'. In K. David and T. Williams (eds), *Health Education in Schools* (2nd edn), pp. 3–45. London: Harper and Row.

—— (1997). 'Health Education as Empowerment'. In L. Jones, J. Katz, A. Peberdy and M. Sidell (eds), *Debates and Dilemmas in Promoting Health: A Reader*, pp. 33–42. London: Macmillan Press.

Tones, K., and Tilford S. (1994). *Health Education: Effectiveness, Efficiency and Equity* (2nd edn). London: Chapman & Hall.

Trigg, R. (2007). *Religion in Public Life: Must Faith be Privatized?* Oxford: Oxford University Press.

Trowler, P. (2003). *Education Policy* (2nd edn). London: Routledge.

Turner, J. (2012). 'Hard Cases mean hard Choices. Like Implants', *The Times*, 11 February.

Ulanowsky, C. (1998). 'Sex Education: Beyond Information to Values'. In S. A. Mabud and M. J. Reiss (eds), *Sex Education and Religion*, pp. 19–34. London: Islamic Academy.

UNESCO (2009). *International Technical Guidance on Sexuality Education. Vol. II: Topics and Learning Objectives*, <http://unesdoc.unesco.org/images/0018/001832/183281e.pdf> accessed 2 August 2017.

UNICEF (2013). 'Child Well-being in Rich Countries: A Comparative Overview'. *Innocenti Report Card 11*. Florence: UNICEF Office of Research.

Vacek, E. C. (SJ) (1994). *Love, Human and Divine: The Heart of Christian Ethics*. Washington: Georgetown University Press.

Van den Brink, G. (1999). 'Was Kuyper a Reformed Epistemologist?'. In C. van der Kooi and J. de Bruijn (eds), *Kuyper Reconsidered: Aspects of His Life and Work*, pp. 158–165. Amsterdam: VU Uitgeverij.

Van der Kooi, C. (1999). 'A Theology of Culture. A Critical Appraisal of Kuyper's Doctrine of Common Grace'. In C. van der Kooi and J. de Bruijn (eds), *Kuyper Reconsidered: Aspects of His Life and Work*, pp. 95–101. Amsterdam: VU Uitgeverij.

Van der Ven, J. A. (1998). *Formation of the Moral Self*. Cambridge: Eerdmans.

VanDrunen, D. (2010). *Natural Law and the Two Kingdoms: A Study in the Development of Reformed Social Thought*. Grand Rapids: Eerdmans.

Van Haaften, W. (1988). 'Can Moral Education be Justified in Moral Education?'. In B. Spiecker and R. Straughan (eds), *Philosophical Issues in Moral Education and Development*, pp. 17–42. Milton Keynes: Open University Press.

Varma, A. (2010). 'Sin, Grace, and Virtue in Calvin: A Matrix for Dogmatic Consideration', *Scottish Bulletin of Evangelical Theology*, 28 (2), 177–194.

Vernon, M. (2005). *The Philosophy of Friendship*. Basingstoke: Palgrave MacMillan.

Verweij, M. (2007). 'Tobacco Discouragement: A Non-Paternalistic Argument'. In A. Dawson and M. Verweij (eds), *Ethics, Prevention and Public Health*, pp. 179–197. Oxford: Oxford University Press.

Vitz, P. C. (1994). *Psychology as Religion: The Cult of Self-Worship* (2nd edn). Eerdmans: Grand Rapids.

Volf, M. (2011). *A Public Faith: How Followers of Christ Should Serve the Common Good*. Grand Rapids: Brazos Press.

Von Wright, G. H. (1963). *The Varieties of Goodness*. London: Routledge & Kegan Paul.

Wadell, P. J. (1989). *Friendship and the Moral Life*. Notre Dame: University of Notre Dame.

Waites, M. (2005). *The Age of Consent: Young People, Sexuality and Citizenship*. Basingstoke: Palgrave Macmillan.

Wakeman, B. (1984). *Personal, Social and Moral Education: A Source Book*. Tring: Lion Publishing.

Weare, K. (2002). 'The Contribution of Education to Health Promotion'. In R. Bunton and G. Macdonald (eds), *Health Promotion: Disciplines, Diversity and Development* (2nd edn), pp. 102–125. Abingdon: Routledge.

Wells, N. (2017). *Unprotected: How the Normalisation of Underage Sex is Exposing Children and Young People to the Risk of Sexual Exploitation*. Ashford: Family Education Trust.

Wells, S. (1998). *Transforming Fate into Destiny: The Theological Ethics of Stanley Hauerwas*. Carlisle: Paternoster.

Werpehowski, W. (2005). 'Anders Nygren's *Agape and Eros*'. In G. Meilaender and W. Werpehowski (eds), *The Oxford Handbook of Theological Ethics*, pp. 433–448. Oxford: Oxford University Press.

Wertheimer, A. (2003). *Consent to Sexual Relations*. Cambridge: Cambridge University Press.

—— (2006). 'Consent'. In A. Soble (ed.), *Sex from Plato to Paglia: A Philosophical Encyclopedia, Vol. 1: A-L*, pp. 184–194. London: Greenwood Press.

White, J. (1989). 'The Aims of Personal and Social Education'. In P. White (ed.), *Personal and Social Education: Philosophical Perspectives*, pp. 7–18. London: Kogan Page.

Williams, R. D. (2002). 'The Body's Grace'. In E. F. Rogers, Jr (ed.), *Theology and Sexuality: Classic and Contemporary Readings*, pp. 309–321. Oxford: Blackwell.

Wilson, J. (1965). *Logic and Sexual Morality*. Harmondsworth: Penguin Books.

—— (1977). *Philosophy and Practical Education*. London: Routledge and Kegan Paul.

—— (1990). *A New Introduction to Moral Education*. London: Cassell Educational.

Wininger, K. J. (2006). 'Nietzsche, Friedrich (1844–1900)'. In A. Soble (ed.), *Sex from Plato to Paglia: A Philosophical Encyclopedia, Vol. 2: M-Z*, pp. 711–718. London: Greenwood Press.

Wolterstorff, N. (1999). 'Abraham's Kuyper's Model of a Democratic Polity for Societies with a Religiously Diverse Citizenry'. In C. van der Kooi and J. de Bruijn (eds), *Kuyper Reconsidered: Aspects of His Life and Work*, pp. 190–205. Amsterdam: VU Uitgeverij.

World Health Organisation (WHO) (1984). *Euro Reports and Studies 89: Family Planning and Sex Education of Young People*. Copenhagen: WHO Regional Office for Europe.

Wolterstorff, N. P. (2002). *Educating for Life: Reflections on Christian Teaching and Learning*. Grand Rapids: Baker Academic.

Wren, T. (2008). 'Philosophical Moorings'. In D. Narvaez and L. P. Nucci (eds), *Handbook of Moral and Character Education*, pp. 11–29. Abingdon: Routledge.

Wright, T. (2010). *Virtue Reborn*. London: SPCK.

Wringe, C. (1998). 'Reasons, Rules and Virtues in Moral Education', *Journal of Philosophy of Education*, 32 (2), pp. 225–237.

—— (2000a). 'Three Approaches to Moral Education'. In J. Cairns, R. Gardner and D. Lawton (eds), *Education for Values: Morals, Ethics, and Citizenship in Contemporary Teaching*, pp. 38–49. London: Kogan Page.

—— (2000b). 'The Diversity of Moral Education', *Journal of Moral Education*, 34 (4), 659–672.

Yankah, E., and Aggleton, P. (2017). 'The Manufacture of Consensus: The Development of United Nations Technical Guidance on Sexuality Education'. In L. Allen and M. L. Rasmussen (eds), *The Palgrave Handbook of Sexuality Education*, pp. 53–67. London: Palgrave Macmillan.

Young, F. M. (2006). 'Towards a Christian *Paideia*'. In M. M. Mitchell and F. M. Young (eds), *The Cambridge History of Christianity Volume 1: Origins to Constantine*, pp. 485–500. Cambridge: Cambridge University Press.

Index

Religion, Education and Values

Debates about religion, education and values are more central to contemporary society than ever before. The challenges posed by the interaction between these different spheres will continue to increase as the effects of globalization and cultural pluralization impact on educational settings. Our radically changed and rapidly changing environment poses critical questions about how we should educate individuals to live in increasingly diverse societies.

Books in this series offer the most recent research, from a variety of disciplinary perspectives, on the interface between religion, education and values around the world. The series covers such themes as the history of religious education, the philosophies and psychologies of religious and values education, and the application of social science research methods to the study of young people's values and world-views.

Books within the series are subject to peer review and include single and co-authored monographs and edited collections. Proposals should be sent to any or all of the series editors:

Professor Stephen G. Parker (s.parker@worc.ac.uk)
The Rev'd Canon Professor Leslie J. Francis (Leslie.Francis@warwick.ac.uk)
Professor Rob Freathy (r.j.k.freathy@ex.ac.uk)
Professor Mandy Robbins (mandy.robbins@glyndwr.ac.uk)

Vol. 1 Jeff Astley, Leslie J. Francis, Mandy Robbins and Mualla Selçuk (eds): Teaching Religion, Teaching Truth: Theoretical and Empirical Perspectives.
293 pages. 2012. ISBN 978-3-0343-0818-2

Vol. 2 Stephen Parker, Rob Freathy and Leslie J. Francis (eds):
Religious Education and Freedom of Religion and Belief.
286 pages. 2012. ISBN 978-3-0343-0754-3

Vol. 3 Ann Casson:
Fragmented Catholicity and Social Cohesion: Faith Schools in a Plural Society.
198 pages. 2013. ISBN 978-3-0343-0896-0

Vol. 4 Sylvia Baker:
Swimming Against the Tide: The New Independent Christian Schools and their Teenage Pupils.
259 pages. 2013. ISBN 978-3-0343-0942-4

Vol. 5 Nuraan Davids:
Women, Cosmopolitanism and Islamic Education: On the Virtues of Engagement and Belonging.
195 pages. 2013. ISBN 978-3-0343-1708-5

Vol. 6 Julian Stern:
Loneliness and Solitude in Education: How to Value Individuality and Create an Enstatic School.
224 pages. 2014. ISBN 978-3-0343-1733-7

Vol. 7 Stephen G. Parker, Rob Freathy and Leslie J. Francis (eds):
History, Remembrance and Religious Education.
423 pages. 2015. ISBN 978-3-0343-1720-7

Vol. 8 Trevor Cooling with Beth Green, Andrew Morris and Lynn Revell:
Christian Faith in English Church Schools: Research Conversations with Classroom Teachers.
205 pages. 2016. ISBN 978-3-0343-1938-6

Vol. 9 Julian Stern:
Virtuous Educational Research: Conversations on Ethical Practice.
258 pages. 2016. ISBN 978-3-0343-1880-8

Vol. 10 Jeff Astley and Leslie J. Francis (eds):
Diversity and Intersectionality: Studies in Religion, Education and Values.
264 pages. 2016. ISBN 978-3-0343-2252-2

Vol. 11 Robert A. Bowie:
Dignity and Human Rights Education: Exploring Ultimate Worth in a Post-Secular World.
314 pages. 2017. ISBN 978-3-0343-1940-9

Vol. 12 Olwyn E. Mark:
Educating for Sexual Virtue: A Moral Vision for Relationships and Sex Education.
254 pages. 2018. ISBN 978-1-78707-128-5

Printed by
CPI books GmbH, Leck